Narrating Evil

NEW DIRECTIONS IN CRITICAL THEORY

Amy Allen, General Editor

NEW DIRECTIONS IN CRITICAL THEORY

Amy Allen, General Editor

New Directions in Critical Theory presents outstanding classic and contemporary texts in the tradition of critical social theory, broadly construed. The series aims to renew and advance the program of critical social theory, with a particular focus on theorizing contemporary struggles around gender, race, sexuality, class, and globalization and their complex interconnections.

Narrating Evil

A Postmetaphysical Theory of Reflexive Judgement

María Pía Lara

Seagull Books
CALCUTTA 2008

Reprinted by arrangement with Columbia University Press

Seagull Books 2008

ISBN-13 9788170463290

Book designed by Lisa Hamm
Cover design by Sunandini Banerjee

Published by Naveen Kishore
on behalf of Seagull Books Private Limited
26 Circus Avenue, Calcutta 700 017

Printed at Rockwel Offset
55B Mirza Ghalib Street, Calcutta 700 016

To Nancy Fraser,

Whose friendship I value as the one true gift from life

Contents

Acknowledgments

This book was made possible through a number of research fellowships that allowed me to complete it after spending some time in those exciting academic environments. I would first like to thank The Fulbright Foundation for awarding me a 2001–2002 fellowship, which I spent as a visiting scholar at the New School for Social Research (now the New School University) in New York City. I want to express my gratitude to the New School for its generous assistance in making my year there a wonderful experience. I also wish to thank the Institute for Research on Women and Gender at the University of Stanford (Stanford, California); the Institute provided a place to start my research as a visiting scholar in 1998–99. I am indebted to my own university—Universidad Autónoma Metropolitana—for giving me its generous support and a permanent place to develop my ideas and interests. For their institutional support in allowing me to finish my manuscript, I owe sincere gratitude to my colleague and friend Rodrigo Díaz, the dean of the division of Social Sciences; to Luis Felipe Segura, the chair of my department; and to Max Fernández , the coordinator of the philosophy departament. And warm thanks to Teresa Luna, secretary of the department, for all her invaluable help, support, and loyalty throughout the years that I have worked at the University.

I am greatly indebted to the Philosophy and Social Sciences Conference in Prague, which provided an important critical forum to debate the ideas in this book. This yearly conference offered me an extraordinary opportunity to meet leading scholars from all over the world. The board of directors, all talented academics themselves—Frank Michelman, Axel Honneth, Jean Cohen, Alessandro Ferrara, Marek

Hrubec, and Peter Dews, as well as the newest appointed directors, Bill Scheuerman, Hartmut Rosa, Rainer Forst, Maeve Cooke, and Nancy Fraser—each, at one time or another, gave me the chance to assist and participate in lively debates. They have enriched my work with helpful commentaries and acute critical suggestions. These experiences have been extraordinarily formative to me. To them all, and to those who regularly attended the conference, my sincerest gratitude and recognition.

I further benefited from the suggestions of other helpful readers and friends who critiqued both earlier and later versions of the manuscript. I am particularly grateful for the support received from Richard Bernstein, Nancy Fraser, Carol Bernstein, Amy Allen, Simone Chambers, Alessandro Ferrara, Ronald Beiner, Robert Fine, Eli Zarestky, and Vanna Gessa-Kurokschtka. I profited additionally from the useful comments of anonymous reviewers selected by Columbia University Press; their careful and respectful consideration proved insightful. Without their invaluable help, this volume could not have been completed.

Needless to say, I alone am responsible for its final outcome. But many thanks are due to my dear friend and talented playwright Kathleen Anderson for her encouragement and technical facility in helping me produce the various English versions of the original manuscript. The last of these was beautifully improved by the skills and professional help of Roy Thomas, my copyeditor at Columbia University Press, who deserves thanks for the care and energy he put into the project.

Special recognition must go to Wendy Lochner, senior executive editor at Columbia University Press, who believed in the book from the start and gave me her unstinting support throughout the completion of the project. I also owe a singular debt of thanks to my dear friend and talented artist Laura Anderson-Barbata, whose beautiful cover design reflects in a perfect way the book's arguments; her generous collaboration on this project is a gift I will always remember. To my student Mario Hernández, who helped me with everything in the entire process of making this book possible, I owe more than I can say with words; without his assistance and enthusiastic attitude toward the whole enterprise, I wouldn't have made it

Deepest thanks must go to my dear friend and colleague Manuel Cruz, whose permanent presence in my life has allowed me to resist and endure its obstacles and hardships.

Finally, I am especially grateful to Nora Rabotnikov, the dear friend who, when we met, made me think for the first time on the issues raised here. She is the inspiration and the soul of this book.

Narrating Evil

Introduction

Why has evil become such a hot topic these days? Although there could be many reasons, it seems to me that the most important one—the most interesting—has to do with our growing concern with how this age-old problem has entered more and more into our consciousness. In other words, in spite of our failure to cope with human cruelty, we possess a clearer, more moral way to analyze what we call "atrocities." Our last century was plagued by horrific actions of human cruelty; nevertheless, something about our understanding has been transformed. This book seeks to explore what has changed, why this transformation matters, and how we can learn from this specific historical development.

The transformation of the way we view cruelty between humans has been the result of collective efforts that have focused on the idea that our moral outlook is constructed *socially and individually*. What this means is that we have recognized that even if we cannot impede other horrible actions from happening, we can, at least, understand why things could have taken a different road. This allows us to design new institutions and collective efforts that can help us prevent such actions from taking place in the future. An understanding of our failures makes it possible to learn from past catastrophes. This is not a triumphant view of human flaws. It is, rather, a way of saying that we can construct a moral conscience through collective efforts of self-examination and that these efforts have allowed us to produce institutions that provide us with the sense that justice can be achieved after we understand the kinds of crimes that we commit against each other. It is no coincidence that the twentieth century was one of genocide. It was also the century during which the real material aspects of international law became more than just mere theory. The tribunals at Nuremberg and Tokyo demonstrate the first stages of our collective efforts to make a connection between a moral understanding of evil deeds and the need to translate that consciousness into crimes committed against humanity. Our moral sense of understanding that what happened in the past can be held as reasons to build political and legal institutions is also another way of recognizing that people who have committed heinous crimes can be held accountable as individuals before their own societies. The fact that we cannot erase our past does not imply that we cannot place our future in a different social setting. This is the most important reason why we now need to focus on what makes these social efforts possible and find a way to put them into motion.

How do societies become conscious of their pasts? That this question might not have a simple answer is, in fact, the point of this book. I make the claim that it has been mainly due to the way some stories about the past can lead to reflection and dialogue that makes it possible to say that those stories have the potential of disclosing the hidden dimensions of human cruelty. The descriptions that unfold in particular stories can first provoke in us a shock. They haunt our consciousness in many ways. For example, when we read certain stories or see certain movies or plays we comprehend something that we could not have grasped before. Clearly, this is because such narratives disclose something that we were incapable of seeing without having them brought to life. These dramatic expressions are disclosive because they trigger our capacity for judgments. Our judgments are moral if we are able to see what is wrong, what is cruel, or why actions like those should not happen. This process might seem deceptively simple. In fact, one can focus on a story because it begins its journey into our consciousness when it is placed in the public world and where, after capturing popular attention, it can be debated. Thus, certain liberties and institutions are needed beforehand in order for spectators to have access to these stories. For this reason we can build social institutions of international law only with the help of democratic countries that allow for open debate about historical cruelties in the public sphere. The public sphere is just one of the main institutions where our freedom is at stake. Thus, a story can be captured by one spectator or by many because it flows freely in the public world and allows us to direct our interest to focus on the importance of the debate. Through discussions, polemics, and the emergence of new stories, we are able to begin the learning process. Again, the role of our judgments seems to be the key for this to happen.

Now the story can begin its own process of disclosure. Its expressiveness takes hold of the people's interest and becomes an undeniable part of their consciousness. This is the illocutionary impact of its disclosive potential. Stories allow us to understand something in a way that is morally filtered. How does a story affect our understanding of the world? This happens, first, when we realize that the story's expressive-disclosive nature makes it deserving of our attention. It must be a powerful description that depicts the deed with clarity. By highlighting the dimension of a moral wrong committed by a perpetrator against another human being, we get a notion of what is *morally* at stake. We can see that a certain way of focusing on an action, combined with a powerful description, can provide us with a view that might allow us to draw our own conclusions of what is morally wrong. Only then are we able to see that the story has become a moral filter—a vehicle that deepens our own understanding about what constitutes a moral wrong. The task of producing our judgment does not stop here, however. Debates are essential to the process, while the contrast between those stories and new ones emerging reveal other dimensions of the same action. At the same time, we begin to construct—through debate—the premises of our moral assessments. Indeed, public debates help us focus on the potential stories that better convey the truth—historical truth. Through them we thematize the way our representations match their data, and the way they become contrasted to other historical data illuminates other angles of the story. These debates shape our public consciousness about how things happened and why such actions are possible at all. Thus, without the public sphere and its spaces of debate, dialogue, and disclosure, we could not exercise judgments. Without stories, we cannot create a space for collective self-examination and self-reflection.

The Public Sphere as Mediator Between Spectators and Stories

There has long been a debate about the way we represent our historical traumas derived from past catastrophes. Holocaust scholars have produced a great deal of literature on this theme. This book focuses instead on the way events, stories, and the narratives of those events (fictionalized as well as historical) have an impact on our societies and on the way their reception has been a fundamental part of our moral consciousness. This has happened because there is a reflexive relationship between historical atrocities, their stories, and the debates generated from them that have triggered a collective self-understanding about those actions. This reflective stage, once it has been set in motion, remains sensitive to revisions and to critical examination.

In my previous book *Moral Textures*,[1] I focused on the public sphere as a stage for self-presentation and the way this stage became an important vehicle for feminist narratives to shape a wider concept of a moral subject by allowing the stories written by women to design a different, wider version of moral subjects. Indeed, visibility and self-disclosure were the effects of stories that women created in order to claim social inclusion. This book deals, instead, with another way in which the public sphere—and publicity—play a role in the political realm. The intention of authors and other thinkers to participate in political, literary, and scholarly debates is to arrive at some kind of agreement about a particular subject. I am interested in showing that certain stories (again, historical as well as fictionalized) give us a point of view about what we should consider when we want to understand human cruelty. In my view, when opinions and debates are developed in the public sphere, societies exercise collective judgments. These judgments are the basis for materializing justice by constructing memory critically, through accountability (international law), and by allowing new narratives to enter the space of public concern. Because of these debates in the public sphere, we have acquired some knowledge about past catastrophes, and we have arrived at some interesting agreements about our need to build up international law and reinforce the capacity of the public sphere to become a sphere of international debates.

What makes a debate possible? Usually intellectuals, writers, or scholars participate in the political public sphere and call our attention to something that they wish the public to understand. Historians and public intellectuals have been essential to our fragile moral consciousness about past catastrophes. It is my goal to show the way their initiatives have allowed us to consider it necessary to revise our past if we are to change our societies. Consider, for instance, Hannah Arendt's favorite quotation from Cato: "The victorious cause pleased the gods, but the defeated cause pleased Cato."[2] This phrase communicates much of what is at stake when we take Arendt's idea of judgment seriously. One of the tasks of a historian is to exercise judgments whose results can give rise to disconcerting truths. Moral understanding compels us to confront those truths, no matter how uncomfortable they might make us. This is why Cato—in Arendt's view—preferred defeat. As a historian, one cannot avoid the quest for truth, but this task is a never-ending one. Nothing offers us the entire truth, as Cato reminds us. Official truths do not always present the full picture, which is why historians strive to share their own views in public debates.

The year 1945 is a watershed in the process of our moral understanding of the Holocaust because it allowed for the construction of international law. The Nuremberg and Tokyo Tribunals were efforts—of *material justice*—to prosecute individuals for atrocities committed during the Second World War. The efforts of these societies led them to consider it necessary to differentiate between the past and the need to construct a different future. All actions taken to build institutions for prosecution of these criminals aimed to produce a new sense of justice. I call these efforts "materializing justice." It is because of public debates that some political agreements have been possible. International law then served as a mediating force to mitigate the dilemma of the rule of law. In this transitional postwar time, the concept of transitional justice needed to justify the legality of retroactivity. Nuremberg and Tokyo were the antecedents to these efforts; we are indebted to them, despite the failures of our present international courts, for positive international legal norms that are now defined by conventions, treaties, and customs. International law offers a source of normative transcendence. We always have at our disposal the example of "crimes against humanity" as a universal response to persecution. Thus, international law enables transitions and transformations.

I claim that the social transformations of our notions of evil are *historical*. We—the historical publics—have been revising our understanding of the catastrophe that we now call the Holocaust. First, historians began to capture the concrete episodes, the possible reasons for such a tragedy, the particular characteristics of Hitler's murderous policies. Once stories from survivors and witnesses started to become public, other issues also began to appear as subjects for new discussions. During the 1950s, people started to understand that European Jews were victims of a genocide. The disclosive term used then was "the Holocaust," though Raul Hilberg did not use it in his very important historical work *The Destruction of the European Jews*, first published in 1961.[3] The process began by finding a way to name the catastrophe, and then to capture what was unique about it, and so on. The *New York Times* first used the term around 1959. By then, many people who had escaped Europe—mainly Jews—were already disclosing stories about their families' losses. Serious methodological questions were discussed publicly and some very interesting shifts in the public consciousness started to articulate a wider space for self-reflection. It took twenty years for the phenomena of the mass murders perpetrated against the Jews to become widely known. This process was triggered by the way stories about concrete people entered into the realm of public consciousness. Indeed, when it happened, we began to see different stories capturing the attention of millions. The 1978 TV miniseries that dramatized the Holocaust (indeed, entitled *Holocaust*) was a turning point because it focused on the fictionalized (but accurately grounded) story of the Weiss family. The Nazi atrocities graphically represented in this made-for-television film indicated that something had changed the larger perception about the importance of this particular historical episode and showed that the public was ready to give the subject wider attention. Statistics proved this hypothesis right, because the show drew a worldwide audience of 220 million viewers, of which no less than 15 million were from Germany (West Germany). The widespread reception from the American public was possible because Americans had been exposed before to other important debates. These debates were not reduced to scholarly exchanges but to a greater participation from other people, who focused on problems that were often related to the social and political spheres. I can provide two historical examples that prepared the American public for a wider debate on the subject. First, in 1961, when the Eichmann trial took place in Israel and the proceedings were televised in the United States. The trial allowed for the disclosure of particular stories from the victims. Around this time, Hannah Arendt, who attended the trial, began to publish her articles about the trial in the *New Yorker*.[4] Her book, *Eichmann in Jerusalem: A Report on the Banality of Evil* (1963), triggered an important debate among intellectuals, historians, and writers, and its resonance in the American public sphere was very important.[5] Films led to a second stage. This happened after stories from the Holocaust had focused on the lives of real survivors. Sidney Lumet's film *The Pawnbroker* (1965) offers the first fictionalized story about the damage done to the identity of a survivor, Sol Nazerman (played by Rod Steiger). Nazerman's tale shows the way that suffering in a concentration camp destroyed his moral identity. Through the film we can see that human cruelty is aimed at destroying the other, and it is this destruction of the identity of humans that I call a moral wrong precisely because it causes "moral harm." In the film, Nazerman utters a mute scream. This scene clearly shows that the horrors he endured cannot be expressed with words—or even with a sound. By the end of the film we realize that Nazerman is a broken person because he has witnessed this catastrophe.

In the late 1970s, *Holocaust* triggered a significant debate in Germany. For viewers in Germany, unlike those in the United States, this provided the initial stage of self-reflection, and their reaction was passionate and multitudinous. German intellectuals were critical, albeit not as intensely as were their U.S. counterparts. The public, however, profited tremendously from these debates. From this point forward, Germans began to participate in their new emergent space for self-reflection. With the public response to this miniseries, we can trace the formal beginning of the worldwide critical debates that triggered the "memory wars" (this issue will be better explored in chapter 4). These memory wars are a product of critical debates, and they also attest to the fact that openness in the public sphere gives place to the disclosure of newer stories and to the enlargement of their critical examination. If such narratives can open our eyes to new ways of recognizing evil deeds, it is because they can help us see the various dimensions of harm and cruelty. They might become a way to keep us ever vigilant.

Another important debate became part of the process of the memory wars in Germany because of the critical response from the philosopher Jürgen Habermas, who questioned the truthfulness of some historical revisionist theories. This episode is called the *Historikerstreit* (i.e., "historians' disupute"), and we will have the chance to focus explicitly on it in chapter 5. Habermas continued debating other historical interpretations of the Holocaust—such as when he agreed to write a foreword to Victor Farías's book *Heidegger and Nazism*,[6] and, later on, when he wrote an introduction to Daniel Goldhagen's book *Hitler's Willing Executioners*.[7] Habermas's important leadership in debates about the Holocaust will be fully examined in chapter 5.

Germany is today in a new stage of critical examination. We can situate this stage historically just after the fall of the Communist regimes in Eastern Europe. It is possible to trace the way different problematic views, at that time, began to pose questions that concern us all. This moral questioning became an important aspect of the memory wars. Bitter memories struggled to gain recognition. The critical questions that were raised dealt with some distressing issues—for example, Which victims and which memories should take priority? Historians have played a positive role in the unfolding of this debate. In the early part of this stage, after 1989, the taboo of comparing communism to Nazism began to crumble. Historical truths are disturbing entities that call our attention to something we could not understand before. It is in this present stage that W. G. Sebald's book, *On the Natural History of Destruction,* has described the suffering of German civilians as Berlin was being bombed by the Allies in 1945.[8] This side—that of the defeated—could not be disclosed before, owing in part to the efforts of the Allies to concentrate on other kinds of accounts. Sebald's impeccable credentials as a writer have made him less vulnerable to being called a revisionist. His work focuses on this important dimension of the defeated—German civilians—whom we were unable to notice before. This theme is reelaborated in the new film *Downfall* (2005). Although the film has been criticized for supposedly humanizing Hitler (played by Bruno Ganz), the fact is that it actually illustrates his horrific *lack* of moral character. Hitler's more general concern for the well-being of his secretary and of his dog, along with his vegetarianism, are portrayed in stark contrast to his total lack of concern about the fate of German civilians. When his assistants explain to him the need to leave Berlin in order to prevent the total destruction of the city, he dismisses their counsel claiming that the "Germans deserve their fate because they have lost the war." He also rejects Eva Braun's plea not to kill her brother-in-law because of his role in the plot against Hitler's life. The agonizing conclusion is that Hitler *knew* Berliners were suffering the most. He was not concerned about civilians—only about the fate of his dog. To complete this critical examination, the recent work of a female German survivor (whose identity remains anonymous) has recently been published in Germany. It has also been translated to English and various other languages. Her diary is called *A Woman in Berlin: Eight Weeks in the Conquered City.*[8] This book could not be published earlier because it is a narration about the horrendous acts of rape perpetrated against her and other German women by Russian soldiers when they entered Berlin in 1945. It is clear that the official truth impeded stories like this to be known, and the fact that the book appears now, with an introduction by Hans Magnus Enzenberger, testifies how much the German public has changed as a result of its open debates in the public sphere.

Eastern Europe had to face its own problems of reconstructing its traces of anti-Semitism. Poland, for example, ignored its own role in the Jewish genocide. As the nation begins to acknowledge responsibility, however, it is starting to see itself in a different light. Jan Thomas Gross's book, *Neighbors: The Destruction of the Jewish Community in Jedwabne, Poland,* describes the way an entire population of Jews was killed by its Polish neighbors.[10] As Poles have been confronted with this horrific truth, the fact that many important political leaders reacted badly to it (Lech Walesa, for example) reveals the complexity of the memory wars. Hungary is now following suit. First, the movie *Sunshine* (1999), directed by István Szabó, exposed the anti-Semitism of Hungarian society and extended his critical view of how little things have changed after the Second World War ended and the Communist regime took over. More recently, Imre Kertész's books about his own experience in a concentration camp are now being publicly reviewed in a much wider international debate, in particular, his autobiographical novel called *Fateless* has been made into a movie with the same name and the film was directed by Lajos Koltai.[9]

Thus, Arendt's quote about Cato is a reminder of the need to keep the critical revision of our past open-ended. The public's views of societies' transformations give the best example of our fragile moral learning and the way these learning processes are historically developed through societies' public efforts at self-examination.

What Is Reflective Judgment?

We have seen that stories and their impact on the public sphere can help societies begin their processes of self-examination. In the critical exercise of revising their pasts, societies can learn to construct their own judgments about human cruelty by focusing on very particular stories. The most important argument of this book tries to illustrate the way reflective judgments can help us notice things we could not otherwise see. It is for this reason that I shall here say a few words about how I define reflective judgments.

In their quests to find meaning for a theory about evil, most philosophers have used *determinant* judgments.[10] I, on the other hand, focus on reflective judgments. This presupposes that only the particular can serve as an example to begin the process of understanding the way certain narratives can disclose hidden dimensions about the cruelty between humans. It is for this reason that stories prove to be fruitful examples of particular actions. Only by finding expressive and original ways to describe those actions can we provide a general concept to describe a historical atrocity. This is what happened when Hannah Arendt used the term *totalitarianism* to describe a state's power to annihilate entire groups of citizens (during the Nazi and the Communist regimes). She showed that the cultural construction of internal enemies was a process of particular actions displayed publicly in order to expel human beings from the realm of citizenship. Once this was achieved, these kinds of states legitimized their own goals of the total destruction of their targeted groups. She called those states *totalitarian* and, as such, produced a reflective judgment.

My theory suggests that we need to reflect on the problems related to human cruelty as belonging to the paradigm of evil. I use the Khunian term *paradigm* to describe the way certain problems related to human cruelty can be organized within a framework of an autonomous sphere of morality. Actions that relate to human cruelty can be considered moral wrongs. They relate to each other only as bearing what Wittgenstein has called "family resemblances." The word *paradigm* also allows me to suggest that there are specificities about what constitutes a moral wrong that we cannot simply describe as injustice. Moral wrongs are the effects of any action that cannot be labeled *only* as a violation of justice. Again, the idea of a paradigm allows us to understand that human cruelty needs an autonomous sphere of morality. The moral filter then makes it possible for us to interpret what is at stake when we find the connection between a specific violation to the integrity of a human being and a powerful way of describing it through disclosive (i.e., expressive) means. These I call "reflective judgments." They are also the result of our collective efforts to understand that the construction of normative terms such as *humanity* were first products of historical descriptions of atrocities that found expressive ways to describe those actions.

In this book I have tried to connect historical and literary narratives to an original idea of judgment. I focus on the way language can be disclosive by shocking us with new meanings and stimulate us to reorient our moral thinking. In this theory of judgment, language plays a pivotal role. My theory of reflective judgment focuses on the notion that disclosive language is an operation of opening up spaces for moral learning (i.e., seeing things differently). In this kind of exercise of judgment there is a conceptual connection between our historical understanding of an atrocity as a particular action (provided by different narratives) and the way we name it with a morally disclosive term. This morally disclosive term is meant to connect the way a word describes a crime to a new sense of moral understanding. The term should have the effect of shocking the spectator. Consider, for example, thc way Raphael Lemkin coined the word *genocide*. He had previously written *Axis Rule in Occupied Europe*.[11] Because the response to his book was critical, Lemkin realized he had to find a new word to describe the tragedy of the killing of millions of Jews during the Nazi regime. He had previously used the word *barbarity* to describe it, but he found that many other historical events could be labeled with such a word, adding no new moral dimension to an understanding of the event. He focused on what made that episode—the massive and careful extermination of Jews—into a particular method of destruction. He wanted to connote not only full-scale extermination but also Hitler's very particular means of destruction: mass deportations, the lowering of birthrate by separating women from men, economic exploitation, progressive starvation, and the suppression of all Jewish intelligentsia from Europe. Thus, Lemkin realized he needed a word that could not be used in other contexts. He consciously sought one disclosive word that could serve as a reflective stimulus to the idea that we must issue an immediate condemnation of what happened there. Lemkin settled upon a hybrid that combined a derivative of *geno*, meaning "race" or "tribe," together with the Latin derivative *cide*, from *caedere*, meaning "to kill." Thus, he coined the word *genocide*. It was short, novel, and it disclosed a reality that produced shock by being morally specific. Because of the word's lasting association with Hitler's horrors (i.e., its historical context), the word is used as a particular term to define a historical episode. Reflective judgments focus on the particular. They generate a general concept, not through subsumptions, as determinant judgments do, but rather by producing general concepts that grasp the specificities of the particular. This is what happened when we started using the term *genocide* as a general concept. What this means is that the atrocity described not only bears certain similarities to Hitler's planned destruction of an ethnic group (the Jews), it also allows us to find further differences because of its contextual and historical specificities. In this way, the word *genocide* becomes a general term that describes similar actions to those performed by the totalitarian German state ruled by Hitler. The general concept means "a coordinated plan of different actions aiming at the destruction of essential foundations of the life of humans conceived as national or ethnic groups, with the aim of annihilating the groups themselves." Thus, the general concept can be used to describe other efforts made by different perpetrators in their attempts to destroy the political and social institutions, culture, language, national and ethnic feelings, religion, and economic presence of ethnic groups and to eradicate their rights in every sense (legal, political, and moral). The completion of the task of reflective judgments presupposes our ability to draw on other differences due to the particularities of any historical atrocity.

With the previous example of the way Raphael Lemkin coined the word *genocide*, I have shown what I mean when I say that reflective judgments first create links between historical descriptions and subsequently capture a description of the "moral meaning" through words created in order to produce disclosive views about the atrocity. These connections are understood as powerful effects produced by the use of disclosive language. The word *genocide* possesses moral disclosive qualities because it allows us to learn about the specific actions that, combined, caused an unprecedented destruction of humans. My theory of reflective judgment focuses on our need to think about the particulars—the atrocities committed by humans against other humans—as historical episodes that provide ways of seeing things through a moral filter. When reconstructed through this moral filter, they can provide a further understanding of the way certain cruelties committed against humans produced specific effects that can be thematized as moral wrongs. Once we use our judgment to find a way to name those actions, then we can say that we have performed a reflective judgment. In other words, we will have generated a concept similar to the one Lemkin found when he coined the word *genocide*.

This theory aspires to give new insights into the paradigm of evil through the notion of moral disclosure based on language and its disclosive meanings. The question, then, is: Who makes the disclosive capacity of the term possible? The answer is: Authors who use creative language to articulate their judgments, but only when those judgments can be validated by the public's understanding of the hidden (moral) dimension of such a catastrophe. This means that the author and the public together generate an "illocutionary action" as a result of their interaction; the act of understanding between ego (author) and alter ego (publics), therefore, produces some kind of agreement. The goal is to provide the illocutionary effect of disclosure (seeing things in a different way). Sometimes the term fails to clear the way for moral understanding, and thus it has no illocutionary effect. An illocutionary effect can only be felt when the disclosed dimension is provided by the description of the name the author uses. At other times the effect is delayed—as in the case of Arendt's use of the term *banality*, which immediately triggered a heated debate. Indeed, the debate led to a critical revision of the use of the term *banal*, and Arendt's various interpreters had to explain the possible novel interpretations of such a word when used to describe the moral character of a perpetrator. These debates allowed the term *banal* to be considered disclosive once it was conceptually defined by Arendt's various interpreters, who influenced the public's understanding. Arendt was not able to adequately explain what she wanted to accomplish; therefore, in order to explain how it was possible, I focus on this example extensively in chapter 4. I argue there that our historical revisions have allowed us to see that she was right, but only after clarifying why her notion of "banality" is the opposite of its ordinary use. Arendt's model of the "banality" of evil is now used by other historians, intellectuals, and scholars of atrocities because of its disclosive capacity. This means that with the help of these specialists Arendt's concept is useful when discussing other similar historical atrocities (this is the main subject of chapter 7).

Representation, Trauma, and the Ineffable: A Postmetaphysical Theory of Judgment

Allow me to address the problem of why I want to situate this theory of evil in the realm of postmetaphysical thinking. I propose that most philosophers have used determinant judgments. Even when philosophers discuss a story, as is the case with some theodicies—Job's story, for example—they focus more on the logical consequences of their arguments (about the existence of God) than on providing us with new insights about what we can learn from the human condition. I insist, however, that the best place to find rich material about human complexities is in the stories themselves. Thus, while these thinkers have used stories only to develop logical arguments that become subsumptions in order to provide for a general concept of evil, I hope to clarify this position by first focusing on certain problems related to questions about representation, trauma, and the ineffable. These three problems are all related to narratives. While addressing these issues, I also hope to clarify why the best way to focus on human cruelty does not rely on metaphysical concepts or in relying on specific religious traditions.

Representation became one of the most important fields of study about the Holocaust. Contrary to the argument that it is impossible to represent traumatic experiences from undeserved suffering, I believe that human cruelty is a problem that has been well thematized in many stories by illuminating the realm of moral responsibility and choice. Thus, my theory of evil is a theory about judgment. Judgments are brought to us by stories through a different method than the one we use when we argue about concepts. One important claim of this book is that judgment and imagination allow us to express the unimaginable by creating linguistic terminologies that can convey the means to express what is unsayable. Indeed, it is the privilege of a well-told story to be able to disclose aspects of the human condition that would seem impossible to translate into pure philosophical concepts. This is why the proliferation of stories about past catastrophes contradicts Adorno's claim that there could be no poetry after Auschwitz. If we focus on what stories disclose, on the different effects they have on societies, as well as on the fact that they are material expressions of the ways societies understand themselves, then we realize that we do not need additional philosophical tools to complete the frame needed for this theory of the paradigm of evil. All we need is to examine different historical episodes—stories as representations—and provide a critical open public sphere where debates can bring us certain understanding about the need to build up international institutions of law.

Second, some good stories of past atrocities prove that human experience can be *narrated.* At the limits of what can be told, we are always confronted with another extreme need—that of sharing with others what has happened. This enterprise presupposes, in my view, that those who have written stories about their experiences, as well as those who find their moral imperative to focus on certain reconstructions of a historical episode, have dealt with the need to build a different moral community as a moral imperative. This moral imperative is directed at making others understand that what happened did not need to happen. Such an understanding of catastrophes forces us to create links between stories and our ability to learn about the ways of preventing future crimes. The idea of questioning the moral role of stories about horrific experiences—because we are bewildered by the permanence of human cruelty—is a stark paradox that this book seeks to put into question. Nothing gives us a clearer sense of the worst isolation between humans than accepting this impossibility as our defeat, because to do so is to accept that we lack the tools to portray the experiences that involve the goal of human destruction. In a way, this entails relinquishing our moral imperative to build up a transformed community with others. Perhaps this is the reason why totalitarian states enforce a silence about their past. In my view, it is because good stories are the result of reflective judgments that can become the chosen means to rebuild communities and envision a different sense of justice. A good story that sheds light on dark episodes of the past is surely the best way to share views that can transform a community. The witnesses who have written their stories, or the stories recovered from others that are gone, may not be redeemed by their efforts. After all, moral wrongs can cause permanent damage to a victim's sense of identity. This is not proof of their inability to become vehicles of moral learning. Indeed, I want to show that those stories have provided us with a moral sense of the need to keep examining the past in order to transform our future.

Third, scholars of the Holocaust have long debated the idea of trauma as an important problem for its representation. Some stories, they argue, can become ways of working through traumas. Though I clearly understand this need to work through traumas, this is not the aspect on which I wish to focus. Rather, I consider the importance of stories—even if repetitive—only when they can trigger societies' critical self-examination. Narratives from the past can also help us build a space for self-reflection. This stage of self-reflection, however, is usually possible because the role of judgment can replace the stage of trauma. This is clearly the case with Primo Levi's permanent quest to tell the same story over and over until he finally reaches a full expression about his experience in the *Lager* (the German word for "concentration camp") with *The Drowned and the Saved* (this will be fully explored in chapter 6).[12]

Fourth, from a postmetaphysical view of evil, religion and morality are two separate spheres. I am aware that many stories focus on the ordeal of doubting the existence of God due to undeserved suffering, or on justifying the existence of a supernatural being in order to cope with our fragility. This is, of course, an anthropological subject, and I am aware that it usually becomes compelling when one faces extreme situations of cruelty. My interest, then, is not religious (though I can accept that many good stories can focus on this topic).

This book deals with stories and the way they help us make judgments; through them, we can depict human actions that aim to destroy others. Human actions belong to the realm of freedom. The moral problem of human freedom presupposes that we need the ability to choose to act or not to act. I claim that it is possible to relate stories to our judgments because we can thematize the concept of action in a normative way. Action is first unfolded through its description as a story. Action is also understood as an interaction between perpetrator and victim. It has an agent and a human target. Narratives here do not refer only to tangible things but to *symbolic* ways of being and of relating between humans. This theory highlights the fact that the interactions in these narrative descriptions should capture those elements of a drama that permeate their descriptions. Even the most subtle dimensions of every aspect of the relationship between perpetrator and victim can be captured through a story. Through our understanding of this expressive description, we are able to begin a dynamic of critical reflective thinking. I argue that it is precisely because of these elements that stories can help us see what we call the "ineffable" (something I previously called the "unsayable"). The ineffable is the territory of human experience that we find difficult to describe only through concepts. When we do, we usually fall into aporias or contradictions. Instead, stories describe actions that disclose some of those hidden angles of our lives through the unfolding of descriptions about our human interactions. Cruelty and suffering are the two dimensions of our human condition that we find difficult to describe with the use of conceptual tools. This is why I describe this theory as postmetaphysical: We do not need to focus on the concept of the intentionality of the subject in order to understand the role of the perpetrator. Nor do we need to measure the amount of pain inflicted on the victim to really understand what is at stake when we say that a certain action has materially or symbolically destroyed a human being's sense of self. By focusing on acts of cruelty, we are able to comprehend why such acts unite the perpetrators to the victims forever. This happens because of the effects of the *inter*action, namely, what I called the moral wrong. It is my claim that we have learned about this not only because of good stories that have described human cruelty, but also because expressive truths expand our sense of reflection when we review them through stories. Then we can begin to interpret them in a different light. Our moral consciousness has helped us interpret those actions in a different way because we have revised them many times, and we have done so because the story can provide new ways of interpreting human complexity.

Some stories are disclosive and, therefore, can help us construct our moral view of the problem. In other words, stories that have certain types of descriptions can provide us with powerful images, metaphors, and tropes, and allow us to fill the void created by our sense of bewilderment. This is the space of the ineffable. Kant, for example, thought about this when he conceptualized the sublime (we will see this more carefully in chapter 3). It was the ineffable that led him to coin the term *radical evil,* even though his philosophical arguments never gave us a clear sense of what it meant.[15] In order to comprehend the darker side of human interaction, we can build a bridge between what is said and what is meant through a disclosive description captured in certain narratives. Consider again the example of the film *The Pawnbroker,* in which we see the image of Sol Nazermann trying to expel his horrific memories of the concentration camp from his soul. In a moment of total despair he wants to utter a loud scream but can only open his mouth to produce a mute grimace. This is a powerful image. What does the silent scream mean here? It reveals that it is possible to bridge the gaps incurred by the ineffable by formulating a connection between what is said or seen (the image) and what is meant. It discloses the meaning of the silence imposed on all those people who perished—who will never be able to scream or say anything because they are gone. It also means that Nazerman did not have the ability to express his anguish and suffering because no words or sounds could adequately express the experience of what he had endured, even after his release from the concentration camp. This is why we refer to that space of nonconceptual understanding as the space of the ineffable. In the film as directed by Lumet, however, Nazerman's mute scream illustrates the ineffable without concepts. It is an image that captures the fact that the people at the concentration camps, now personified by the concrete figure of Nazerman, were forced into isolation. Their suffering is symbolized by the mute scream. It is a metaphor that most effectively captures the way an awareness that their society did not care—that people outside the concentration camps were incapable of listening to what was happening inside—was the worst punishment they had to endure. Thus, the scream becomes a horrific soundless grimace. This example allows me to say that instead of revisiting the logical argument that these experiences are not communicable at all, I prefer to use particular stories to show the very opposite of this claim. Stories are expressive vehicles that better allow us a glimpse of some truths without the use of conceptual tools. Confronted with the difficulty of communicating the radical gap between our expressive means and our experience, I suggest that we continue to insist that there are efforts to revise what happened, and through those stories we can change our views of those atrocities. Those stories are also expressions from witnesses about their struggles, and they illustrate the need to tell a story as a moral imperative. Rather than declare that we cannot simply conceptualize questions regarding the most obscure complexities of human behavior, we should insist that literary and historical contributions carry significant insights between what we mean and what we want to say.

Finally, with language as the basis of the creation of meaning, I step away from metaphysical theories and focus on what we can learn from those stories and their powerful descriptions. The literary effect of metaphors and of naming can disclose the hidden truths (the gap between what we need to say and how we need to say it) as morally compelling signs that require all our attention.

The View from the Forest

This book is organized with this introduction, nine chapters, and an epilogue. The following chapters are developed by connecting important insights from the works of Kant, Arendt, and Habermas. The concepts that link my choice of these authors are: reflective judgments, public debates, public opinion, the open public sphere, and understanding past catastrophes. Our constructed sense of moral understanding will be examined in the first chapter. It is in this first chapter that we will also be able to see the historical images that different stories have built in terms of their contextual conceptions about evil. Since the idea of using stories is tremendously significant for this theory, in chapter 2 I bring up Hannah Arendt's ideas about judgment, representation, and stories. In chapter 3, I show that Kant was the first philosopher to think about judgment in his *Critique of Judgment* (1790) and discuss why the connection he made with the aesthetic realm is vital for my construction of the concept of reflective judgment as being linguistically interpreted.[16] In chapter 4, I go back to Hannah Arendt because of her need to recover Kant, although she left us only with her lectures on Kant's political philosophy and did not develop a more systematic theory about them. Since no true connection has been established between Kant and Arendt that could make some of the nuances relating Kant's interest in aesthetics to develop Arendt's theory of politics explicit, I wanted to develop this *missing* connection. I do this by focusing on the idea that reflective judgments use language in its expressive dimension, and I connect Kant to Arendt in a way that has not been done before—through the Heideggerian notion of language and the concept of disclosure and through Benjamin's philosophy of history. This idea of reflective judgment is the explicit connection I develop between Kant and Arendt. All my arguments here are aimed at showing the possibility of recovering Arendt under a linguistic view. In chapter 4, I establish the links between Kant and Arendt by showing the way she changed some of his views in order to fulfill her need to think about catastrophes. She took Kant's concept of reflective judgment, not by using the idea of exemplarity in a positive way—namely, as giving us a good moral example—but as using the idea of exemplarity to portray evil. Either by describing the way political institutions were built in a totalitarian state and the efforts that these processes entailed, or by showing us the lack of moral character in a perpetrator (Eichmann) who committed one of the worst crimes of our times, Arendt gave us an idea that reflective judgments can provide us with the negative notion of exemplarity that I want to make apparent.

In chapter 5, I establish a connection between Arendt and Habermas. Arendt believed that our most important task was to revise our past. I claim that no one exemplifies this effort better than Habermas, with his interventions in the public sphere. With his inspirational use of the concept of the public sphere, as well as with his concept of the place of the intellectual with regard to societies' need for critical self-examination, one can see how it is possible to stir up a debate through his critical interventions. I also appropriated his concept of "learning from past catastrophes" to define the process of establishing a connection between the collective critical examination of past catastrophes and the learning processes in which societies engage. These efforts have given us an opportunity to build up international institutions of law.

The remaining chapters form the second part of the book, which relates to different narratives and the way they help build up conceptual arguments about the whole theory. In chapter 6, I use one of my favorite examples of a good narrative. I present Primo Levi's *The Drowned and the Saved* as a story that captures the very interesting nuances of exercising reflective judgment. In a way, Levi's story *is* a story about judgment. The possibility that Levi's arguments are demonstrated by his narrative technique gives me the opportunity to fully explore the disclosive capacities of his expressions. It is also a very good example of the way a narrative can undergo a process of self-reflection through different attempts to transform the process of trauma into a process of judgment. Precisely because Levi's story is a story about judgment, I want to focus on its subsequent stage by showing that his narrative has given way for a further examination of the same catastrophe. This is why I have chosen to focus and relate it to the work of Giorgio Agamben—notably, *Remnants of Auschwitz*.[13] I take Agamben's tale to illustrate that Levi's coined concepts (i.e., "gray zones" and the *Muselmänner* or "the Muslims") allow him to be revisited through his descriptions in order to expand the original judgment. While it does so, one could say that Agamben's narrative is an important commentary of Levi's work. It is also a powerful expression of what can be accomplished with words, and it articulates his subsequent judgment as a very original commentary. I also wanted to focus on Agamben's conclusions about the historical episode of the Holocaust because I see them as inaccurate. It is important to develop my argument of what is wrong in Agamben's conclusions in order to better clarify why an overgeneralization is the opposite exercise of reflective judgment. Agamben's conclusion deals with the idea that contemporary politics is an extension of the way power was used in Auschwitz. Naked power then becomes Agamben's notion of biopolitics. I see this not as an example of reflective judgment but as one of determinant judgment. The state of emergency cannot be a definition of politics since the particularities of the use of this notion are what made the idea of Hitler's use of politics pathological. It is my claim that we should be careful when using a category that we consider disclosive about a particular episode. I have also argued that some disclosive categories can lead us to use them as disclosive concepts in a general sense (recall the example of Lemkin's word *genocide*) by finding new particulars that relocate the historicity of the term. I do not think we can use a concept like "state of emergency"—created by Carl Schmitt to define Hitler's politics—to define *all* modern politics. This is not a reflective judgment but a determinant one. It is also particularly relevant for me to be able to show this shifting exercise in judgment as a description of the wrong turn that Agamben takes.

In chapter 7, I aim to show that we construct political reflective judgments. I chose to use the metaphor of Conrad's novel, *Heart of Darkness*, because its disclosiveness is still expanding its meanings.[18] In my view, Conrad's novel is a contemporary way to describe our notions of recent historical evils. Conrad's metaphor had already caught Arendt's attention. Nonetheless, I believe it is important to explore the idea that in *totalitarian states* it is easier to choose to do evil than to refuse to do it when laws are reversed or do not exist at all. I take Hannah Arendt as an example of the notion that we can interpret her reflective judgment by using the word *totalitarianism* to describe Hitler's state and policies as a place where laws were reversed and choices seemed to disappear. Kurtz's figure will be interpreted not as portraying the intelligent, talented creature that underwent a transformation in a place where no laws existed. Rather, I argue, it is because it takes great effort to choose not to do evil under these circumstances that we can say that only brave, morally conscious people refuse to become alienated by their social environment. My interpretation of the way Arendt used the figure of Kurtz is not traditional. I claim that she used him as an example of the way one can relate easily to the social practices of *totalitarian politics*. He is no better than his accomplices, though Kurtz becomes a brutal killer by his association with others. Conrad describes his immersion into the heart of darkness as the "the horror," that is, as entering into a void of darkness where there are no moral reasons why one can justify one's own actions. In this interpretation, Kurtz does not represent a monster. Rather, it is his inability to resist evil that makes him like any other ordinary human being. Though the seed was first planted with Kurtz, Arendt later perfected this idea when she focused on Eichmann (as its opposite). The chapter delves deeper on the way other historians and political scientists have used the concept of totalitarianism as a term to describe other atrocities and to develop further particular concepts through it. In a way, it is the reverse of the previous chapter. The chapter also focuses on the way we construct our enemies through language and the way language becomes the institution of different culturally dehumanizing processes.

Chapter 8 focuses on a story that illustrates the concept I call the "moral wrong." I use Roman Polanski's film adaptation of *Death and the Maiden* (1994), from a play by Ariel Dorfman. The second part of the chapter analyzes the way the story of Paulina Salas (Paulina Escobar, in the film) provides another way to explain the paradoxical choices made by Chilean society in order to articulate its transition to democracy. A type of amnesia was orchestrated by Pinochet's elite in order to prevent Chilean society from revising its recent past. Despite stories like Dorfman's, this goal was never fully achieved and the memory wars began only after the story had already *represented the mute voices of Chilean society*. Writers like Dorfman found ways to express themselves in the literary public sphere.

In chapter 9, I explore Walter Benjamin's metaphor of his "Angelus Novus." It is interpreted as if the angel materializes in our moral consciousness. Just as the angel is condemned to live between catastrophes, so are we forced realistically to situate ourselves between catastrophes. The key here is not to forget that as long as we are humans, there will be new ways for people to choose to harm others. Like Benjamin's angel, we need to have our faces turned back to the past, not to reify it but, rather, to understand our human flaws. This revision of our past places collective self-examination and judgment as one vital process that helps us change the way things are understood when we are able to learn from past catastrophes. For Benjamin, it was the solidarity with those others that facilitated his connection to the past. For the rest of us it is our moral imperative, a collective consciousness that leads us to struggle in order to build a different future. For both Benjamin and ourselves it is here that memories collide, where we attempt self-examination in order to get things right, which will allow us to transform our societies. Linking past with future is the major task of judgment. For this reason I discuss here that the paradigm of evil relates to the paradigm of justice. They do so by materializing justice in our collective efforts to revise our past catastrophes.

Finally, in the epilogue, I try to give a general conclusion about the whole theory. The aim of the book has been to seriously consider Hannah Arendt's desire to develop a theory of judgment. The key is to relate the theory to our contemporary concerns and to insist that understanding evil is no simple matter. The question of why I call my theory a postmetaphysical one is answered there: it is because I use stories and our critical debates about them, and because these two dimensions have helped some societies initiate the process of building social institutions of international law.

PART I

The Concepts and the Tools

CHAPTER 1

Why Do We Need to Create a Moral Image of the World?

The history of freedom begins with evil, for it is the work of man.
—*Immanuel Kant*[1]

Kant was well aware of humanity's propensity for evil. Much has been written on the subject, yet we hardly understand it. That humans are capable of harming other humans, and of choosing to do so, is still one of the most puzzling questions—dramas—that we must still confront. This problem has lately been addressed by several philosophers who have reexamined previous attempts to consider these issues.[2] I, on the other hand, will employ a different view as my point of departure. As I explained in the introduction, I wish to address the problem of evil as a moral problem in a postmetaphysical paradigm. By using the term *evil*, I will present a paradigm that encompasses all our historical experiences in which human cruelty against other humans has been the defining experience of a specific type of act. In other words, the word *evil* cannot and should not be used in political or religious terms, as well-known politicians have recently done. Instead, I will clarify the importance of this paradigm by relating historical atrocities in which humans have willingly participated and propose that our moral theory of evil is a product of what Habermas has called "learning from catastrophes."[3] Within this moral view, "learning from catastrophes" means that societies confront their past as they come to critically understand what has happened. In the first stage, we have acknowledged that actions once thought to be performed only by nonhuman forces because of their horrendous implications are now considered a significant aspect of human behavior. With the second step, we arrive at the certainty that evil needs its own paradigm. Indeed, by distancing ourselves from the idea that those actions can be grasped only within the realm of justice, we seek to provide an autonomous sphere in which to thematize this type of act. In the last stage, evil can be related to the paradigm of justice only once it has shifted from the moral to the legal point of view. That is, we can locate the actions as crimes against humans once accountability and responsibility are the suitable notions where individuals can be held accountable for their deeds. We have learned about the positive normative aspects of human features only after we have dealt with their violations. This is what learning from catastrophes means. Thus, this theory highlights that even when normative definitions of the good have existed before in moral and legal paradigms, we learn about their true content only if some important catastrophes make us aware of them because these notions were violated in the empirical actions of cruelty between humans. Such is the case with the term *humanity*.[4] We can realize that the term is a historical construct that has allowed us to build on new normative contents only once we see what human beings are capable of doing to others in order to harm them. Our notions of evil are all historical, which is why literature is a good example of how actions that were not conceived as evil in the past can now be reassessed as such because of our historical moral understanding of those catastrophes.

I also emphasize our awareness of the notion that evil deeds cannot be properly comprehended within the simple context that suffering possesses some kind of moral meaning outside our moral consciousness. If suffering is such an important dimension of our awareness of evil, it is important to stress that it is we who attach the charge of constructing a *symbolic meaning to all our experiences of suffering*. This is an anthropological need of humans when confronted with cruelty.

Thus, in the use I will give the term *evil*, we should distance ourselves from traditional religious or political connotations. I propose, instead, that we use the term in its disclosive capacity so that we can take advantage of what literature and stories can offer in terms of moral knowledge, namely, that stories clearly reveal the darkest sides of human nature without the need to offer conceptual developments. Stories describe how our actions can illustrate human beings' capacity to hurt and destroy one another. They force us to learn about this type of activity by exercising judgment. Stories do not replace moral knowledge. Rather, we gain knowledge only if we are capable of exercising judgment. When facing events that we might eventually define as "catastrophes," we rely on powerful historical accounts that name events in a certain way and set forth their description with its new conceptualization to the open public. This is what I have called the disclosive-critical capacity of language. Such was clearly the case with the word *Holocaust*, [5] a term used by historians to define the catastrophe inflicted on Jews by the Nazi regime. The *Oxford English Dictionary* dates "the specific application by historians" to the 1950s. As Tim Cole notices, "The word itself did not appear in the *New York Times* until 30 May 1959, and interestingly was not used at all by Hilberg in his classic *The Destruction of the European Jews*."[6] It is when a historian or a public figure uses her judgment to name an event that the phrase or word is reappropriated by the public because it defines the specificity of the event. The meaning of being a good exemplar—its disclosive capacity—becomes validated by the public when it is accepted as a *moral filter* to define a catastrophe. It is in this sense that Cole adds, "Around 95 percent of Americans have heard the term and 85 percent claim to know what it means," allowing him to conclude that the "word entered our vocabulary and an event entered into our consciousness"[7] after some important contributions from historians' narratives. If we are aware that historical accounts have interpretative views, then we must conclude that there is no single, clear, determinate understanding we can draw from the past. But if historical understanding depends on social and historical contingencies, we meet our moral responsibility to past catastrophes in our efforts to build up a moral image of the world by adopting a critical view that is open to revisions. We do so when we can deliberate openly about different accounts of the same events—when we have a critical examination of the data and can highlight what makes a story a good example of a moral view of the problem. This historical process requires collective memory to become a critical vehicle of self-examination through the recovery of stories that show examples of evil. It is for this reason that the socially constructed understanding of evil needs the rule of law to reconsider links between collective memory and accountability. The pivotal role in shaping social memory can be played by the law, as Ruti Teitel has well argued.[8] These historical narratives possess justificatory *epistemes* that can define the ways in which our future can be shaped.[9] This is why we must link the idea of collective memories to accountability: it is through the framework of law that language, procedures, and vocabularies of justice can play an important role in shaping our public opinion. Accounting for the past affects and constructs a distinctive view of justice. Learning from catastrophes relates the paradigm of justice to the paradigm of evil as they converge within the realm of law.

The last stage of our ideas about learning from catastrophes can be completed if we stress that only within our historical assessments, by way of connecting our imagination to our moral understanding, can we build a model for our reflective moral judgments. These judgments will constitute the final stage of this postmetaphysical theory of evil.

The Historical Understanding of Evil Through Literature's Devices

In the past, *evil* was a term widely used to describe human suffering, natural disasters, and metaphysical fears related to the existence or the absence of God. Theodicies were the narratives chosen by the traditional philosophy because, by creating them, philosophers sought to relate their concerns about evil with the task of arguing about the existence of God. Their attempts to explain the existence of evil actions and human suffering, while maintaining that it was possible to justify God's existence, were driven to focus more on the logic of the argument than on the capacity to disclose a hidden dimension about evil interactions between perpetrators and victims. If we focus the attention on the cruelty of human actions, then, we can begin to situate this problem as related to responsibility and choice. Thus, the problem of inflicting suffering through cruelty belongs to the realm of morality, and it should be restricted to moral agency. After all, evil actions only concern human deeds. If we can understand this much, then we are capable of assuming our tragic fate—the realization that our most basic right, human freedom, can also be our worst dilemma. This much was clear to Hannah Arendt, who understood that Kant's greatest achievement with regard to this matter was his proclamation that evil is a problem related to humans, and that in defining the core of human action we are only concerned with freedom and our capacity to exercise judgment.[10] This crucial connection led Arendt to conceive her idea about a postmetaphysical paradigm of evil by relating human freedom to the judgments of our actions. Arendt also clearly separated an understanding of evil from obscure ideas about psychology, from metaphysical theories about the existence of evil, from concepts such as perverted ill will, and even from the idea that a treatise of evil envisions a realm in which the moral subject is still immersed in the philosophy of consciousness (Kant). By rejecting all of the above, Arendt allowed us to create a new postmetaphysical framework for the problem of evil.

Thus, we must begin by thematizing human cruelty and our capacity to choose to act cruelly in terms of actions exemplified by narrated stories. We highlight how *emplotted* actions are unfolded as stories that disclose their moral content—not only through the interconnection with our understanding about the complexities of human beings but also because those actions help us configure our moral identities by teaching us to form moral judgments reflectively.[11] These stories become the material sources by which we can frame our historical perspective. Because we can recognize in stories the concrete meanings of our evil deeds, this process gains a dimension of moral understanding. I use the notion of "historical understanding" much in the same way that Gadamer used it with his concept of "*Wirkungsgeschichte.*"[12] In other words, "effective history" is built on the interpretation of a past event as conditioned and valuated through its reading in the present. This important interplay between past and present leads us to make historical judgments by a type of "fusion of horizons" between past and present.[13] This normative condition also speaks of the impossibility of declaring something evil if it is not reconstructed in light of these two historical stages and with the contrast gained through applied judgment along with our moral imagination. Learning from catastrophes gives rise to a dynamic—a dialectic movement—with our effort to understand what happened in light of the present stage. In that same effort, we gain a space in which to develop our reflective qualities, which allow us to become autonomous moral beings. If we look at the past, we see that in ancient literature, for example, an act such as rape meant something entirely different from what it means now. In Homer's stories, for example, when the Greeks or the Achaeans won a battle, the spoils of war included the right to take women and rape them (Euripides' tragedy *The Trojan Women* illustrates this point). Only through the evolution of our moral and historical understanding are we able to think of rape as a weapon of war to destroy other humans. We recognize this now because we have heard about the way Serbs raped Muslim women during the Balkan war[14] and that many of these acts were committed during and even after the Sebrenica massacre.[15] Furthermore, because we have made moral judgments about those kinds of actions, we are able to discuss in the public sphere why it is possible to translate the moral meaning of wrongdoing into a positive legal framework within the realm of international law.[16] With our historical understanding of what happened in the Balkan war, we can define rape as a crime against humanity.[17]

Let us take a closer look at the way narratives have offered us different notions of the meaning of evil. If evil was ever characterized in ancient times, it was through the idea of Greek tragedies. The notion of evil that these plays reflect is still tied to a metaphysical idea of evil. Tragedies relate to the *daimon*, emphasizing the relationship between the divine and the human and their inevitable links.[18] It is for this reason that Bernard Williams argues that "tragedies involve supernatural conceptions, in particular of necessity."[19] Evil, in Greek tragedies, is seen as the product of destiny. It is interesting, however, that Greek tragedy is concerned mainly with action. This dimension deals in one way with what Williams calls "our historical notion of responsibility," and, on the other hand, with understanding how Greek tragedies became so important to understanding the complexity of human actions. This is why Aristotle believed that such complexity could be shown only through the literary devices of the genre of tragedy—that is, through a plot represented in action.[20] It is already known that Martha Nussbaum's interpretation of Aristotle's ideas about tragedy emphasizes the role of judgment. According to Nussbaum, tragedies represent action well because one can see the characters choosing and doing (379). She argues that pity and fear are emotions spectators can feel because they understand that our world is fragile and that anyone can make mistakes without necessarily being evil. Pity is the response to witnessing an action of undeserved suffering, says Nussbaum, while fear is produced by the idea that such terrible suffering could occur to any of us (385). In Nussbaum's interpretation, both pity and fear are "sources of illumination or clarification." Thus, the representation of actions depicted by Greek tragedies portrays some important knowledge (388). The idea of evil, nevertheless, comes out of the complex web of necessity and chance—out of divine and human sources.[21] Things happen to the characters or they are driven to some kind of action that is already predestined to be their fate. This concept of action is an important source for the more general historical understanding that sees evil as a paradigm that includes both dimensions—metaphysical and natural disasters—along with our human mistakes and our human frailty.

It is for this reason that the complex relationship between literature and evil can be historically thematized based on how much we have learned about humans from the ways poets and writers have written about them. In this sense, no one has more fully developed the complex idea of modern subjectivity than William Shakespeare. This is also why Harold Bloom has argued that Shakespeare invented the human.[22] We see that Shakespeare's characters "develop, rather than unfold, and they develop because they reconceive themselves" (xvii). The questions arise: Why is the development of characters the result of the process in which they struggle against evil? And how do they redefine themselves after such struggles? Consider, for example, Shakespeare's historical evolution through his characters Richard III and, later, Macbeth. The first is a true villain. He is portrayed as the premodern notion of the demonic. He has no doubts, he excludes "piety," and his naturalism "makes us [aware that we are] all beasts" (65). Richard III has no goodness in his soul. He personifies, or rather simplifies, our view of human character. This play already involves a stylistic change in Shakespeare's approach because of the new rules that the character establishes with the audience. What is strikingly new about this character is that he is the first to consciously establish an intimate relationship with the audience (70), as if he were its moral conscience. We do not need a chorus, as in Greek tragedies, to make us participants in the performance as witnesses and judges. We are now in a position to establish our dialogue with the main character. Thus, when reading *Richard III*, we learn about ourselves as we become aware that we are "incapable of resisting Richard's terrifying charms" (71), which are displayed consciously in front of us—indeed, directed to us—addressing us with his evil self-assurance. He is, nevertheless, a transitional figure of Shakespeare's modern notion of evil.

Macbeth, on the other hand, is considered Shakespeare's greatest evil character. As Bloom explains, "In the Renaissance sense of imagination (which is not ours), Macbeth may well be the emblem of that faculty, a faculty that must have frightened Shakespeare and ought to terrify us" (17). Macbeth dreams about his future and imagines how extraordinary it could be if he takes the steps required to transform it. Freedom appears here as the main element of his choosing to do evil. We know that Macbeth "suffers intensely from knowing that he does evil, and that he must go on doing even worse" (517). Thus we are confronted with our own ambitions and must question the way certain goals in our lives can lead us to be self-deceptive by compelling us to avoid any moral consideration in order to achieve our ambitions.[23] "Our identity with him is involuntary," argues Bloom, "but inescapable" (518). Only literature can bring us to the idea of visiting the other's mind as if it were our own.[24] We have to concur with Bloom that by "working against the Aristotelian formula of tragedy, Shakespeare deluges us with fear and pity, not to purge us but for a sort of purposiveness without purpose that no interpretation wholly comprehends"

(518). Here we can see clearly what the concept of the ineffable means. Shakespeare has bridged the gap between what is said and what is meant by describing the inner tragedy of the mind when it confronts the most basic dimension of the human soul, that of our freedom. Herein lies the space of self-reflexiveness of the modern subject—that which makes us aware of the hard fact that we have to choose in order to become human. There can be no understanding of evil without the complexity of our choices in the context of our particular moral crossroads and in the defining ways that we justify ourselves. People always have "reasons" to do evil—this much Shakespeare knew about our human condition, and it is well reflected in Macbeth's character.[25]

Shakespeare, however, developed the concept of evil as a result of the passions of human beings—as a force that controls human will. Indeed, as Agnes Heller argues, "Shakespeare's most interesting characters throw themselves into a stream where they courageously swim towards their goal, or where they will eventually be carried away toward self-destruction."[26] Some of the most interesting characters of the best Shakespearian plays—like Macbeth or Hamlet, for example—are men and women in love; they are guided, in part, by this passion as a condition of possibility to commit an evil crime.[27] Without love for Lady Macbeth, Macbeth would not have murdered King Duncan. Without Gertrude's silent complicity, there would be no reason for Claudius to wish for and commit the murder of the king and usurp the Danish crown. Other characters—like Iago in *Othello*, for example—are filled with envy. Though Shakespeare deals with these kinds of passions, he also defines existential beings and their moral decisions as new important spaces for the self. Nevertheless, Shakespeare gives significant weight to the fact that passions dominate human decisions and make people their slaves. Kant feared that by giving so much importance to passions, we lessen the significance of freedom. Perhaps one can say that it is really in the combination of passions that Shakespeare makes a valuable contribution to the modern thematization of evil. We see this, for example, not only in Lady Macbeth's passionate love for her husband but also in her boundless ambition to see her husband become king. These passions turn the struggle of human decision-making in a moral crossroad a tragic one. Such a view was the prevalent concept of evil throughout many centuries. Shakespearan plays are extraordinary vehicles for the exercise of judgment because his plays never provide specific causes for an evil action. Indeed, as Agnes Heller has rightly noticed, "He does not represent causes—as [Georg

Lukács] observed—and brings together different characters in extreme situations to find out for himself how the chemistry among them will develop and what actions will occur as a result, that so many different interpretations of 'causes, motivations' can be made equally plausible."[28] This is why there are so many interpretations of Shakespeare's dramas. His great achievement in portraying evil actions is that he was mainly interested in actions as such, and that he was quite aware of their historical contingency. Perhaps this is the reason Shakespeare's characters invite us to think about freedom differently than Kant. If Shakespeare believed everyone has a soul, then "the voice of conscience sounds"[29] in every moral crossroads that humans confront in a very different way, and, thus, freedom is still the most important category related to evil. This time, however, it is expressed as the choices we make in becoming human with our unique way of reacting when facing moral dilemmas. Shakespeare's most mature characters undergo this process when they are forced to overhear themselves "as the royal road to individuation."[30] Indeed, Shakespeare's characters create the space for self-reflection because they don't justify themselves. Instead, they struggle over "statements about the meaning of the larger world within which the self finds itself, larger than moral, political, natural, and divine orders within which the self finds its place."[31]

Most recently Shakespeare has been used as an example to contrast our modern legal notions of crimes. This is clearly the case with the work of Theodor Meron, a professor of law, who has analyzed the works of Shakespeare specifically because they deal "with crimes and responsibility" and "they touch the intellectual genealogy of our modern humanitarian law."[32] Meron discusses Shakespeare's dramas in order to provide a careful examination of the way we have begun to see certain dimensions of responsibility and accountability which can be traced back to interesting historical contrasts and similarities in Shakespeare's accounts.[33] In a previous work, Meron analyzed the play *Henry V* in order to revise our transformed notions of pillage, rape, just wars, and compelling obedience by destruction.[34]

Following the previous examples of how we can find historical notions of evil in major works of literature, I want to suggest that one of the most interesting contemporary examples of an evil character is portrayed in Joseph Conrad's novel *Heart of Darkness*. The metaphor of a human immersing himself into the heart of darkness discloses the idea that the socially constructed ways in which certain actions of human cruelty occur can be captured through the concrete example of

Kurtz's story. Kurtz represents the individual who faces the dilemma of choosing not to do evil when everyone else embodies the practices of cruelty and murder. Indeed, the social orchestration of evil in our contemporary times relates more to these kinds of social situations where totalitarian states reverse laws or where there are no laws. Through understanding how the web of political strategies and social complicity appear in front of those who resist evil, we gain knowledge of what is at stake when we say someone possesses moral character. Complicity and totalitarian politics are the two sides of the coin that facilitate the lack of moral character. When confronted with their deeds, militaries always reply that they were only "following orders"—obeying their superiors or the totalitarian law, or just doing what everyone else did.

Narrating and Judging Evil

Thus, by narrating evil deeds, we will reassess why judgment is connected to an interrelationship between ethics and aesthetics in a different way than I have described in my earlier work about the public sphere.[35] Literature makes it possible to capture the historical differences between the past and the present. Yet it is only through our moral application of reflective judgments that we are able to recover those stories as tools that help us learn about our evil deeds. When the story provides us with its own reflective judgment by using a powerful description of the event, we are led into a second stage of reflexiveness. This is where we are able to grasp the moral dimension of the story once we can frame it in disclosive terms, which will allow us a critical and moral perspective. The disclosiveness of the descriptions of actions relate to the aesthetic realm because they are well-constructed *expressions* that make us see things in a way that we were not capable of seeing before. With this conscious move, I mean to connect a disclosive view of language that affects both realms to the aesthetic qualities of an expression and to the moral capacity of immanent critique while using certain expressions in an original way to communicate something. It is only after we consciously offer the possibility of publicly debating the moral contents of a story that we can arrive at this second stage to exercise some kind of judgment. For this reason the public sphere becomes an important historical mediation that allows us to understand the moral construction of our reflective judgments. These judgments become historical stages of our critical understanding of the past. Through dialogical efforts to grasp our past legacy of horrors, stories must be submitted for public scrutiny in order to gain the recognition of their critical moral worth. With this normative condition, we establish criteria by which stories should submit their *possible* moral content to public scrutiny. The more we understand ideas about moral wrongs through these criteria, the more likely they will become good examples of reflective judgment.

I have argued elsewhere that it is impossible to thematize evil through abstract theories or by giving it a single definition.[36] The best approach is through a description of such acts within the context of stories. Our understanding becomes clearer when we realize that evil actions cannot merely be considered problems related to justice. We cannot say that mass killings, genocide, or ethnic cleansing are simply violations of justice. We need a different type of paradigm with which to categorize those actions. We can also call this evil paradigm "the atrocity paradigm"[37] in order to clarify the dimension of human agency involved in those actions. Arendt gave us valuable insights when she described the multiple aspects of humanity that Jews were denied in Nazi Germany. She clearly understood that something she considered "unprecedented" required a different kind of category. She even comprehended that, for the first time, we were dealing with normative conceptions of humanity by learning how these features associated with humankind could be erased from the lives of individuals. Dignity, spontaneity, freedom, and plurality—all of these categories—became relevant as soon as she saw that they constituted that which makes our lives specifically human. We can grasp what that means only because of the calculated efforts by the Nazis to erase them from the lives of millions who were secluded by force in concentration camps. By offering us a story of what she called "totalitarianism," Arendt framed her narration according to the moral view of what constitutes an evil deed in light of its historical uniqueness. Furthermore, she used a new political disclosive term—*totalitarianism*—to define the historical comprehension of what was happening then as well as what made it a totally new effort requiring new categories. It was then that she thought of linking action to judgment. The challenge lay in what she thought it would mean to understand that evil deeds only concern human actions. This understanding led her to focus increasingly on the idea that we have the moral capacity to grasp why moral agency is always involved when we decide to perform some acts instead of others. Rather than to focus on the subjects' intentions, Arendt opted to tell us the story of Adolf Eichmann. For the first time, she saw evil as the most ordinary achievement attributed to a human being. Eichmann was not an extraordinary man. His capacity to understand what he had done lacked the clarity of what is at stake when we deal with moral judgments. He was only capable of conflating the Führer's orders with his moral duty.[38] There was no depth to his thinking. Thus, Arendt thought to describe him as an example of the "banality of evil." With this telling phrase, she thought again that the critical view of her judgment should allow us, her readers, to understand what she meant when she portrayed evil in the persona of Eichmann. She concluded that the most ordinary of men committed the most extraordinary of crimes. The darkest side of evil, she claimed, remains in our incapacity to see why certain kinds of actions can have no forgiveness. Arendt was not understood in her time, as we have seen before. It was only once we started to discuss her views in public, and by debating her ideas and stories over and over again, that we have been able to understand why she chose to entitle her polemical judgment of Eichmann the "banality of evil." By allowing us to immerse ourselves in the deeply entrenched corners of those kinds of human actions, she produced, in her long journey of the historical experiences of her time, two significant historical judgments. These judgments were historically situated and politically significant in terms of allowing us to think about those experiences with new categories and with a new learned moral understanding. She had finally laid down the basic insights of her theory by enabling us to understand the interconnections between human freedom, responsibility, and moral judgment. Thus, she made the first contribution to this theory of postmetaphysical reflective judgment.

Contrary to the belief that only suffering defines evil,[39] it is my claim that evil is best understood in terms of narrated actions, which moral actors strive to comprehend by thematizing the stories unfolding the complexity of evil deeds repeatedly in public debates. I move away from psychology, metaphysics, and transcendental theory in order to arrive at a postmetaphysical theory of judgment that stresses the importance of a historical public discussion in which to begin the exercise of a collective moral judgment. This theory of reflective judgment deals with the way human actions—which depict cruelty—are established between victims and perpetrators. Thus, if cruelty is an undisputable element of those actions, it cannot disclose the complete dimension of these specific kinds of human actions because we can also exercise cruelty against animals—yet animals can be cruel to other animals without being evil. The missing element in what I refer to here as "evil" is not only related to the way our actions aim to destroy others by inflicting pain but also to what we have learned about the symbolic content of those sufferings because they are meant to infringe a permanent moral wrong that destroys a person's identity forever. It is for this reason that our duty to reconstruct their stories in light of a public debate must focus on the idea of moral wrongdoing. These kinds of actions deal with a specific type of moral agency related to our freedom and to the specific choice to inflict permanent harm on others. We can say that those humans aim to destroy others' humanity. In other words, we have learned that the choice and meaning of inflicting a permanent moral wrong on others connect the perpetrator to the victim forever.[40] Such are the conclusions derived from our historical comprehension of those stories. They have taught us why we were so horrified when these actions were committed by other fellow humans. We dreaded imagining that such behavior was possible and learned that they were not caused by the existence of a supernatural being, but by other humans like ourselves, who allowed such things to happen. In learning from catastrophes, we have reached a new stage of historical consciousness. What makes us appear inhuman is the dimension of our actions, which illustrate our very capacity to do evil. The only way to return to our historical understanding about the idea of moral responsibility lies in the idea that even if those actions are performed by someone who seems not to be human, we are in fact the only ones capable of performing them. Both Kant and Arendt took hold of this moral understanding. They crafted it carefully in their distinct ways of establishing the interconnections between freedom and moral choices. They agreed that they did not want to make evil appear otherworldly. Rather, they preferred the idea that evil relates to moral agency and that moral choice must be situated within a paradigm of moral judgment. This is why a notion of evil cannot be fully comprehended without a proper notion of freedom and of judgment.

Moral judgments, however, cannot be arrived at by isolated agents. This theory stresses that moral learning is tied to a historical collective reconstruction. With it comes the conception of our simultaneous efforts to build moral autonomy as the other side of responsibility. Such consciousness of a historical understanding is stimulated only when the collective task of learning from catastrophes makes us aware of the intimate connection between autonomy and responsibility. This effort also implies that it is necessary to submit those stories to a public debate—to discuss them critically with others. This is a necessary step that leads us to an open debate about what makes certain acts morally important in our historical understanding of those past atrocities. By revising and contrasting them again and again, we can begin the collective process of reflective judgment, which is articulated in historical stages. It allows persons to internalize them, and in this way we learn about the past experiences of others. With them, we gain important new insights into what it is that makes us truly human. Judgment here allows us to remove ourselves from all essentialist understandings of evil. Through our historical debates, and with the long critical interaction between different views, we put into play a set of contrasts that only our imaginations can crystallize into new meaningful claims. We are also forced to create moral identities by means of self-reflection. These debates articulate the mediating role of the public sphere in allowing us to connect our socialization and individuation as two simultaneous processes. The plurality of points of view allows for the emergence of the detached critical debate, in which we can begin to see things differently. When reflective judgment is built through the disclosive capacities of our moral understanding, we are able to bring a moral quality to our judgment, and with it we can produce an "illocutionary" effect. *Illocutionary effect* refers here to our capacity to understand and build consensual steps for the future. This is the stage in which our understanding of moral wrongdoing can be translated into the realm of the law as typified crimes. It is the stage that exposes our moral capacity for judgment; it requires that we effectively construct the positive basis for protecting the moral contents of the term *humanity* and develop the positive steps that can translate the moral content of our understanding in terms of laws.

When Arendt thought to revise our historical traumas, she claimed that "mastering the past" was a necessary step if we were to begin anew. This does not mean that we become capable of erasing the evil aspects of our humanity, but rather that perhaps, because of a learned understanding from catastrophes, we can create laws and acquire important moral knowledge about our self-binding choices. After all, such knowledge implies that we are aware of what it means to be truly human. In this theory, then, I stress that the task of becoming thoroughly human is equal to the building of our moral selves. It is a construction—a process. This historical understanding of what it means to be human is only possible in part after we learn to make reflective judgments about evildoing.

It is my claim that we can only give our understanding of such an action its moral code by linking the perpetrator and the victim when examining any action. As we have seen, stories by themselves are not enough for this connection. We need the interaction between stories and our historical understanding of those stories. We can only have both when our reflective capacity for moral judgment makes us see why such an action described by a story can be thematized as moral wrongdoing—that is, as evil. One must approach this issue by connecting stories, where the perpetrators are related to the victims by the aim of inflicting permanent harm on them so that it is possible to recognize these perpetrators as agents of certain actions which imply the aim of moral wrongdoing. We cannot describe these actions unless we enter the very paradigm of our historical understanding of the reason moral wrongdoing means permanent harm to one's identity. This is true because such an action permanently damages a person's most basic sense of self. Thus, we learn that those stories acquire their potential moral qualities by allowing us to understand these kinds of moral wrongdoings through descriptions that involve new disclosive terms. They show those actions that lead us to think of a need for a new political term to describe them. There are two different ways that language becomes the important site that gives struggles their disclosive meanings. On the one hand, take the case of the way the word *genocide* was coined. As I noted in the introduction, this term was first created and used by Raphael Lemkin.[41] He used a hybrid combination that combined the Greek derivative *geno*—which meant race or tribe—with a Latin derivative *cide*—which meant killing. Thus, with the fusion of the two terms Lemkin created a word: *genocide*.[42] A second example comes from a totally different way of ascribing meaning to evil actions: Totalitarian regimes develop their own personal language (as we shall see in a later chapter) and carefully craft their words to distort reality by expressing metaphors of "cleansing" or erasing the humanity of their enemies. For example, when the Argentinian military used the word *subversives* to justify its abductions, resistance groups started to use the noun *desaparecidos* ("the missing") to refer to the people who had been taken (and murdered) by the military in broad daylight and "disappeared" without leaving a trace.[43] Historians and political theorists continue to use these kinds of words in order to allow us to see a hidden dimension of the terror created by totalitarian regimes. Only after such a translation can those political terms allow us to articulate a new positive understanding of a moral wrong in terms of the law.

Such have been the cases involving genocide, ethnic cleansing, rape, and crimes against humanity.[44] We can see that a story can provide a moral judgment for the same reason that it can articulate the historical defining features of a certain action by using a disclosive term or by developing a valid theory for why such crimes involve important new moral assessments of wrongdoing. We create a specific language to describe those actions. When we understand the relevance of those very words—when we use them to describe those actions—they will disclose the moral dimension of our judgment. This view of critically horrendous deeds described in a story compels us to pay full moral attention to them. If such an exercise can capture our moral attention, the public will press for a relevant way to use the moral contents of our judgments to find a proper definition that suits the requirements needed to be translated into the realm of law.

If Kant was the first to understand that the problem of evil was a human problem, Nietzsche clarified that our need to relate suffering to some kind of meaning was our constructed way of believing that suffering needs to be connected to a transcendental order. After all, Nietzsche claimed, what seems unbearable is to live with the idea that human suffering has no meaning at all. This postmetaphysical paradigm of evil asserts that there is no essentialist meaning of suffering. If we search for transcendence, it is because we need to construct ways of bearing undeserved suffering. All suffering produced through cruelty is undeserved. Human suffering is a subject that concerns us because we are the only responsible perpetrators of those cruel actions. This important insight—that is, Nietzsche's understanding of our constructed views of the meanings of suffering—became apparent only when the tragic events of the Holocaust illustrated that there could be no causal connection between the victim and the cruelty of the evil actions performed by the perpetrator. Indeed, this historical understanding became apparent, for example, when Primo Levi narrated his own story and by the way he confronted this brutal knowledge in light of witnessing so much undeserved suffering. He, like Jean Amèry and many others, began to question the very existence of God because of his experience in the Nazi *Lagers*. We do not need to develop theories about suffering as if they were the only defining means of what constitutes evil. Stories give us infinite ways in which to look at this problem. Through them, we gain the historical consciousness that leaves us with the harsh reality that it is we ourselves who make our human world a cruel one. It is entirely our human responsibility.

An awareness of how humans stopped constraining themselves because of the metaphysical "death of God" (Nietzsche) was perhaps the harshest conclusion of our learned experiences from the Holocaust. This is why Susan Neiman insists that the Holocaust is the defining moment of all contemporary evil.[45] This is also the historical beginning in our need to reconceptualize the postmetaphysical paradigm of evil. Such a task first emphasizes that if we pursue a path to a historical reassessment of atrocities, it will have to differentiate itself from the way both traditional philosophy and theology have done it in the past. If I succeed in recovering the term *evil*, it is because I find no disclosive substitutes for such a term. I pursue my task only by providing certain kinds of historical judgments about our recent past. The twentieth century is a century of genocides.[46] I can only find examples of evil acts through the stories we recover that provide an outlet for a moral dimension that allows us to become responsible and exercise our duty to express why we need moral judgments to be the material sources of our moral identities and the new basis for an international order. These efforts should allow us to connect those stories to a whole new understanding of ourselves.

It is by family resemblance, to put it in Wittgensteinian terms,[47] that I wish to accomplish the task of providing negative examples of evil deeds. I will connect the universality of our understanding to those deeds thematized as examples of evil. Yet, as in each historical example, I will be able to provide the specific characteristics that make such a particular historical event an atrocity that fits the paradigm of evil. The success of our moral judgment should help us recognize what needs to be done so that the story will not repeat itself. We can accomplish this task only by thematizing the story in the diverse stages of understanding that undergo critical scrutiny in the historical public sphere. If the story gains consensus about its moral qualities, then the judgment will allow us to translate the realm of a good example of reflective judgment into a typified crime in the realm of law.

If I can show that the dimension of evil is best explained in particular stories that provide us with the material that relates their concrete actions to a universal paradigm of a moral kind, I will then prove that there has already been a resemantization of the term *evil*. In many of the stories that I will be analyzing, we will see that the term *evil* plays an important role. It is the filter that focuses our attention on permanent moral wrongs and guides us to consider the story an important vehicle for collective self-reflection. This term is not used in the political sense, but within its moral disclosive capacity. I will use examples that will help me illustrate how the stories about evil actions have reappropriated the term in light of our historical efforts to connect our ideas about certain kinds of human actions to the historical account of the paradigm of evil.[48] This paradigm relates these actions to our moral learning from catastrophes. I can say that our historical judgments can accomplish our moral duty by recovering evil as an important moral dimension of constructing our moral identities, and of our collective moral consciousness of what happened in the past. It will also provide us with a normative term of humanity, which must play a significant role in international law. This normative term of humanity, as a social construction, has allowed us to understand the internal connections between violations and the normative notions that we need to create in order to prevent future catastrophes. Many of the most interesting reflective judgments have been offered by some of the stories from the critical witnesses of the past century.

CHAPTER 2

Storytelling

[The Disclosive Dynamics of Understanding and Judging]

One of my previous books develops a narrative theory.[1] I would now like to focus on Arendt's narrative perspective in order to show how she used narratives to understand evil. It is worth noting that Arendt believed storytelling provided her a better way to cope with crisis and with concrete problems than did the use of abstract and systematic theories of the political. Narratives provided her with an original method for political theory, which is why I wish to revisit some of her ideas on the subject.

Hannah Arendt pioneered the use of literature and storytelling as important devices for political and moral thinking. Because this interest in stories permeated every problem she tackled in her passion for politics, Arendtian scholars have recently begun to focus on this dimension of her work. Arendt was clear about why stories gave her a better chance to articulate her own historical understanding of the political. On the one hand, the structure of the plot and its particular conventions allowed her to develop her arguments using this device. Stories are always concrete. They can share similarities with other stories, but they are always original because they are immersed in finding the particular view of a storyteller. She also wanted to provoke the reader—to make readers aware of the necessity of critical thinking. The interpretation of events are judgments and if they possess a moral filter then they can be original. This might be why Lisa Disch suggests that Arendt thought of "storytelling [a]s a kind of judgment."[2] Arendt was very aware that judgment is found in the way plots unfold *disclosively*.[3] Because the storyteller is already exercising some judgment, it is the process of understanding that allows the complexity of any action to be interpreted in different ways. Arendt demonstrates that when we need to understand something complex and even difficult to express, we can use storytelling as a bridge between imagination and understanding.[4]

Life stories can help us reconcile human burdens, Arendt tells us, because "even in the darkest of times we have the right to expect some illumination, and that such illumination may well come less from theories and concepts than from uncertain, flickering, and often weak light that some men and women, in their lives and their works, will kindle under almost all circumstances and shed over time span that was given to them on earth—this conviction is the inarticulate background against which these profiles were drawn" as narratives.[5] Human understanding depends, according to Arendt's concept of the use of storytelling, on giving meaning to our actions, on training the imagination to go visiting. It is not as a way of reconciling the past, but rather, a way of demonstrating that those actions have a permanent significance that allowed a single story to enter into history,[6] and that such stories have allowed us to assume that the active role of understanding means transforming ourselves. Arendt argues that we are constantly "preparing the way for poetry" because of its human potential—"in reification by the poet or the historian, the narration of history has achieved permanence and persistence."[7] Furthermore, storytelling reveals meaning without erroneously defining it.[8] This is the reason why Arendt turned to Kant's concept of reflective judgment rather than on his concept of determinant judgment. Arendt conceived action with relation to her basic categories of natality, plurality, and narrativity. Thus, Arendt's concept of action dynamically links it to the idea of the disclosure of the self.[9] In this chapter, I want to show that by linking action to judgment through *narratives* we can see why reflective judgment consists of two different moments: The first happens when the spectator or reader issues a judgment about what is happening in the representation, where she considers the idea of a spectator who sees action with an impartial detachment.[10] The second moment occurs when spectators engage in understanding action, to pursue new paths to transform themselves. Then the viewer becomes an actor. In deliberating with others, then, spectators see themselves as persons whose responsibility toward their community needs to activate their collective judgment in order to create a sense of community. Communicability using this process of deliberation in the public realm brings political understanding.[11] This is why it is so important to thematize evil by examining actions as they are narrated through stories. Action produces stories, and those stories give meaning to our deeds. It is most interesting, however, that the only way to mediate actions with judgments is to narrate them. Arendt knew that narratives are always open to reinterpretations, and that by retelling them to new audiences we pave the way for possible new meanings. Since narratives are always open to new interpretations, they are never final judgments. The idea of their possible revision is implicit in their characteristics because they are open to new ways of describing the same actions with a different perspective.[12] Narratives describe a complex web of human interactions, and their need for subsequent interpretations relies on any given interpretation's powerful expressiveness. They set in motion a plural process of understanding that allows many perspectives to be presented and configured in the dynamics of the public sphere. It is only after understanding these basic links in Arendt's theory that we have come to realize why she chose the concept of reflective judgment as her last subject of interest. The story proves fruitful when it triggers critical thinking. In basing our judgments on an enlarged mentality,[13] we provide the missing conceptual link between action, judgment, and narration.

Arendt, however, for various purposes has many different views about the role she wants to assign stories. Her unsystematic view has led Arendtian specialists to focus on some of those dimensions without clarifying exactly which function she attaches to them at different moments.[14] It is for this reason that I wish to discuss some of those functions—already mentioned by her scholars—to see the role that stories play in her more particular view of evil and judgment.

If we recall Arendt's judgment that "the spectacle before the spectator—enacted, as it were, for his judgment—is history as a whole," then we can recognize that "the true hero of this spectacle is mankind as a whole."[15] As she realized this to be true, Arendt became a special kind of historian, one that would consider herself closer to poetry than to traditional historians' views.[16] This is why we should begin by studying Arendt's thoughts on stage plays. The link we should establish here is with Kant's ideas about judgment as an aesthetic dimension that entails community practices as products of shared experiences. As Robert Pirro has pointed out, this is where spectators join to configure judgments together.[17] She was not simply interested in conceiving Greek tragedies as narratives that provide us with examples of intense suffering, but also as stories that allow us to put imagination into play and, by deliberating with others, establish a sense of community.[18]

This is the place where Arendt transforms the concept of Kant's concept of the sensus communis as the intersubjective experience of critical thinking. For Arendt this was an important category inspired by Kant's own ideas. It is clear that she was thinking about them when she began her research for a theory of reflective judgment.[19] It is no coincidence that Robert Pirro argues that "to the extent that intuition is felt to originate within rather than from without, aesthetically activated or supported membership would be founded on voluntary commitment, rather than (or, in addition to) being founded on submission, utilitarian calculus, or habit."[20] This interpretation by Pirro allows me to show you why Arendt saw aesthetic pleasure as a strong tie that relates to a community by sharing an intersubjective judgment about the complexities of human life.[21] It also makes us aware that when Arendt chose Kant's aesthetic theory of taste to develop a connection to politics,[22] she was doing something much more complex than purely translating from a theory of aesthetics to a theory of politics. She was thinking about how to build up a sense of community, and how expressive devices helped a great deal to achieve this. The intersubjective feeling that an audience experiences by simultaneously sharing the critical-rational and the emotional sides of a play allows us to build up a sense of community, which comes from the internal and structural conditions of that shared knowledge that only a drama can activate.[23] Stories possess the potential of expressiveness through language.[24] Spectators can see the hidden dimensions of complex human interactions through those very same descriptions that are captured intersubjectively.[25] There is no clear example of something like this happening in the political realm. Thus, Arendt understood the importance of creating a sense of intersubjective judgment about certain human actions through an aesthetic-moral device—its expressive description—which allowed a place for an enlarged mentality as its result.

Judith Shklar, another political theorist who is often compared to Arendt, also feels that novels and stories illustrate the irrationality of human conduct. Without the mediation of rational explanations, stories would not complete their task. They require the skill of novelists—their *judgment*—to illuminate these kinds of actions. "Illumination" is the concept she uses, and it deals with the idea that we make sense of the world when we read stories because they activate understanding "by removing the covers we may have put on the mind's eye."[26] The aesthetic device of "illumination" connects with Arendt's idea of increased knowledge and adds to the quality of our imagination.

Lisa Disch has focused on the idea of spectators learning to develop their critical role when hearing stories. In Disch's view, this role leads to a viewpoint that is captured by the work of the imagination. She argues that "the work of the imagination in visiting is twofold. It distances me from the familiar and takes me to standpoints that are unfamiliar ... The visiting moment fosters a practical equality of concern by multiplying the stories in which I imagine myself to be an actor."[27] From my perspective, however, Disch's interpretation also strengthens the conceptual basis for the use of storytelling because, as she tells us, "storytellers need not withdraw altogether from the condition of plurality in order to practice their art and indeed cannot if they are to have material for it."[28] This conclusion will help me show that Arendt's concept of judgment need not make a separation between the judgment of the spectator and that of the actor.

Arendt makes reference to literary characters and stories from works of fiction as well as biographies. First, she told us the story of Rahel Varnhagen[29] and connected it to what was wrong with her fate as a Jewess and as a woman.[30] This was not simply a historical account of the *salonnière*, it was a political argument about the conditions one would need to become an active participant in dark times. Arendt also employed different narrative devices, as we can see in her work *The Origins of Totalitarianism*.[31] The first time we see this is in her narration of her theory of anti-Semitism through the exploration of the life of Disraeli as well as the Dreyfus Affair. Later on, when she describes the events of the Eichmann trial, she narrates different stories, which she recovers from the trial and the historical data of real people.[32] She also tells the stories of persons she finds morally exemplary, as we see in *Men in Dark Times*.[33] In *The Human Condition* and other works, she describes the nature and meaning of historical events and periods by narrating stories she has recovered to illustrate what she means.[34] Nevertheless, it is only in *The Human Condition* that she thematizes the idea of narratives in a more systematic way.

There are four specific ways in which Arendt establishes her strong connection to narratives: (1) through the literary works themselves and their relationship to her ideas; (2) through her practice as political theorist, which uses narratives as literary devices to illustrate her work; (3) through her use of personal references; and (4) through her concentration on literature, which is linked to concreteness, particularity, and the permanent element of contingency in human affairs. Thus, her self-conscious way of using material in narrative codes gives her the strength to pursue a path other than that of an abstract theory.

Most recently, Robert Pirro has explored Arendt's intense relationship to narratives through her connection to Greek tragedy. He clarifies that Arendt's notion of Greek tragedy came not simply from the German tradition, but from her very particular way of understanding them. Arendt was interested in developing her idea of freedom and linked this concern to the concept of the disclosure of the self by focusing on what individual action means.[35] She develops this theory in *The Human Condition*, where she attaches it to the category of natality, so closely associated with her notion of freedom. What interests me here is the way Arendt's perception connects action to theater and, in particular, to Greek theater. Dana Villa has also focused on this dimension of Arendt's work.[36] The novelty of Pirro's interpretation lies in linking political freedom to tragedy. It is through the recovery of Gotthold Ephraim Lessing's idea of the tragic, and in his understanding of Greek tragedy in particular, that Arendt thematizes political freedom. Indeed, as Pirro argues, "Arendt notes Lessing's Aristotelian approach to evaluating poetry in terms of its effects on the audience," which is why "Lessing's theory of tragedy provides Arendt with a conceptual framework for thinking about the nature of tragic storytelling and its relevance to the crisis of the political that, in her view, afflicted contemporary times."[37] When written tragedies express the depth of human actions by disclosing diverse angles of cruelty and suffering, we find the need to connect to others with this gained knowledge of who we are and why we care for our world. Indeed, in her essay "On Humanity in Dark Times: Thoughts About Lessing," Arendt explains that it is the aesthetic pleasure we feel at a play that makes us capable of an "intensified awareness of reality," and, "not even the knowledge that man may be destroyed by the world detracts from the 'tragic pleasure.'"[38] Arendt argues there that Lessing's aesthetics is different from Aristotle's, for he is trying to strip fear of an escapist aspect in order to save it as a passion, and passion, she believes, is what affects us because we are only affected by other people's sufferings. Furthermore, for Lessing the "essence of poetry was in action,"[39] Lessing coincided with Aristotle in thinking that it was in the representation of a story where one could see the effects that we share with other spectators in relation to our world. Thus, Arendt uses Lessing in order to show us that her concern about the tragic effect is not simply an interest in the aesthetic device but, rather, in how the effects configure ways in which humans begin to sense the need to share the world with others. She also uses Lessing's interest in criticism in order to claim that in representations of theater plays, people learn to exercise their understanding along with their judgment.

Arendt knew that not all stories are able to affect audiences the way she wanted; only some can provide the desired "tragic effect." This "tragic effect" should lead audiences to question why some actions in particular have taken place at all. The ability to understand something as tragic is the result of the ability to recognize that things could have happened differently. Freedom is the underlying concept behind Arendt's idea of judgment. Freedom can also be an essential part of our tragic condition as humans. When we learn from stories in which those actions seem inevitable, we also learn that they could have happened otherwise. The possibility exists, then, to understand that nothing is determined, that there is no causal way of understanding human action. Only when a story can provide this kind of understanding can it trigger sound judgment in the audience. This is where we begin to see why a judgment coming from a spectator can later become a key in choosing a path to any future action. Thus, actor and spectator shift roles with anyone capable of exercising judgment.

Arendt: The Historian, the Storyteller

This long preamble can help us now reconsider that Arendt had an underlying view of storytelling that she never fully expressed—namely, that tragic stories have the capacity to produce reflective judgments. This is its reconstruction. Stories play more than just an important role in Arendt's entire work, as I said before. They are her method. Her stories are important vehicles for understanding, and they are the thematization of human freedom. Arendt also saw an important aesthetic-moral device between certain ways of telling—the poetical disclosive device—and a certain moral way of narrating a story.[40] When she deals with this connection, she not only considers action, natality, and the disclosure of the identity of the actors. She also takes into consideration the ways literary devices can help us capture moral issues that cannot be properly described without the help of expressive, creative, or poetical terms. This connection between aesthetics and moral devices that comes through language produces the greatest effects on an audience when judgment is needed. Language and the methods we use to make our stories communicate certain ideas are put in place in order to seek a specific connection to the audience. This is the reason why Pirro linked Arendt's ideas about storytelling with Greek tragedy.[41] It is also for this reason that, by shaping our notions of what is valuable and what is good, *Men in Dark Times* has been such an important source of inspiration, because of the kind of examples about how stories might have a special place in our cultural background.

The significant conceptual connection between narratives and judgment comes from the critical view that judgments provide an audience. When viewers are able to understand what happens, they can see that thinking and judgment are not only "prophylactic faculties"[42] but also moral critical ways to establish the normative criteria for new courses of action. A theory of reflective judgment can offer the possibility of reconstructing Arendt's experience as a spectator and as an actor during the Eichmann trial.[43] It is not an accident that Arendt begins her description of the Eichmann trial as being situated in an auditorium that resembled a theater.[44] The judges are the actors in the trial,[45] and the spectators[46] (Arendt among them) are those who attend the trial. Arendt is the main narrator of this story. The metaphor of the theater emphasizes the notion of represented actions as the witnesses recount—disclose—their stories to the public. Leora Bilsky has already written about this with much eloquence.[47] With this story, we can begin to solve the riddle about the differences between the role of the spectator versus that of the actor, if we take Arendt as our empirical model. Bilsky, for example, argues that it is possible to think of Arendt's conception of judgment as a dialogic one, by situating it as a dynamic "in between actors and spectators," or as "an ongoing dialogue between actor and spectator."[48] As I argued in my previous book on narratives,[49] actions are thematized as narratives; actors' deeds affect the audience because they capture the *meaning* of these actions.[50] When the past is unmastered, as is usually the case when we face past atrocities, we need to understand what happened and to endure the knowledge that comes from those two processes. Again, in "Humanity in Dark Times: Thoughts about Lessing," she gives us a clear example of what she means by this idea. She explains there that after the First World War it took many years to "master" such a past; indeed, it took thirty years to achieve this through a work of art—Faulkner's *Fable*—because he was capable of bringing the "tragic effect" which makes one capable of accepting the fact that something like that could have happened at all. Only when we are capable of experiencing a second time, are we capable of providing the space of memory as a site of reconstruction; it is a site for critical recollection.

And it is in *Eichmann in Jerusalem* that Arendt becomes conscious of the strategies societies build up in order to initiate the process of understanding and judging. Here, too, spectators could distinguish the negative "example" of Eichmann, during his questionings, from the exemplary actions of the judges, who represented a sense of communal identity. In Arendt's narrative, Eichmann becomes the example of a shallow human being, and "on trial are his deeds, not the sufferings of the Jews, not the German people or mankind, not even anti-Semitism and racism."[51] We, the readers, see the example in the particular moral description of him that she gives. Then we have to form our own judgments. Clearly, Arendt designed the setting for this drama. She was not only the author of the narration but also the most critical spectator in attendance at the Eichmann trial. Arendt is clear about the dangers implicit in this kind of exercise. She knew it could be exploited for political purposes, which would impede it from being a just trial. She was also aware, however, that if successful, the trial could help us strengthen our views of justice. This is why Arendt seemed so critical of some of the measures taken by the Israeli government during the Eichmann trial.

In Arendt's narrative of the trial, Eichmann is the lead actor. He is the perpetrator of the action of this drama, which begins and ends with him. Arendt proves that she is conscious about the strategy of making the trial into a "show-play" for the purpose of defining what was done and how it was done in terms of a new understanding of justice. The story, as she narrates it, shifts from an earlier emphasis on theodicies, or traditional views of perpetrators as monstrous, and focuses instead on the kind of action that Eichmann was capable of taking. "A trial resembles a play," writes Arendt, "in that both begin and end with the doer, not the victim. A show trial needs even more urgently than an ordinary trial a limited and well-defined outline of *what was done, not for what he has caused others to suffer*" (emphasis added).[52] We can also see here that she failed to concentrate on the sufferer; she is more interested in describing the kind of person Eichmann was—his lack of character. The reason Arendt introduced this conceptual shift is that, in court, the deeds of the doer have to "serve the purpose of *illuminating* some aspects of his actions" (emphasis added) as moral violations.[53] The metaphor of the theater highlights the relationship between spectators and actors through the mediating role of the collective exercise of judgment. Let us look closely at the idea that judges are also the actors of this drama.[54]

The most important question was whether the judges were aware that their actions would be taken as an essential element of a critical process of defining a new sense of justice through enabling collective memory. Keep in mind that I have called the critical periods of accountability through trials as transitional periods where justice should be redefined. Eichmann's trial was meant as a well-orchestrated representation and dramatization of a criminal past. This is why the spectators' attendance at the trial allowed them to become a political community. Bilsky highlights that the judges at the Eichmann trial could behave either by following previous written scripts (what Kant would call making a "determinant judgment"),[55] or by finding new resources to produce their own script in accord with the evidence shown at court (which would mean making a reflective judgment).[56] This interpretation makes it clear that legal justice is achieved through the process of disclosive stories presented in a legal court. It is a forum for developing a reflective judgment about international justice because such stories help to frame in broader terms our sense of understanding and responsibility. When judges are able to develop their own scripts to typify a new kind of crime, they provide us with a reflective judgment based on the filters of the paradigm of evil to the paradigm of justice. Because Eichmann's crimes were novel, the judges' task was challenging. After all, they could not rely on traditional legal categories.[57]

Arendt's narrative offers us a new concept of evil through her idea that Eichmann was a banal moral agent.[58] Arendt went against all traditional conceptions of evil. She understood that by focusing exclusively on the doer, she was bringing accountability and moral responsibility to the forum. She also demonstrated that, by focusing on a perpetrator and showing us his lack of conscience, she could offer a description of the means by which totalitarian regimes silence the voice of conscience "by making reality appear behind a wall of *language codes*" (emphasis added).[59] Thus, Arendt's "phenomenology of evil actions," as narrated in her *Eichmann in Jerusalem*, is a reflective judgment. She stepped away from traditional ways of understanding evil and created a new term, *banality*, to disclose the nature of this kind of moral actor—a new type of criminal who is a bureaucrat.[60] There are two sides to her reflective judgment: the moral dimension, with its description of Eichmann's lack of moral consciousness represented as the figure of banality; and the legal dimension, emphasizing the claim that this new type of criminal could not be judged according to the normal standards of criminal justice. In this way, Arendt grasps our need to conceptualize the idea of crimes against humanity as an opening of a new chapter in our understanding of justice. Arendt seeks to highlight this dramatic moment of awareness with her own narrative. On legal grounds, she knew that if these crimes were unprecedented, we would need a new set of concepts for dealing with them. For Arendt, crimes against humanity needed new disclosive terms—a language capable of making us understand that, for the first time, here were crimes committed with the very public intention of erasing from existence (humanity) a large group of human beings. Out of this concrete example she drew the concept that is produced by her reflective judgment.

On the other hand, Bilsky's interpretation strengthens my own when she seeks to explain a way out of Arendt's circular problem concerning the roles of the spectator and the actor. Bilsky interprets them as a dynamic interaction set by the public drama between the spectator and the actor. Arendt personifies the role of the distant and critical spectator, while the role of the actor is to be the judge. After all, they perform actions when they enact laws. Thus, Bilsky's narrative of the drama of the Eichmann trial allows one to interpret reflective judgment as practiced both by actors and spectators simultaneously. Arendt showed that the negative exemplarity that she sought in describing Eichmann's deeds could be possible. She knew that she had to distance herself from Eichmann when judging his actions. Her narration of Eichmann's flaws and his lack of true moral character are evidence of this distance. However, by limiting her role to that of spectator, Arendt confronted another problem: she also had to detach herself from her own community. This position made her an extremely harsh critical observer of the other side. Bilsky argues that this move made Arendt forget her role as an actor "in the Jewish community."[61] Here the condition of impartiality was lost. Arendt gave an accurate account of the existence of the Jewish police in concentration camps, yet she failed to contrast other important questions which impeded sufferers to react against the threat of evil deeds. What she lost was the ability to depict the moral wrongdoing that harms the sense of self and makes persons incapable of reacting against evil. In *The Origins of Totalitarianism*, Arendt saw this type of harm—moral wrongdoing—as the most extreme original condition produced by totalitarian regimes. The act of stripping the humanity from any person is a permanent wrong.[62] Because she did not introduce these kinds of moral disclosive descriptions about the roles of the sufferers, Arendt lost the needed conceptual connection between perpetrator and sufferer in an evil interaction. Thus, she seemed to condemn the sufferers' inability to react and did not create an account to describe the ways in which crimes harm the sufferers at extreme levels. Primo Levi gives us a better perspective with his narratives about the complex interaction between doer and sufferer. Bilsky argues that Arendt failed to meet the challenge of becoming simultaneously a spectator and an actor in this drama. Indeed, "she fails to practice *enlarged mentality* in relation to her own spectators, [and] in particular, the Jewish victims. Second, anxious to render an 'objective' judgment, she seems to forget her own role as an actor in the Jewish community."[63] In order to avoid this problem, Arendt would also have to present a moral account from the point of view of the victims. Unfortunately, she chose to leave out her main arguments about them in this story. This is why many of her critics focused on the negative descriptions she gave of the victims and on the limited space she allowed herself to explain the complexity of the victims' behavior. In this way, Arendt forgot her own lesson, "that she herself is a spectator among spectators and that her judgment will be judged by others not only for what it says but also to disclose who she is."[64] More importantly, by using such a strong critical term to define the perpetrator's lack of moral character in the subtitle of her book, she seems to have made a final judgment of the whole historical event. Thus, her disclosive term became obscured.

In failing to develop a dynamic movement of her reflective judgment, which could have allowed Arendt to shift back and forth between her roles as spectator and actor, she seemed to prioritize only the role of the spectator.[65] Furthermore, without these kinds of dynamic shifts, she could not thematize both sides of evil actions—that is, of the sufferer and of the doer. Therefore, in my theory of evil we cannot dispense with either side.

Arendt made one last mistake, which I have already analyzed elsewhere:[66] she was not able to clarify her own method once the polemics started. One of her greatest achievements was that she set the debate in motion for the public sphere. She made many conceptual mistakes, however, when narrating what she was trying to accomplish. It is only after we understand the entire discussion that came afterward that we realize how much she had already achieved. Arendt's most original idea in her use of Eichmann's case was to make him a particular negative example.[67] With this move, she made it possible to connect her narration to judgment and to use the metaphor of the theater when she attended the trial as if it was a play where past actions were revised by the world community. Her work *Eichmann in Jerusalem* is a narration that is linked to her judgment, and this judgment has become a hallmark to be debated by future generations because she set a process of debate and reflexivity into motion. It was an act of participation that depended on its public nature. It entailed a sense of responsibility to the community, and it is for this reason that Arendt felt Kant best understood why a shared aesthetic sense of community can be the result of the way we experience the idea of bonding through our collective judgments while attending an aesthetic-moral drama.

CHAPTER 3

Reflective Judgment and the Moral Imagination

Central to the moral imagination is seeing what is humanly important.
—*Jonathan Glover, Humanity*

Stories perform many functions for those who read them and those who write them. In this sense, we should first focus on what makes a story an important model for reflective judgment. I will argue that processes of aesthetic apprehension are created by the work of the productive imagination of some moral experiences. This makes stories important vehicles of reflective judgments. Through their written expression, moral stories have demonstrated that, in spite of many theorists' skepticism, they capture the "ineffable" characteristics of evil actions.[1] In works of fiction as well as in historical stories about evil acts, the "ineffable" seems to have found many different and variegated ways that are expressed communicatively due to the interrelationship between the aesthetic and moral spheres. As Albrecht Wellmer has persuasively argued, even though "there is an unbridgeable gulf between what is meant and what is said-that is precisely what the word "ineffable" means. But we do know of a paradigm in which this gulf is closed in that it is, so to speak, transferred to the interior of the image, and the *claim* to be saying something with the image disappears." This is where the disclosive dimension of "the aesthetic image" presents itself.[2] The interweaving of the way language finds its moral expression by reconfiguring itself into new metaphors and tropes, and the way those disclosive images in stories provide new methods for moral understanding,[3] constitutes the horizon of my theory of reflective judgment. My thesis proposes that stories can create these links between language and moral understandings through the work of the productive imagination understood as disclosive imagination.

In order to explain what I mean by "disclosive imagination," I must first address Kant's original idea. Kant was the first to consider this category aesthetic. I would like to bring this interconnection to your attention to ask why we humans, seeking to morally interpret our historical experiences from the past to configure a new understanding of our present, need to bridge a conceptual link between moral meanings coming from suffering—i.e., experiencing cruelty—into what I have already called in the first chapter "learning from catastrophes." The efforts to reach a new and deeper understanding of such experiences are perceived by the sufferers, and by the readers, as the realm of the "ineffable" translated now as the most salient characteristics—disclosive images—of evil deeds appropriately captured by those written stories.

I have examined Arendt's notion of storytelling. I believe that her underdeveloped notion of "storytelling" can be connected to a moral frame through which we can reflect on the meanings of evil actions. I must first address the need to describe the moral framework being considered here, for stories alone cannot provide such a reflective stance. There are stories of victims and perpetrators, as well as stories about persons who seek to configure a tale or myth of an exclusionary group that justifies violence against others because of the way those others have treated them in the past. It is important to stress that stories can only provide a limited moral understanding of the phenomena of evil. They are justified by a claim of validity—an illocutionary force—which is a universal recognition of their moral worth in helping us understand the "moral wrongs" of human experiences. This is because those stories strive to present the ways in which we humans have excluded others from being considered fellow humans. Otherwise, the term *evil* could be used to describe anything we hate, dislike, or regret. Stories can lead to distortions, exclusions, and hatred. Therefore, in order to be useful within the context of my theory, a purely aesthetic tale cannot capture the ineffable of human cruelty. In order to do so it must provide a filter through the historical reconstruction of its moral frame in which the moral lesson from past actions of suffering and hatred demonstrates how and why we humans have harmed others whom we excluded from the realm of humanity. What we might consider here, then, is that not all stories can teach us something morally valuable about wrongdoing, cruelty, and hatred—only stories that disclose a specific connection between the moral to the aesthetic imagination (capturing the features of the ineffable) and offer a universalistic claim which can describe the meaning of "moral wrongdoings." The paradigm of evil can help us clarify why, by using concepts such as "humanity" understood as a "moral category," we can recover the ineffable into a moral understanding of what has happened. It is only through this filter that we can obtain moral knowledge about ourselves—about our frailties and flaws. This dimension of evil, which Kant named the expression of our "wicked heart," is the realm of the paradigm of evil. It is possible to trace those experiences of our actions by coming to terms with the way the productive view of moral imagination links itself to a historical and moral interpretation by providing us with the features of its "exemplarity" reconstructed in our judgment of the story. This can lead us to a conscious understanding of moral wrongs, which would in turn allow us to begin a process of moral *Ausbildung*. The act of exercising moral judgment was, for Arendt, the only way to stand before those actions and interpret them as our ways of coping with our darkest sides and learn from this stage of consciousness about the human cruelty captured by those tales. I will call it a "moral reflective stage." To understand why we are capable of moral wrongdoing against other humans, we must enter into a reflective stage on the subject of evil. This is the reason Arendt used storytelling in her postmetaphysical theory of evil. It is only possible to speak of the connection between stories and their moral framework with the help of reflective judgment. In order to develop this interconnection, however, I should first explain my conceptual tools. We need to understand that the interpretation and the structural critical organization of historical events must be confronted with the help of a moral analysis that can only be provided by collective efforts to frame our stories in the public sphere. They can provide or help us construct an imaginative expression as seen in our reconstructive view of moral harms through the exercise of reflective judgment.

I would like to focus on the need to develop a theory of reflective judgment by entering the specific moral and aesthetic interconnections within the task of interpreting "evil actions" as a hermeneutical task of understanding our moral capacities and our moral flaws. In order to do so, I must first develop a specific theoretical connection to Kant in order to illustrate better the idea of moral imagination, which is basic to a theory of reflective judgment.

Reframing the Kantian Legacy of Reflective Judgment Through the Use of the Concept of Moral Imagination

It is already known that Kant and Arendt were thinking in very different ways about reflective judgment as a tool for moral knowledge. The fact that Arendt chose Kant's theory of judgment must not be trivialized, even if we assume that she used it in a rather creative, unorthodox sense. We must recall a few important theoretical aspects of Kant's theory so we can see the clear connections that led Arendt to view this as fruitful territory in which to build her own concept of judgment.

Kant connected the aesthetic and moral dimensions by relating his idea of the aesthetic imagination (and taste) to the moral imagination (and to moral feelings), and from the latter to a subsequent stage. There were plenty of reasons to do so, as various experts on the work of Kant have demonstrated. Henry Allison, for example, has even claimed that Kant's theory of reflective judgment is part and parcel to his concept of radical evil. Key to this understanding is the fact that Kant had conceptually linked taste to the experience of beauty and morality.[4]

Kant laid out one of the best-known dimensions of this interesting connection with his idea of "taste," which entailed an intersubjective capacity[5] that we all have in common and that allowed for a public discourse.[6] The second was his idea of "*sensus communis*" or common sense, which again is related to some specific kind of knowledge that we are all capable of exercising and sharing. The most important category, however, is Kant's idea of our productive capacity for imagination. Indeed, as Allison has well argued,

> the imagination in its freedom (from the laws of association) links the thought of something supersensible with a wealth of sensible representations or images, which does not amount to a logical expansion of the concept (through additional predicates), but does constitute an "aesthetic expansion" [a *disclosure*], through the interconnection of the core concept (say, that of God or eternity) with these sensible representations that call to mind related or associated thoughts. These, in turn, may be said to "prompt much thought" (presumably concerning the concept in question), and therefore lead[s] to an expansion of the mind, albeit in an indeterminate manner.[7]

Kant used the idea that supplementary representations which are involved in the aesthetic expansion can lead not only to analogies but also to differences from the logical predicates that result from cognitive, synthetic judgments. Kant wanted to explain why a specific type of reflection that involves a transition from the sensible to the supersensible, or as Allison puts it, "the transition effected through reflection on the beautiful is not itself a transition to morality," although "it does facilitate that transition."[8] Kant, therefore, understood that this process of reflection both distances one from all sensuous sides of the self, while at the same time allowing oneself to be thought of as part of a community, that is, "as a member of an ideal community subject to a universally valid norm."[9] In this way, the concept of imagination was connected to the concept of taste as *sensus communis*. The two categories together configured the centerpieces of his theory of the universalistic features of the judgments of taste.

Richard Kearney, who has focused extensively on the concept of imagination, claims that in modernity, mostly because of Kant, the paradigm of productive imagination replaced the paradigm of mimetic imagination.[10] Kant's radical interpretation of the creative powers of imagination produced a Copernican revolution. Kant's efforts replaced the idea that imagination is only reproductive or mimetic because he understood that imagination is one of the very sources of knowledge.[11] It is an active faculty (*Einbildungskaft*). And if imagination possesses rules, these rules are self-imposed. Furthermore, Kant believed that judgments of taste produced by the productive imagination can be made universal because of its "universal communicability."[12] The imagination not only produces its own laws, but rather, it produces knowledge.[13]

On the other hand, there are several important aspects related to my goal of further developing Kant's insights on the concept of moral imagination for my own theory of reflective judgments. Before focusing on Kant's ideas, I must first clarify that while Kant thought of the relationship between aesthetics and morality in terms of positive exemplarity, I still need to develop a view in which exemplarity can be considered in its negative sense. According to Kant, aesthetic ideas would be translated into the moral realm by educating the moral soul. His concept of exemplarity was based on the idea of beauty as perfection. My theory of reflective judgment, however, presents the idea that art can provide us with a negative version of the concept of exemplarity. The link here is through the concept of imagination. Imagination will be understood not only as the power to convey images but also as the power to produce emergent moral meanings in language. Imagination will be conceived in this paradigm as a dimension of disclosive language. In order to strengthen my thesis, I will use the example of two different theories—one provided by Rudolf Makkreel and another by Paul Ricoeur—based on the idea that reflective judgments can be conceptualized as processes of linguistic innovation and that the exemplarity needed can come out of such a linguistic paradigm.

We can return now to Kant's theory of reflective judgment. In Kant's view, the first characteristic of reflective judgment is that it allows us to draw fields of concepts and to seek a connection of those concepts into a leading path where wide problematic views are grouped into a single unity.[14] Indeed, as Peter Strawson argues, Kant "declares the schema to be a product of, and also a rule for, the imagination, in accordance with which, and by means of which alone, the imagination can connect the particular image or the particular object with the general concept under which it falls."[15] The second aspect shows how the empirical relates to the conceptual in Kant's own theory of moral judgment.[16] And third, we have Kant's way of first introducing two different kinds of judgments, then attributing reflective judgment within a wider territory in order to solve all kinds of problems.[17] A fourth element, and perhaps the most relevant for my theory, is the idea that Kant conceptualized the intersubjective validity of aesthetic judgment as "exemplary ... because everyone ought to give the object in question his approval and follow suit in describing it as beautiful."[18] It was here that Kant linked judgment to creating a sense of a *community*. In this respect, the universality of an aesthetic judgment is its imputability or the acceptability of all judges or subjects. Ultimately, the determining ground of all aesthetic judgment lies in the concept of the "substrate of humanity," which is tied to the idea of *sensus communis*. These four elements of Kant's own theory are important in further developing my concept of reflective judgment. In order to do so, however, we must transform Kant's idea of exemplarity to a negative one.

For now, it is sufficient to say that even if we consider Kant's ideas to be incapable of providing us with the concept of negative exemplarity, it is possible to rework his views if I transform their basis. Take, for example, the concept of the sublime.[19] If I substitute the idea of the beautiful with the idea of the sublime, I might allow exemplarity to confront its negative aspects.[20] The sublime and the beautiful differ essentially in that the sublime stimulates awe and admiration, whereas beauty triggers joy and pleasure (78). The sublime is not necessarily linked with the beautiful, and Kant sees it as something superior in quality (80–81). The sublime is divided into three kinds: the terrifying, the noble, and the splendid. Most interestingly, however, is that Kant thought about the sublime not only as an aesthetic category, but as a human feature—a component of the person (87). The feeling of the sublime is complex. In his *Critique of Judgment*, Kant further explains that the sublime "proves that the mind has a power of surpassing any standard of sense."[21] He also claims that the feeling of the sublime makes "the mind feel agitated" (115), not restful in contemplation (as it did with beauty). It is an agitation that rapidly alternates between "repulsion from, and attraction to, one and the same object" (115). This is also a good definition of the ineffable. Here, the imagination is afraid of losing itself and falling into an "abyss" (115). Kant says that with the sublime, reason and imagination work "by their conflict, namely, to a feeling that we have of a pure and independent reason, or a power for estimating magnitude, shows superiority [which] cannot be made intuitable by anything other than the inadequacy of that power which in exhibiting magnitudes (of sensible objects) is itself unbounded" (116). Again, what comes to mind here is the idea of the *ineffable* and how certain descriptions in language might allow us to understand what seems incomprehensible. Earlier, Kant portrayed three versions of the sublime. I suggest that we focus on the idea that the sublime can produce a terrifying feeling. In this way, we can rescue Kant's concept of the sublime to expand my aesthetic notion of exemplarity into a negative one.[22]

We need to conceptualize "evil" as a "field of problems," and understand that "evil actions" can be conceptualized as particulars related in a nondeductive way to our universal understanding of moral wrongs. With most complex actions where humans have destroyed other humans, it is difficult to conceptualize the different empirical and cultural actions of destruction, which in themselves seem to be definable only with the term "ineffable." To frame our collective understanding of human cruelty exercised against other humans, we must employ intersubjective standards of moral judgment. A similar argument has been developed by Peter F. Strawson in his work "Freedom and Resentment," where he claims that imagination can be linked to "our power to recognize different (and sometimes very different) particular objects falling under the same general concept."[23] It is only through specific uses of language in the recovering of those experiences that we are allowed to reenter the territory of understanding the inexplicable and frame it into a new moral perspective. James E. Young, for example, has eloquently argued that "writers grew increasingly frustrated and dissatisfied with their traditional lexicon of destruction" after the Holocaust. Young argues, however, that "they became more likely to figure the most horrible events not in terms of the ancient past but in the tropes of their current disaster."[24] The use of language provided a new moral framework and, with it, a new understanding of the unprecedented historical destruction.

Let us return to Kant's ideas so that we can connect the previous paragraph to Kant's views. Since Kant developed his theory of reflective judgment in his *Critique of Judgment*, he claimed that "judgments of taste" were of a more general type, which he called "reflective judgments." The reason for this connection, as Paul Guyer has argued, is that his theory of reflective judgments contains the foundations for his theory of taste because it leads to the idea of the "harmony of the imagination and understanding" and "provides an important clue to its interpretation."[25] That is the reason Kant seemed to be pointing out the importance of imagination as the basic mediating function between sensibility and intellect. By focusing on the role of imagination, which Kant was so interested in elucidating, he intended to show its connection to the idea of "free-play," that is, to put it in Kantian terms—that reflective judgment "schematizes without a concept." Kant's basic idea was that judgment is the "capacity for the subsumption of the particular under the universal." For Kant, the principles of judgment draw a "territory," in other words, "a field of objects that apply without being legislative." When differentiating between determinant judgments and reflective judgments, Kant argued that the former refers to our capacity to apply concepts already given to appropriate particulars, whereas the latter is our "capacity for reflecting on a given representation according to a certain principle, to produce a possible concept." To exercise reflective judgment seems to be a capacity that goes beyond the comparison and combination of given representations. Furthermore, reflective judgment puts the imagination in the lead role, while creating its own ideas to organize our experience as if it was a purposive system. As Rudolf A. Makkreel has argued, "by a transcendental principle of reflective judgment," Kant draws a principle of constitutive and regulative "applications" of the imagination.[26] The imagination's function, however, becomes creative, for Kant now thought of the imagination as a productive tool that "mediates between understanding and sense to apply the transcendental unity of consciousness to 'all objects of possible experience' " (29). The novel idea is that

Kant believes we can only achieve a productive synthesis of the imagination by combining understanding and sensibility.

Revising Makkree's Novel Interpretation of Kant's Legacy

Makkreel's interpretation of Kant is useful for my purposes because he takes Kant's idea of productive imagination to highlight the need for a concept of interpretation. First, Makkreel claims that Kant's concept of distinguishing epistemology from psychology conceived "the contents of consciousness in terms of formal mathematical relations that are constitutive of intersubjective experience" (38). Makkreel adds that what allowed Kant to add a "conventional linguistic dimension to epistemology," and thus to think of imagination as assuming "a quasi-linguistic role" (38), was the fact that he thought of this formal analysis of consciousness. With this twist, Makkreel concludes that the so-called "synthesis of apprehension" runs through "particular words to project an indeterminate whole," and then it is determined "by the more deliberate synthesis of reproduction and recognition" (39). The operation that Makkreel has displayed with his interpretation entails that there is a crucial dimension added to Kant's original idea, namely, that by introducing the idea of the "metaphor of reading" he has introduced the idea of "meaning" (39), which allows us to transform reflective judgment into a specific kind of interpretation. If this is correct, and I assume it is, I can use the idea that stories provide a field of comparative situations and widen our understanding of evil by introducing new meanings of moral wrongs. Furthermore, only stories can disclose our historical understandings of reconstructions of how we distinguish moral wrongs from evil actions. James E. Young, for example, describes Elie Wiesel's appropriation of biblical stories as a novel way of conceptualizing evil. Through "such a rereading informed by the Holocaust can he [Wiesel] find in Cain and Abel the 'first genocide.'"[27] For Young, Wiesel must first understand the particulars of the legend, and then inform his "own experience" by introducing a creative term that gives the past myth a renewed meaning in light of our present understanding of the word *genocide*. Young, in fact, shows us that Wiesel produced a reflective judgment by linking the old biblical tale of Cain and Abel. It is by reconfiguring the meaning of the word *genocide* in light of Wiesel's own experience of the Holocaust that he was capable of recovering an ancient story to give new insight into moral wrongdoing. Wiesel's exercise of reflective judgment illustrates the mediating role of the productive imagination that took the form of a linguistic innovation. There was also a connection between past and present that led him to a specification of an evil image—genocide—rather than a simple exercise of schematizing.

This is why it is important to recall that, according to Kant, reflective judgment might be concerned with certain relationships between objects which are not immediately evident in the pure or empirical concepts applicable to them. This notion of judgment allows us to stress the idea that imagination plays an important role in relating a field of concepts. It also highlights the imagination's role in relating and connecting to understanding, as they are the two basic categories needed for a theory of hermeneutic interpretation. Furthermore, reflective judgment proceeds "tectonically," to use Makkreel's geological metaphor, or, if we use Wittgenstein's idea of family resemblances, we might say that by linking different historical experiences, we can use a concept that provides us with an understanding of why it isn't only the similarities shared by those experiences of evil actions that allow us to understand their specificities, but also that the differences make us conceive of new meanings with which to interpret past moral wrongs. The idea of moral imagination as productive and disclosive—that is, the connection between the aesthetic and the moral realms—is possible because the mind seeks to work through the experience of the "ineffable" regarding human behavior. Through a process of free association between our sensibility and imagination, we can create a reinterpretation of past experiences in light of present ones by symbolically articulating old meanings into new ways of describing present understandings. Thus, the aesthetic dimension unites itself to the moral realm through the use of the disclosive imagination. This is because it develops its own logic to complete the understanding of a singular event by developing a connection to past experiences—to ancient stories—and to the idea of an intersubjective recognition of moral wrongs. Once we connect those past experiences with new ones, we can unfold new meanings for our present experience through the use of new words, new metaphors, and new tropes. Our judgments describe the ways in which evil actions are framed and how we comprehend them through a collective historical reconstruction of the past and the present.

We are now in a position to adjust some of Kant's insights for my own theory of reflective judgment. I will use the term *illocutionary force* to distinguish the reflective moment when the connection between the linguistic expression or symbolic articulation relates to the moral frame through the work of productive disclosive imagination and to produce an "exemplary" story of evil. This brings to light specific knowledge from the moral content of the story tied to its expressive, disclosive device.

On the other hand, Makkreel, who has argued in favor of using Kant's theory of reflective judgment as a hermeneutic theory, allows us to connect Kant to Arendt by relating "Kant's analysis of reflective judgment to characterize the hermeneutics of facticity of Wilhelm Dilthey and Heidegger where the concern is to understand the individuality and historicity of the particulars of experience" (113). The most interesting feature of this interpretation connects Kant's concept of aesthetic ideas to the transformative processes led by the potential of our imagination. This is why the imagination can change our experience, and why the most important insights provided by stories about evil become such vital tools for reflective judgment. Aesthetic ideas can surpass and transform our experiences when we share them publicly. They can enlarge our given concepts. Furthermore, aesthetic ideas can become tools of interpretation because they help us find forms of expression, not by following certain rules but by free association in the imagination as it recaptures our experiences of suffering. As Makkreel argues, "aesthetic ideas can add a moral dimension to the meaning of experience" (122). Makkreel's interpretation is in agreement with Allison's views on Kant's theory of reflective judgment. Makkreel claims, as Allison did before, that it is precisely because of "the expressions of aesthetic ideas to the symbolic presentation of moral ideas of reason" that Kant related his theory of reflective judgment to the model of aesthetic apprehension.

We are now in a position to go back to our discussion at the beginning of this chapter. I might say that aesthetic ideas challenge the fact that certain experiences are not capable of being translated to words. It is through the creative capacities of the creator, the artist, or the "genius" that we can understand something that seemed impossible to communicate through other means than its own expressive ones. When reading a text—a novel, a poem, or even a historical narrative—the ineffable is communicated by expressive disclosive means.[28] Kant's idea of genius is, therefore, necessary in order to understand why we can capture the ineffable within an aesthetic expression. Genius, for Kant, expresses the "ineffable state of mind by a certain representation" and "makes it universally communicable" (C3, §49, 161). Makkreel's interpretation of Kant has provided us with clues for a hermeneutic approach that appeals to this connection between aesthetic ideas and the work of the productive imagination. It is here that the aesthetic imagination allows us to articulate our moral imagination into what I have called the "disclosive imagination" (and the moral feelings attached to this productive center). Imagination functions as a "mode of *Ausbildung*," Makkreel argues, and it "produces an aesthetic idea that gives an intuitive approximation of the totality of reason" (123). Imagination functions as a process analogous to the symbolic formation "of the rational idea" as expressed in "its symbolic or linguistic analogue" (123). My theory of reflective judgment stresses, then, that we can recover Kant's use of the concept of imagination in its function of expressive language as key to understanding how language connects the spaces of the ineffable to its moral dimensions by creating different moral meanings of past events. Thus, *representations of our experiences of evil* are possible, and we can provide multiple examples of stories that have achieved the unthinkable, as for example, Primo Levi's experience in Auschwitz.

In relating judgment and hermeneutical interpretation, Makkreel makes another significant contribution to my theory, which is helpful in furthering our understanding of reflective judgment. He suggests that when Kant discussed the concept of the "aesthetic normal idea," he understood that the role of the imagination was to read between the lines of the ordinary experience and produce archetypes (C3, §17, 71). Arendt, too, used those archetypes to consider important events in her life. Makkreel argues that archetypes appear as "the image of the whole race, which hovers between variously different intuitions of individuals" (V, 234ff.). In a similar way, Northrop Frye describes "archetypes [as] associative clusters" that "differ from signs in being complex variables." The "complex is often a larger number of specific learned associations which are communicable because of a large number of people in a given culture [that] happen to be familiar with them."[29] It is interesting to use Frye's notion of archetypes, along with those envisaged by Kant, when thinking about "the aesthetic normal idea" and its relationship to individuals and intersubjectivity. The plots of stories are derived precisely from those figures—images of archetypes—that relate to everyone's intuitions and have played a major role in narrating our experiences of evil since ancient times. Greek tragedies have been the subject of philosophical, literary, and psychological research because of the universal and explanatory powers of archetypes.[30] The interesting connection here, however, is provided by the important consciousness of many specialists who have highlighted the particular characteristics of the symbols that capture the "ineffable" through the production of archetypes. This is why Frye claims that "the symbol may be best called the image."[31] Recall that Wellmer also referred to the image in the citation I used at the beginning of the chapter to explain why the ineffable is best captured by an aesthetic image. Young's study of Holocaust writers, for example, bases its conclusions about the enlightening ways in which these authors express themselves and their experiences on their use of Jewish archetypes as a reflective technique. Thus, Young claims, "neither Wiesel's nor [Tadeuz] Borowski's case" made "a calculated effort to find equivalence between past and present stories, but rather only the reflexive equivalence created once they review antiquity through eyes now informed by new experiences that are so strong as to overwhelm and displace other figures" and have produced a new impact in our moral understanding. Experiences, stories, and texts about ancient times remain the same in themselves, but it is in the symbolic recovery of our particular present that we infuse those stories with new meaning. In Young's words, "Their echoes, causes and effects, and their significance all changed with the addition of new experiences in the lives of these texts' interpreters."[32]

The Disclosive Imagination

In a similar manner, Paul Ricoeur has used the idea of disclosive imagination with his idea of the hermeneutical imagination. In his view, the role of productive imagination emerges with the idea of how we connect new meanings to our understandings. Imagination becomes a dimension of language. Richard Kearney has drawn attention to Ricoeur's important contribution to the idea of imagination, particularly when he conceptualized imagination "as an indispensable agent in the creation of meaning in and through language."[33] Paul Ricoeur has called this process "semantic innovation." In fact, for Ricoeur, it is only because hermeneutics has the power of "deciphering" meanings that imagination acquires the role of transforming meanings into new ones. His hermeneutics attest to the notion that imagination is primarily verbal, and this is why a verbal metaphor in poetry can be considered exemplary of the idea of productive imagination.[34]

Kant's old schematization acquires a new complexity in this view, for Ricoeur develops his concept of semantic innovation by linking semantic fields not considered identical. It is a "semantic shock," produced by these two dissimilar semantic fields, that allows the creation of a new meaning. By reconciling opposing meanings, we can forge an unprecedented semantic understanding. With this hermeneutical move, Ricoeur provides us with a disclosive view of language, which is much closer to Arendt's views of reflective judgment. Ricoeur is able to capture the important links between Kant's productive imagination and connect it to his own semantic clashes between dissimilar meanings. Thus, language allows Ricoeur to set forth a new course for productive imagination. For my idea of reflective judgment, the concept of disclosive imagination can be accepted as an important tool that responds to a demand for novel meaning, while assessing moral wrongs that need emergent realities to be described in different disclosive ways. When Ricoeur allows the possibility of understanding imagination in its linguistic paradigm, he also lets us visualize the disclosive capacities of linguistic imagination. Such an imagination opens up innovative moral worlds. By providing original meanings of moral wrongs, this understanding can allow us to project different modes of action. Ricoeur's paradigm of semantic innovation provides us with an important view of moral transformation.

In *The Poetics of Imagining*, Richard Kearney focuses on Paul Ricoeur's important contribution to the systematization of Kant's original idea of productive imagination. According to Kearney's study, Ricoeur provided us with four concepts of productive imagination that are worth careful examination.[35] Kearney classified them as the symbolic imagination, the oneiric imagination, the poetic imagination, and the social imagination. The first, *symbolic imagination*, deals with the power of archetypes. Myths like those of Prometheus or Adam enable us "to disclose the symbolic relation" of human subjects to meanings.[36] Ricoeur gives us an understanding of myths as ways of exploring human meanings and the creative power of imagination in providing us with symbolic significance that can be applied to our lives. Here, symbolic imagination is also linguistic imagination. Its expressiveness conceives language as providing us with "double meanings." These double meanings are explored through the concept of myth. Ricoeur chooses the strategy to dissociate myth from gnosis (a strategy similar to that of Kant himself when allowing imagination to acquire the status of knowledge by creating its own rules). Only by separating myth from gnosis can Ricoeur lead us to the concept that symbolic order "opens up and discloses a dimension of experience that, without it, would remain close and hidden."[37] Ricoeur connects the notion of the symbolic order to narrations because "what is essential to us" now "is to understand why that consciousness, structured lower narration, any fable or legend, nevertheless breaks out into language under the form of narration," and why, in order to understand it, "we shall follow the opposite course from the pre-narrative consciousness to the mythical narration, where we will discover the 'enigma of the symbolic function of myths.'"[38] Myths are expressions of language, and, at the same time, they take the form of symbols. It is precisely for this reason that the power of the symbolic opens up the field of hermeneutics to the important task of thematizing evil. Evil can be seen as a primary source of our historical understanding of symbols. Ricoeur argues, for example, that in "imagining monstrous defilements in legendary criminals, poets opened the way to a symbolic of impurity."[39] With Ricoeur's recovery of symbolism, then, we even become capable of understanding the origins of a pessimistic anthropology that saw humans mysteriously linked to evildoing, and that their stories are tragic accounts of their inevitability.[40]

With the second type of imagination, which Kearney calls *oneiric*, Ricoeur establishes important connections between his hermeneutical position and the studies of the unconscious based on psychoanalysis. Freud and Jung become his partners in dialogue. Ricoeur is capable of providing us with an intepretation of the psychic function of the imagination and its power to create symbolic meanings.[41] Psychic life unfolds its expressivity through language. The cosmos and the psyche are one and the same. Ricoeur explores Freud's theories through his hermeneutic view and sees psychoanalysis as also needing its own narrative interpretation. Dreams are like myths and poems—they possess double meanings. Dreams need to be told as narratives, and in their need to be told we revisit the importance of telling them—of the power of recounting our own tales. Ricoeur has the advantage of understanding that images are not only about disclosure but also about *concealment*. As Kearney reveals, "the work of dream images provides ample evidence of the fact that the symbolic levels of sense are far more complex and oblique than the traditional models of analogy or allegory would allow."[42]

Ricoeur searches for a critical hermeneutic interpretation of psychoanalysis that combines a hermeneutics of suspicion with one of affirmation. Ricoeur focuses on our ways of disguising truth and of confronting the fact that meaning can emerge from self-disclosive devices provided by dream images. Ricoeur even discovers that Freud developed a cultural interpretation of the death instinct because "culture now represents the interests of Eros against myself, the center of deathly egoism; and it uses my own self-violence to bring to naught my violence against others."[43] By critically targeting the problems of psychoanalysis, Ricoeur can give us an extended view of symbolic meanings and of our need to unfold their layers of meanings through past and present. At this level, we find that the oneiric imagination possesses a symbolic scale similar to that in art, where we see the possibility for language disclosure, distortion, and revelation. He makes us aware that psychoanalysis can be seen as a hermeneutics that can map the way symbols involve a development of individuals and societies, as well as how their use of symbols discloses or disguises, projects or suppresses, our moral and psychic trajectories.

Poetic imagination is the most significant dimension of productive imagination. It is here that Ricoeur connects himself closely to a systematic view of imagination. Within its poetic function, language is always in the process of evolving. It creates and re-creates meanings. In his most accomplished work, *Time and Narrative*,[44] which I have analyzed and referred to elsewhere,[45] Ricoeur explores the power of narrative and the way storytelling provides us with more than just meanings—it incorporates us into the very process of understanding ourselves. In this stage, we see clearly that Ricoeur's idea of imagination is a semantic theory that links itself to his Kantian roots. As Kearney says, "treated as a schema, the image presents a verbal dimension," because instead of becoming the "gathering point of" perceptions, it situates itself as the place where different meanings "emerge."[46] The metaphor works through schematization. Just as Kant had previously thought of a schema, Ricoeur puts forth the same idea. Instead of compiling the similarities of semantic pertinence, however, we dismantle them through the networks of other semantic fields by the imaginative power to elicit shock. This violence is generated by contradictory methods such as the example of the metaphorical use of seeing x as y. Thus, the metaphoric function of the imagination exerts its power by grasping identity through differences. Schematizing here means that we set our disclosive imagination to produce figurative meanings from an interplay between identity and difference. The operation does not end here. Rather, as

Ricoeur acknowledges, images are needed and can only be provided with an account of the way verbal imagination is connected to the idea of disclosure. "Seeing-as" is the "only sensible key of poetic imagination," for it contains its "ground, foundation," and even its process of "resemblance." As Kearney argues, "Ricoeur can conclude that seeing-as plays the role of the schema, which unites the empty concept and the blind impression."[47] By grasping the most important aspect of Heidegger's view of language, in which it becomes the house of being, Ricoeur claims that the metaphorical imagination produces new meanings centered around the idea that "semantic innovation" opens up our worlds. We find ourselves becoming new beings only when we begin to narrate ourselves. We have reached the level at which the power of emplotment is our power of self-creation. Just as we gained our own historicity and the power to begin anew, with the power of our imagination, we also insert ourselves into other persons' narratives. Schematizing is then understood as the capacity of our imagination to provide us with our own narratives, for as Kearney well realizes, "the narrative act of emplotment, which configures a manifold into a synthesis, enacts what Kant had defined as the productive power of transcendental imagination."[48]

Finally, we arrive at the level of the *social imagination*. Ricoeur makes a new synthesis of all the other ideas of imagination, which can now crystallize at the level of the shared sociopolitical "*imaginaire*." We find here the place of utopia as well as the place of ideologies. We must confront tradition and innovation, or better, continuity and transformation. Memory and recollection play significant roles in this social space. Our collective imagination is again a script to be filled with our tales. It is where we must confront the critical ideas of who we are and where we want to go. The issue is not only about our past and our future, but about transformation or forgetting ourselves. Confronted with this dilemma, we again need Kant's idea of schematization. We must aim to build up our social imagination as a process of establishing a dialogue between ideology and utopia. By making choices, we emerge with the strong characteristics of our moral selves.

I can now conclude that Kant provided us with an important step for a moral theory of reflective judgment. He conceived of judgment as the capacity to bring together universals and particulars through the joint efforts of our moral understanding and our productive imagination. With his theory of taste, he also provided us with the means to judge, through an open understanding, our moral feelings provided by the free association of our imaginations rather than the conceptual knowledge restricted by rules that determinant judgments need to follow. The concepts of communicability and of *sensus communis* allowed him to set the groundwork for the "ineffable," captured only by a complex process between the aesthetic and moral realms—which are fused in the concept of disclosive imagination—now linked to a collective idea of intersubjective judgment. Finally, with the help of two very important interpretative theories—those of Makkreel and of Ricoeur—based on Kant's ideas of the productive imagination, I have given sufficient evidence to regard Kant's legacy as a good point of departure for my renovated version of a theory of reflective judgment.

Coda: Imagination and Representation

"If We Remain Silent about the Holocaust, the SS Have Won"
—Emmanuel Levinas

We have seen in the first chapter that mythology's representation of evil came from the Greeks in order to explain the origins of the cosmos. They offered us plots in which they represented evil as monstrous. I concluded that mythological dramas from ancient Greece represented the ideas about moral choice as inextricably linked to cosmological cycles of fate and destiny. They represented evil as a force that predetermined human action.

In biblical narratives, we see the representations of evil that focused either on suffering evil (the story of Job) or in doing evil (the story of Cain and Abel). These narratives differentiated themselves because they represented the enduring of pain, or the idea of actively committing a crime. Beyond their differences, however, we find the idea that victims and perpetrators were used in order to raise questions about evil. It was a device that helped humans raise their concerns to God, and they used those narratives to relate humans to God in their quests for understanding.[49]

With the genre of theodicies, evil became a subject of speculative discourse. *Theology* was its center. From Augustine's idea of evil as the privation of the good, to the historical explanation given by Hegel, most philosophers who engaged in creating their theodicies articulated the concept of evil as a paradoxical exercise of reasoning between the extremes of human experience. This systematic speculation led to the development of determinant judgments instead of providing us with the tools for understanding different dimensions of human cruelty. No version of theodicies seemed to provide us with a convincing answer to the problem of undeserved suffering or of extreme cruelty. Kant's greatest intervention on this subject put the question of evil in its rightful place.[50] He separated the problem of evil from speculative reason and situated it in the realm of the practical—the moral sphere. By understanding evil as linked to the contingency of human action, Kant was able to articulate the problem of evil as one of human responsibility. He also warned us from the idea of mystifying it by categorizing it as an external demon or a deity. Kant knew that we humans tend to anthropomorphize God before the question of evil by trying to understand his nature. Kant, however, was not blind to the aporetic dimension of human evil. He called this inscrutable characteristic "radical evil."[51] This is where the problem of the ineffable reappears, and it has raised many questions about the possibilities or impossibilities of representation and interpretation. The question, then, is whether we have the proper instruments to meet this challenge. I conclude that we do if we recover Kant's great insight of linking his idea of moral imagination to our judgments.

Let us consider some of the problems associated with this task. The problem of representation became the subject of scholarly thematization after the traumatic events of the Holocaust. The term *ineffable* reappeared, associated with the impossibility of representing suffering, trauma, and extreme pain or cruelty. Many theorists sacralized the historical atrocity of the Holocaust and insisted on the impossibility of representing what happened then.[52] A key work illustrating this view was Claude Lanzmann's movie *Shoah* (1985). Lanzmann's theoretical explanations about his work,[53] as well as Shoshana Felman's classic interpretation of his movie, became the hallmarks of this position.[54]

Recently, however, there has been a further stage in this discussion about the representation of evil as something impossible to accomplish. Richard Kearney has called this critical group of authors the "postmodern *teratology of the sublime*."[55] The approach of some of these scholars has removed evil from the realm of possibility for any interpretation. Instead, they associated it with "horror," with "unspeakability," with "abjection," and with "nothingness." These postmodern thinkers have focused on Kant's idea of the sublime in a rather different version from mine. They conceive of horror as the ineffable[56] and they conclude that, for that reason, it cannot be represented.

In my theory, on the other hand, horror is one of the dimensions of the ineffable. Yet we have another dimension—moral imagination—in which communicability is achieved through the disclosive tools of the expressive power of language. Together, they enable the faculties of sensibility and understanding to produce reflective judgments. I have shown here how language becomes a key concept in this situation. These postmodern thinkers, on the other hand, refuse to accept that it is possible to find expressions to describe or interpret our darkest human experiences. With this position against representations, they leave us helpless when facing the challenge to understand atrocities. They also claim that the need to interpret the Holocaust should be taken as an exemption of human historicity. In a way they regard this event as a "sacred one."[57] They conceive of evil as an absolute event of strangeness and monstrosity. Thus, they end up saying nothing meaningful about it. Authors such as Julia Kristeva, Jean François Lyotard, and Slavoj Žižek are good examples of this position.[58]

Julia Kristeva, for example, defines the "abject" as "edged with the sublime" in her work *Powers of Horror*.[59] Kristeva uses Kant's idea of the sublime as something aporetic and describes it as "objectless." She goes further than Kant, however, because she proceeds to link the sublime experience as an experience of the abject, and interprets abjection as a *perversion or transgression*. In this interpretation, "We encounter evil portrayed as the sublime admixture of horror and exuberance ... so excessive and transgressive that it passes *beyond* being altogether [and, therefore, paradoxically, we arrive at] the very core of modern nihilism."[60] Kristeva's view of evil as the sublime leaves us with no space for moral understanding. We lose our capacity to pose questions about responsibility and accountability.

Lyotard's version of the sublime is more aesthetic than psychoanalytic. Again, the sublime appears as the unnameable, the uncommensurable, defying reason and reducing our human understanding to the space of silence.[61] With Lyotard's version of the sublime we see the concept of imagination being dissolved, and our capacities for representation as impotent. Thus, we are left helpless before the task of raising any moral claims about certain moral complexities when facing historical atrocities.

An even more radical concept of the sublime is offered by Slavoj Žižek, who argues that what appears good in a humanistic perspective of modernity is in fact evil.[62] He uses Kant's original concept of the sublime to illustrate the presence of apocalyptic heroes such as Milton's Satan, or Conrad's Kurtz succumbing to horror, or Melville's Pip in *Moby-Dick*. These monsters emerge as self-fulfilling prophecies of modernity, according to Žižek's concept of the return of the repressed. The representational and interpretative tasks are now developed by a death drive, a compulsion of an imaginary, which refuses to deal with the real. Again, we are left at the end without any possible inquiry about the problem of evil.

Against all these recent interpretations, I claim that we must relocate this discussion by insisting that representations of evil are possible within Kant's paradigm of moral imagination. As I have stressed before, the idea behind Kant's reflective judgment is to have a capacity for imagination from the point of view of others. Putting ourselves in the place of others is not an impossible task, despite the difficulties it brings. An enlarged mentality allows us to travel with our imagination and enter into the realm of seeing others' realities from their perspective. Disclosive language makes it possible to enter into a realm that we could not have imagined had a description not disclosed those dimensions that we could not see before. The bridge between what is said and what is meant is now captured through the images that represent the unfolding of a narrative order. Those very words can transport our hearts and minds to the realm of the horrible. The image discloses the unthinkable because of our need to redescribe something that seems to escape our understanding but defies our conceptual categories. People who have suffered or witnessed evil can never stop in their attempt to say something meaningful so that others can understand. This is a creative task (a work of genius, in Kant's terms). I can offer the example of the trajectory of Primo Levi's narratives. Throughout all his life, Levi continued to explore the uncertain meaning of the experience of evil (for him, through his survival). In this ordeal, he developed a great depth in his moral reasoning. His judgments were not created to give us a unique account of his personal strength or his courage. Rather, his stories revealed that he felt ashamed of what he had learned. His ideas were morally disclosive because he seemed to have understood cruelty and suffering as the two sides of moral destruction. In the various images he offered us we find the hallmarks of a moral definition of "shame." This image appears in *The Truce* (1963) and reappears again in *The Drowned and the Saved* (1986). He knew that the most distinctive feeling of shame was the result of an inability to forget that the struggle for survival meant forgetting all standards of good moral behavior. For this reason, he ends *The Truce* by recalling his dream of the *Lager* as the only certainty in his life.[63] The dream provides him with a dialectic of reality and dreaming produced by horror. The *Lager* showed him characteristics of humans that are hard to accept as truthful, even though they are real. Nonetheless, he realized that this truth was the starkest image that remained in his consciousness for the rest of his life. He was haunted by this dream. Levi once explained to his doctor (before undergoing surgery) that the only true sickness he endured was symbolized by the numbers printed on his wrist. He kept going back and forth from his experience of the past to his need to write about it. Perhaps it is clear to us now that he never felt satisfied. Over time, however, his views became more mature. They grew into deeper descriptions about the extreme difficulties endured in Auschwitz. It is interesting to note that he became more and more interested in the importance of language. He gave us several descriptions of the *Lager* as an insistent way of translating Auschwitz into terms unfamiliar to our native ear. If naming stabilizes reality, continual renaming unsettles it. The deeper meaning of Levi's babel of tongues rests in his chilling descriptions of Auschwitz, where "*not only verbal but also moral values mutate in this volatile realm.*"[64] Finally, the gap between what was said and what was meant closed, even if only for an instant. Then, a clearer picture emerged from *The Drowned and the Saved*. Communication, after all, is a never-ending series of attempts to narrate what has taken place. Levi spent the rest of his life exploring the meaning of shame and judgment and brought us the image, in Langer's words, of a "gray zone where man's vaunted moral self has lost its dignity and never found a way to reclaim it."[65]

Literature has given us plenty of examples of these kinds of illustrations. Poetry, with its disclosive capacity, is one of the greatest vehicles of language that connect us to the moral imagination. Paul Celan provides an example of my version of the sublime. In his most famous and anthologized early poem, "Death Fugue"[66] (which he later refused to recognize and tried to ban—apparently unsuccessfully—from reprinting), language becomes the key to his point of view. Celan transposes his personal experience into distanced imagery. He connects it to a musical structure—the fugue—so incompatible with reportage that a kind of echo affected its rhythm through the "terrible beauty" which came from its images of horror. The power and pathos of the poem arise from an extreme tension between the horrific material and its pure poetical form. Shoshana Felman has given us a good description of the poem's working dialectic of illumination:

> The performance of the act of drinking, traditionally a poetic metaphor for yearning, for romantic thirst and for desire, is here transformed into the surprisingly abusive figure of an endless torture and limitless exposure, . . . the perversion of the metaphor of drinking is further aggravated by the enigmatic image of the "black milk," which, in its obsessive repetitions, suggests the further underlying—though *unspeakable and inarticulated*—image of a child striving to drink from the mother's breast. (Emphasis added.)

But the denatured "black milk," tainted possibly by blackened, burnt ashes, springs not from the mother's breast but from the darkness of murder and death, from the blackness of the night and of the "dusk" that "falls to Germany" when death uncannily becomes a "master."[67] Here we see the clear construction of a language that has bridged the gap between horror and experience. Its communicability is an act of moral construction and of imagination.

There is no naïveté in saying that even if traumatic episodes oblige or force the subjects to insist on repeating them through different versions of what happened, with time and in returning to those events, we are capable of giving finer descriptions. We can always find a better language, as the examples of Levi's work and of Celan's poetry both illustrate. Levi became a rigorous moral thinker who crystallized his view in narratives. Celan most radically revolutionized poetry after Auschwitz. Disclosive imagination in both worked as the creator's most expressive tool in constructing good moral judgments.

The power of imagination lies also in the reader's capacity for a wider perception of historical atrocities and suffering (enlarged mentality). Language then can go beyond the silence of the horrible and make it a disclosive expressive space for the ineffable. The sublime shock of evil does not mean that we have no human responses to it. Understanding is the first stage of our moral duty. Judgment –as it is communicated to others--is the second. The best way, therefore, to issue a response is to challenge the view of things as incomprehensible. *Understanding what happened does not mean erasing the past.* Rather, we are forced to see that things could have been different. With this critical view we learn that we are the ones who change. Evil becomes our problem. It is our ordeal. Nothing is causal, and no progress is assured by our human knowledge of those atrocities. But *imagining* and *thinking* give us a space—a moral critical space—where we can begin to deliberate if we are capable of transforming ourselves. With it, we acknowledge that a story can never be replaced by a concept, but "the kind of moral mindfulness needed here is one which tries to remain faithful to the testimony which the story of evil relates,"[68] namely, that we are forced to bear the responsibility of being human, and that by listening to those humans who have suffered under extreme cruelty we provide for a new sense of the community we want.

CHAPTER 4

Hannah Arendt and Negative Exemplarity

{The Moral Paradigm of History and Its Particularity}

It is our great misfortune that Hannah Arendt did not live to explore these matters and it is our great fortune that she pointed the way.
—*Michael Denneny*[1]

Much has been written about Hannah Arendt's reflections on evil and of the particular way she analyzed her two different conceptions of evil—radical evil and the banality of evil—in her works *The Origins of Totalitarianism* and *Eichmann in Jerusalem: A Report on the Banality of Evil.* I myself have explored some aspects of the theories within these two works in the introduction to my edited book *Rethinking Evil: Contemporary Perspectives.* I will not repeat those arguments here, nor do I wish to recall the many different and contradictory interpretations of her contributions on the subject of evil. Since the purpose of this book is to develop a theory of reflective judgment to rethink issues concerning evil acts, I would like now to turn to her ideas about judgment, a subject about which much has already been said. The main conclusion that can be drawn from those studies is that Arendt had two different and contradictory views of judgment.[2] In order to question this already-accepted view of her work, I would in this chapter like to develop a three-part argument. In each part I will illustrate the balance in Arendt's work between Heidegger and Walter Benjamin as her main sources of influence. The result of this fusion is an original concept of judgment. In the first part of my argument, I will develop a hermeneutic approach to her ideas about judgment. I will demonstrate that history, storytelling, and the role of the spectator are subjects she cleverly brings together in a highly original fusion of Benjamin's views and Heidegger's sources. In the second part, I will develop the argument that Arendt's idea of disclosive language was taken from both Heidegger and Benjamin, and that her notion of historicity—combining Benjamin's views with Heidegger's—led her to formulate a concept which I will call "the negative exemplarity of reflective judgment." In the last part, I will draw conclusions by showing the way Arendt's ideas can be turned against her, in order to reconcile the contradictory views of actor and spectator when considering reflective judgment. In order to avoid the problematic stance of envisioning two different kinds of judgments—those of the spectator and of the actor—we can think of reflective judgment as comprising two very different, albeit linked, tasks. Both entail a resonance between individual and collective judgments. Moreover, a mediating stance between these two dimensions lies in the fact that they are related through the role of the public sphere. The public sphere is a vehicle that allows for moral learning and the critical construction of memories. The idea of publicly discussing stories will also allow me to show that "learning from catastrophes" is a process of moral learning.

Judgment and Storytelling: The Role of Historians and Storytellers

What I want to do, then, is bring to light some aspects of Arendt's ideas about judgment that I think have been missed in the fine works of scholars dedicated to interpreting her work. I will establish the structural axis of my discussion around the concepts of the historian as judge, of storytelling as the vehicle for reflective judgment, and of moral and political judgments as two different moments of the same process which I have earlier called "learning from catastrophe." If we consider her idea of the public sphere, these three concepts can be linked structurally. Hannah Arendt presupposes that published works—such as stories—need spectators to judge them, for without them, "the world would be imperfect." Thus, "if there were no spectator to look out for it, admire it, straighten out the stories and put them into words," there would be no real political world.[3]

First, I would like to make these connections and relate them to two quotes that she loved and cited often from Cato. Both quotations appeared together in the last paragraph of her postscript to *The Life of the Mind*.[4] It is no coincidence that they appear together there, since both epigraphs form the basis for Arendt's work about judgment. The most well-known citation states: "Old Cato, with whom I started these reflections, [claims] 'never am I less alone than when I am by myself, never am I more active than when I do nothing,' [and he] has left us a curious phrase which aptly sums up the political principle implied in the enterprise of reclamation. He said: '*Victrix causa deis placuit, sed victa Catoni*' ('The victorious cause pleased the gods, but the defeated one pleases Cato')" (216).

We must first focus on the role of the historian. In *The Life of the Mind,* just before Cato´s citation, Arendt introduces her idea about the historian's role, but not as one would normally imagine. Rather, she envisions someone closer to Homer—a poet—instead of a traditional historian. She explains her preference by turning to the origin of the word *historian.* Arendt explains that the Greek word for the verb "to historicize" is derived from the Greek word "historein," which means, "to inquire in order to tell how it was." Arendt reminds us that, in the "Homeric tradition," the noun "history" means to "judge" (216). Therefore, Arendt concludes that if "judgment is our faculty for dealing with the past, the historian is the inquiring man who by relating it sits in judgment over it." Thus we see why a historian who is more like a poet can play a central role in Arendt's view about who is better equipped to make judgments.

But how can a poet—a storyteller—become a judge? Arendt replies that it is because "bards," like Homer, "straightened the story" with "magic words," and because "they did not merely report, they also set it [the story] right (*orthosas*)" (132). Consequently, if stories can "set things right," then poets must use their judgment to provide an understanding of the meanings of these stories. Such an idea brings us back to Arendt's concept that narratives are the sources from which historians find the needed tools to make judgments. She explains that in the *Iliad* Homer recovered "the fear and grief on the hearts of men," and by doing so he wished to educate us (106). Moreover, Homer could trace the hidden aspects of stories because they articulated "human experience" (109). Arendt's belief that Homer exemplified a special kind of historian illustrates why she feels that this process requires spectators, not only because they need to learn the skills of judgment through these stories but also because they add the important political dimension that allows for real learning. This can be demonstrated through her poetic account of Thucydides' response to the Greek question, "Who becomes immortal, the doer or the teller?" (133). Though the answer might never be settled, Arendt tells us, we need only focus on Pericles' funeral speech in which Thucydides realizes that the answer lies in the "imperishable monuments"—the stories—left behind (133). These "monuments" make up the identity of the polis; they share characteristics with society and serve as a reminder of what is needed.

Now we must turn our attention to another type of historian—one who is also a critic: Walter Benjamin provides the model for this kind of scholar. Arendt again connects historian and storyteller, using as inspiration Walter Benjamin's idea of history, his criticism of the concept of progress, his idea of the power of storytelling, and his comments on the moral role of the historian. It is true that some links to Benjamin's legacy have already been documented by Seyla Benhabib[5] as well as by Ronald Beiner in his critical essay included in the book (which he edited) about Arendt's lessons on Kant's political philosophy.[6] What I would like to stress, however, is that Arendt connects Benjamin to her view of history and to storytelling because of his critical view of history, of the concept of progress, and of the role of the historian as the moral mediating force between the public and the stories. These Benjaminian concepts lead her to connect history to its moral dimension, on the one hand, and critical thinking to political judgments on the other. Both of these moments belong to a single process. She accomplishes this by showing that historians can rescue stories by means of their expressive (or aesthetic) devices and critical efforts, resulting in the creation of spaces to interpret the events that have taken place. One can see that Arendt understood stories, as witnesses' accounts, to be necessary components in the process of critical revision within the public sphere. In order to begin anew, we need to understand what has really happened. One can only arrive at a reflective judgment after collective and critical deliberation about the meaning of a story.

On the other hand, I wish to argue that Benjamin also led Arendt to rethink Heidegger's ideas about language as connected to its dimension of expressive disclosure. Without this kind of connection Arendt could not have drawn a particular view of critical thinking and of language as possessing disclosive capacities. Heidegger's legacy, along with his contribution to a theory of language, created an expressive device through the concept of disclosure. It provided Arendt with the view that poetic language could play a role in her theory of judgment. In order to illustrate this connection between Benjamin and Heidegger,[7] Arendt writes that

> In Heidegger and Walter Benjamin, the old sight of metaphor has not altogether disappeared but has shrunk, as it were: in Benjamin truth "slips by" (*huchst vorüber*); in Heidegger the moment of illumination is

understood as "lightning" (*Blitz*), and finally replaced by an altogether metaphor, *das Geläut der Stille*, "the ringing sound of silence."[8]

Arendt felt that Benjamin thought by means of the "poetic." She clarifies, however, that he "was neither a poet nor a philosopher."[9] Rather, he was a critical figure—one who, "as an alchemist," practices "the obscure art of transmuting the futile elements of the real into the shining, enduring gold of truth." Arendt attaches to Benjamin's concept of language a disclosive view, especially after she clarifies it with his interpretation of "the historical process" conceived as "magical transfiguration."[10] Benjamin makes us see things in a different way (recall the image of the pearl diver). Arendt saw Benjamin as a special kind of critic—or better, as a real historian exercising the judgment of his times. When Arendt describes Benjamin's most important critical contribution, she understands that Benjamin's expressions opened up the path to the idea that images can disclose a tragic view of his time. He allows us to see that, through the idea of world disclosure, understanding can come out of the ineffable image of an artistic work. Benjamin uses Paul Klee´s "Angelus Novus" to disclose his critical idea of history. Benjamin's description of the "Angelus Novus" sets forth the concept of "the angel of history."[11] In Benjamin's view, Klee's image is fused to Gerhard Scholem's poem,[12] and together they found their moral resonance within one another. Benjamin explains that when the angel turned his back to the past, he could only see a pileup of "wreckage upon wreckage."[13] This angel, Benjamin explains, would have liked to "awaken the dead," but instead was compelled by a violent force that led him to the future—a future that could only disclose the real meaning of that historical time as a vision of terror. The image of the storm embodies what we call "progress." By allowing us to understand what the angel saw as the "ruins of the past," Benjamin connected for the first time the past and the future as a single process.[14] He endowed the textures of history with a moral quality. His awareness of this wreckage—the sight of these ruins piling up—informed this angel that human actions can cause disasters: cultures destroy other cultures, and civilization is based on barbarianism. This consciousness—the active aspect of memory—is the reason we cannot forget what lies behind us. It is precisely because Benjamin worked through these connections that he can provide "a moral connection" between history and judgment. That Arendt regarded Benjamin's conception as essential to her own ideas can be demonstrated by the fact that she sent to Heidegger one of Kafka's aphorisms,[15] which bears a similar description to that of the "Angelus Novus." This reference appears in her letter written to Heidegger on September 24, 1967.[16]

Benjamin's angel stands in the historical time known as the *jetztzeit*. He bears the weight of our moral responsibility because of the way that the past is now linked to the future. Arendt concludes that Benjamin most surely was more comfortable "with poets than with theoreticians,"[17] because of his ability to draw the metaphorical innovations that led her to compare his efforts to the works of the Homeric tradition.[18]

In the essay entitled "The Pearl Diver,"[19] Arendt recovers Benjamin as a historical figure because he "knew that the break in tradition and the loss of authority which occurred in his lifetime, were irreparable, and he concluded that he had to discover new ways with dealing with the past" (193). His new methodology is illustrated in the famous quotations now known as his original method. Arendt explains that he was most concerned with the idea of "transmissibility" (196), and he found this idea of communication within the realm of the aesthetic (just as Kant had done in the past). Benjamin, for example, analyzes Kafka's work because it illustrates that "by making decisive changes in traditional parables or inventing new ones," he was able to destroy his tradition. This is why Arendt argues that Benjamin's critical views of tradition and his ways of seeking new forms of telling were more similar to Heidegger's than to anyone else's (though this might seem paradoxical, since Benjamin considered himself a Marxist) (203). Thus, Arendt connects Benjamin to Heidegger's idea of disclosive language when she describes Benjamin as a "pearl diver." She explains that Benjamin not only quotes, he names, "and naming rather than speaking, the word rather than the sentence, bring[s] truth to light" (203). Arendt argues that this is no coincidence, for Benjamin always had a special interest in language, and even if he did not read Wittgenstein, he knew that the problem of truth deals with the concept of "revelation." This concept of language as revelation "comes quite close to Heidegger's position" (204), because both understand language as an "essentially poetic phenomenon" (205).

Historicity and Exemplarity

As we have seen, Arendt shares a perception of history similar to that of Walter Benjamin. It is a view that connects the past to the future with a moral thread placed in the hands of the historian. By means of a judgment, we are able to move from the present to the past. It is imperative that we return to the past and consider those who have experienced suffering. We owe it to them. It is the only way to build a future—to begin anew. This is where a mediation of the moral interpretation, based on the judgments of historians, takes hold. Recall that Arendt reminds us that Cato was more concerned with defeat. Not all historians are able to make true reflective judgments. Only those concerned with our past catastrophes have that capacity to grasp that actions of human cruelty entail an open ended process. When making judgments, historians must perform two tasks: one concerns the moral duty owed to those who have disappeared from earth, the other demands that historians/judges powerfully communicate their messages in order to free us from the burden of our past. A historian must play a similar role to that of the genius, in a Kantian sense.[20] It takes a great deal of imagination to communicate what seems ineffable. Arendt's idea appears now connected to the Kantian concept of imagination and of its free-play. This type of exercise in imagination, however, implies that, along with aesthetic expressiveness, there is also a moral streak because the imagination brings others to that same space. This is also a dimension in which plurality gives rise to the possibility of a "critical discourse."[21] Different viewpoints allow us to see other perspectives. Then, to critically examine them, we are forced to deal with contrasts and criticism.

Arendt develops her ideas about reflective judgment only by basing it on historicity. Each particular moment of an event is grasped by historians as they define the characteristics of the event's particularities as exemplary. Only historical judgments, or judgment of taste, can provide us with an idea of exemplarity. This is the reason Arendt needs Kant. As we have seen, however, Kant shows exemplarity only in its positive view, a perspective based on his idea of beauty. Arendt, on the other hand, has to transform the concept of exemplarity into a negative one. She does so only by demonstrating the way positive examples of the exercise of judgment—like Benjamin as a critical thinker—face the challenge of thinking about the critical aspects of his times. Dealing with this, and doing it critically, allows her to transform the idea of beauty into one of horror (recall the idea of the sublime in Kant). The historian, either as poet or judge, critically recovers her times, and in so doing she faces the past and transforms her critical views of those features into a model of exemplarity conceived now as negative. Thus, the wreckage of our past is always brought back when we reply to the challenge of our times with a critical judgment. This judgment might allow us to understand what happened. We need the moral force of the critical effect of the interpretation from the spectators in order to complete this collective task of understanding.

Like Benjamin, Arendt was against the idea of progress.[22] She also believed, like Kant, in the possibility of freedom. She rejected the idea that history was or could ever be conceived as a "rational" force of humanity. Heidegger also influenced Arendt's idea of time. When connecting her Heideggerian roots to her own concept of time, she revisits Benjamin's influence in order to arrive at a concept of history as a new moral space in which to frame our human connections to the shared world of politics. These links are expressed in our moral duty to understand what has happened. It is here that Arendt comes to the understanding that storytelling and judgment coincide. For the first time she begins to see herself as that kind of historian. In her search for her own theory of reflective judgment, Arendt describes her times critically, drawing the characteristics of the unique phenomena of evil acts committed during the twentieth century. In systematically recovering Arendt's insights, Seyla Benhabib, for example, finds that Arendt's work has four distinctive themes that make her work on exemplary validity appealing: (1) "historicization and salvation," (2) "the exercise of empathy, imagination, and historical judgment," (3) "the pitfalls of analogical thinking," and (4) "the moral resonance of narrative language."[23]

Once we understand Arendt's concern with judgment and narration and their historicity, it becomes clear that she believes a "historical narrator" re-creates a shared reality from the standpoint of all concerned. Storytelling also provides us with knowledge about ourselves. As Martha Nussbaum has argued, "Storytelling and literary imagining are not opposed to rational argument, but can provide essential ingredients in rational arguments."[24] By using stories about evil as vehicles of interpretation and understanding, Arendt shows that her work is inspired by Benjamin as well. Arendt not only thought of Benjamin as a "pearl diver"; she also cites that Benjamin's own account of the power of storytelling is best illustrated in his essay on Nikolai Leskov,[25] which bears significant resemblance to Arendt's ideas about storytelling and the role of historians. Like Arendt, Benjamin also cites a historian—Herodotus—as the first storyteller (89). Just as Hannah Arendt cites Cato and Homer as the best examples of historians, Benjamin also recalls the importance of the historian—Herodotus—when recovering the power of stories. In this same essay, Benjamin explains why narratives achieve "an amplitude that [pure] information lacks" (89). A story, Benjamin explains, is "capable of releasing [its strength] even after a long time" (90). For Benjamin, stories are the best source of collective memory, and they force listeners to integrate them into their own experience because of the need to reproduce them, to retell them to someone else. Consequently, "the more self-forgetful the listener is, the more deeply is what he listens to impressed upon his memory," and "when the rhythm of work has seized him, he listens to the tales in such a way that the gift of retelling them comes to him all by itself." Thus, Benjamin concludes, "this is the nature of the web in which the gift of storytelling is cradled" (91). This is the reason "historiography and epics share a common ground" (95): both deal with the way we see things. We manage to make our interpretations as "embedded in the great inscrutable course of the world," and when "the storyteller keeps faith with it," he deals with "death" as "the last wretched straggler" (97). In the connection between epics and history, we find him rescuing memory as "the epic faculty par excellence" (97), for "it is only by virtue of a comprehensive memory [that] epic writing absorb[s] the course of events on the one hand and, with the passing of these, make[s] its peace with the power of death on the other" (97). Herein lies the moral dimension of the power of judgment. Memory is the moral texture of history. In his essay on Leskov, when Benjamin refers to the power of the story to move us, he insists that even if we find the force to make a judgment, or our own interpretation of it, others instill in us a moral need to appropriate it. For him, certain stories possess a moral power because they make it possible to bring those others to our lives. If stories help us bring those others back to our present, in the same act of retelling those stories we engage in our moral duty to create a collective site for memory. Only by honoring our duty to remember them does a story liberate us from the burdens of the past. Here, then, appropriation—the process of retelling—means also being able to think in terms of moral responsibility.

Sharing a Community of Spectators and the Role of the *Sensus Communis*

On the other hand, when Arendt recalls Cato's dictum—"Never am I less alone than when I am by myself, never am I more active than when I do nothing"—she clarifies why his sentence is the very source of her inspiration about her idea of a historian. Only when judgments are developed can the historian realize that the presence of those others is best captured through his story. This is why one is never alone. Because Kant thought of imagination as the vehicle with which to bring the others' viewpoints to a judgment, Cato's sentence illustrates Arendt's concern for recovering it. This connection fully restores Kant's own concept of sociability (*Geselligkeit*), which is the reason Arendt loves to quote his *Critique of Judgment*. Kant had appealed to the concept of imagination as an important way of having others always in our minds—to be always with them. The moral idea of autonomy is also a key to this concept of imagination. Recall the categorical imperative. Kant had already developed his idea that the ability to think with others was a valid criteria on which to base morality. When one is able to imagine what others think, one develops a moral point of view. Arendt sees Kant's concept of imagination as a valid reference for understanding her ideas about sociability. For Kant it is in the judgments of taste that we find our "ability to look at the same thing from the perspective of other people," and "we do not judge as they might judge," but rather, "we judge from their point of view." It is because of this "mysterious power of the imagination"[26] that we are capable of visiting other viewpoints in our process of forging our judgments. It is no coincidence, as we have seen, that Arendt adopts Kant's idea of imagination. Kant links aesthetics to ethics. Both realms are fundamental sources of human values.[27] It is for this reason that Kant's idea of imagination allows Arendt to seek an important transformation of the concept of reflective judgment by articulating an intersubjective concept of the sensus communis.

If Benjamin is a key figure who portrays the poet as judge, Socrates is an apt figure to portray the philosopher as a thinker. Both regard their times critically and face a crisis of their traditions. If we return now to the second part of Cato´s dictum, in which he refers to the idea of thinking alone as the paradoxical place where one can find oneself with those others, then the idea of critical thinking is best exemplified by Socrates. He experienced his time as one of crisis and as a clash of moral values. By bringing Socrates back into our historical time, Arendt wanted us to be conscious of a challenge that should not be missed. The key to facing such a challenge is the exercise of real critical thinking. When Socrates finds himself "knowing that we do not know, and nevertheless unwilling to let it go at that," he makes of "his own perplexities" an opportunity to build his judgment. He stood still and "paralyzed himself." Arendt clarifies that we cannot fail when we "look [at] paralysis from the outside [recall Cato's phrase]"—and feel that it is "the highest state of being active and alive."[28] On the other hand, perplexities for Socrates were not to be avoided or feared; he understood that the only thing we can do at such moments is "share them with each other."[29] As Dana Villa explains, "Thinking prepares for judgment in a largely negative fashion: it purges us of 'fixed' beliefs and habits of thought, ossified rules and standards, through it, we find again an open space 'of moral and aesthetic discrimination and judgment.' "[30] Both Villa and Denneny[31] insist that Arendt writes of the aesthetic space as one that enables and provides a sense of particularity, of discernment, and of novelty. She uses two examples to illustrate the idea of critical thinking. One is Walter Benjamin, as we have seen, and his inspiration about historicity and the idea of disclosive language (which he shared with Heidegger). The second is Socrates, because she needs to illustrate that real critical thinking might force us to stand still rather than act, making our inaction a true radical political answer to the challenge of a critical time. As Arendt explains, "When everybody is swept away unthinkingly by what everybody else does and believes in, those who think are drawn out of hiding because their refusal to join in is conspicuous and thereby becomes a kind of action."[32] Furthermore, to initiate the process of judgment requires a negative force, a "purging component of thinking," which "is political by implication" (192). By thinking critically, the philosopher—in this case Socrates—makes possible "the faculty of judgment, which one may call with some reason the most political of man's mental abilities" (192) to become another kind of action. The fact that thinking and judging must coexist can be explained by pointing out that they are morally bound to one another. This is why Arendt saw the two interrelated in the same way that "consciousness" is related to "conscience" (192). Their manifestation becomes crystallized as the capacity to "tell right from wrong, beautiful from ugly," and in those "rare moments when the stakes are on the table" (192), it is, indeed, possible to prevent the catastrophes that we face. Socrates did not miss the challenge of his times: he chose to exercise his critical thinking, and death was his punishment. He has been rescued, however, by our collective memory. Arendt argues that it is important that others bring back Socrates's story to the public sphere, for it is only because we have it in the public sphere that we know who Socrates really was.

"We know much less of Socrates," explains Arendt, "who did not write a single line and left no work behind, than of Plato or Aristotle, [but] we know [him] much better and more intimately" because "we know his story."[33] This example reminds us that in the public sphere we find that stories play an important role as moral mediations between spectators and the stories' witnesses. It is here that we build a common world and allow the political methods of making judgments to become real actions.

One cannot forget that another of Arendt's favorite philosophers missed such a challenge. Indeed, Heidegger's failure was his incapacity to make a moral judgment of his times. As Dana Villa reminds us, "If we put Arendt's tribute essay together with the lengthy Heidegger critique found in the penultimate chapter of *The Life of the Mind*, we see that what at first glance appears to be an apology is, in fact, an indictment."[34] According to Arendt, both Socrates and Heidegger share many favorable attitudes, but there is "one crucial difference." While Socrates activates the faculty of judgment with his "voice of conscience" (this is the moral dimension), Heidegger's thinking "is utterly divorced from the world of appearances, and the world of politics."[35] From Arendt's point of view, Socrates faces his perplexities as successfully as Benjamin did. Both allowed their critical thinking to become a "prelude" of "genuinely reflective" judgments—that is, as the moral space in which to "exercise of judgment."[36] Yet the real process is not complete. Rather, in the case of Socrates, because his inaction became a kind of action—a good judgment—his story was recovered in the public sphere as an example of good reflective judgment. We have learned about the moral quality of his judgment through his example. It is only when "pure thinking" remains alone (as it was in the case of Heidegger), that we find "the death of judgment."[37]

Key to Arendt's idea of reflective judgment is her concept of negative exemplarity. In her case, the key to understanding evil is related to her concept of the negative use of "exemplary validity." While appropriating the term from Kant, she argues that "Kant accords to examples the same role in judgments that the intuitions called schemata have for experience and cognition." She then goes on to state that "examples play a role in both reflective and determinant judgments, that is, whenever we are concerned with particulars." As we have seen before, Arendt links judgment to understanding by means of language. While many theorists have focused on the link between interpretation and understanding in Arendt's work, and many of them have pointed out some of the difficulties in her concept of "schemata" and "exemplary validity,"[38] I still believe we can recover some of Arendt's main assertions. Thus, what I want to highlight is that by studying judgment through the perspective of language it is possible to avoid the problems set by analogical thinking and schemata, and, at the same time, the notion of "exemplary" can be connected now to a theory of imagination and the sensus communis. As we have seen, Arendt's concept of language emerged from Heidegger's theory of language. Language allowed her to restore the need for autonomous thinking—that is, reflective judgment—as a condition for developing a groundbreaking interpretation that would allow us to see things differently. Second, by describing symbols and images linguistically, Arendt develops a highly original idea of reflective judgment. It is a technique that attaches violence to ordinary language. It is another way of saying that by altering the semantic meanings of ordinary expressions we find novel ways of describing human actions. The negative sides of actions that are thought to be unprecendented become the material for judgments. For example, take Arendt's idea of the banality of evil. Calling something "banal" which cannot possibly be "banal" provokes a semantic shock—a violence. Consequently, through the shocking use of the word *banal*, we begin to understand that it has ceased to mean what it means in ordinary language. Rather, the shock makes us conscious that there is an implicit criticism in this way of expressing it. Such a way of describing an absence of moral character is obtained through the introduction of this term with the description of someone who was capable of sending more than six million people to the gas chambers without offering any reason for doing so. Eichmann's lack of moral character is now described as "banal" and represents a typical figure of the history of his times. By calling him "banal," we also understand that there is no real identity between that which is expressed through moral character and the incapacity to offer reasons for doing evil. They can never be together in our ordinary language. The expression "banal" is meant to produce a semantic shock, such that those who hear this usage reflect on the way the term is critically situated. Arendt articulated her idea of imagination to the role of the spectators as reacting critically because of their need to deliberate about an interpretation through the story (such as her own story on Eichmann).

In her essay "Understanding and Politics," for example, Arendt claims that "the result of understanding is meaning."[39] The way language creates new meanings through its disclosive capacities is best described by Dana Villa, who argues that "the poetic capacity to bring something radically new, that was not contained, in potentia, is that which already is." "Poetic," in this sense, means "radical *poiesis*."[40] Like Benjamin before, Arendt strengthens the idea that the aesthetic dimension of language is its *subversivness*. Thus, the question for Arendt is how to establish a link between understanding and judgment to allow for the creation of meaning in what seems to possess a "horrible originality."[41] If disclosure means bringing truth through language, then knowledge should achieve communicability through the semantic shock that produces critical thinking. While Heidegger "insists upon seeing communicative and world-disclosing speech as antithetical," Arendt unifies them through the mediating force of reflective judgment.[42] What Heidegger's theory of language lacks is the way disclosive intersubjective and communicative powers can also provide a critical and reflexive space for understanding. This is why Seyla Benhabib argues that "*Verstehen* is a form of judging."[43] James Bohman has also argued that this disclosive view is critical. He states that "the concept of disclosure is a certain way of talking about changes in cultural codes and understandings."[44] Shocking uses of language produce new expressions that disclose a critical moral understanding and help us—through this violence—to forge the idea of judgment by means of a critical examination. The use of ordinary language to describe something completely unprecendented becomes innovative once we understand that in such a description "*x* is only identical to *y*" as a violent semantic shock. The task of reflective judgment depends on the fact that innovation in poetic language demands the rearrangement of a framework to describe those new experiences with our ordinary language. Understanding, then, becomes the other side of action, which, for Arendt, now means the possibility of coming to terms "with what irrevocably happened," and with "what unavoidabl[y] exists."[45] Arendt concludes in a Kantian vein that "we may call the imagination the gift of the 'understanding heart,'" because "imagination is concerned with the particular darkness of the human heart and the peculiar density which surrounds everything that is real" (322). It is because of the faculty of imagination that we are able to avoid "vicious circles" in our quest for meaning. Through it we might "catch at least a glimpse of the always frightening light of truth" (323). This technique of "distancing of some things and bridging abysses to others is part of the dialogue of understanding," and the faculty of imagination becomes our very own process of "understanding" (323).

When Arendt found words to describe new forms of domination by describing those political actions as "totalitarian," she provided us with new meanings for cruelty. In the same way, by creating a specific account of certain actions as cases of exemplary validity, the historian or storyteller provides new meanings even to old terms. In the Germany of the 1930s and '40s, the word *Jews* became a description of a group that was considered nonhuman. Violent events like *Kristallnacht* were named during a historical moment. Although we understand the word out of its ordinary use, it has become a description of a very specific historical stage of horror. Terms like "Judenräte," "concentration camps," "extermination," and "Final Solution" were all resignified in stories written after the war ended—once persons other than the perpetrators started to learn about them and began to describe those facts. These stories have caused ordinary terms to mean something completely different.

Arendt reworked the terms "radical evil," "absolute evil," and "the banality of evil," to give new meanings to our traditional way of understanding them. By expressing clearly that a concept such as "radical evil" seemed at odds with our rupture from our philosophical tradition, she seeks a way out of the impasse by using her imagination as a primary tool to create new concepts where there are no rules. We cannot provide reasonable causes to our understanding of evil actions. We have to grasp what precisely is at the core of human cruelty when "we actually have nothing to fall back on in order to understand a phenomenon that nevertheless confronts us with its overpowering reality and breaks down all standards we know."[46] There was only one thing to do in a system where all men "have become equally superfluous," and that was to find out how the negative features of some actions led to the stripping of the humanity of a particular group of persons. This idea led her to explore the negative exemplarity of totalitarianism as a systematic way of destroying humanity.

Such an understanding of the unique horrors performed by one group of men against another later led Arendt to accept the challenge of becoming a witness of the Eichmann trial. It was in Jerusalem that she realized how the evil she had decribed earlier—as stripping away the essential features of humanity—needed to be seen from a different perspective when focusing on the moral point of view of a moral subject. In Eichmann's case, evil was caused by shallowness and rigidity—by what she conceptualized as an "exemplary case" of the "banality of evil."

Arendt not only gives us two possible paradigms of evil, she even creates her own vocabulary that describes them as two different stages in the understanding of the stories about the Holocaust. In *The Origins of Totalitarianism*, she narrates what happened to humans qua humans in the sequence of terror that stripped away individual identity. The loss of plurality erased the humanity of individuals. In Jerusalem, she came to see Eichmann as one of the perpetrators of what she thought was the most heinous act ever done, and found that he had no comprehension of the moral meaning of his own deeds. The result was *Eichmann in Jerusalem: A Report on the Banality of Evil*. Arendt's biggest mistake was to use the word *banality* in her title, for it is only after one has carefully read the whole text that one is able to grasp what is meant by such a term. The complexity of her judgment is visible when one focuses on Arendt's almost physical description of Eichmann. Everything about him is described as vulgar, clichéd, and deficient in nobility and moral character. Eichmann was taken as the perfect example of what had happened: a "German society of eight million people had been shielded against reality and factuality by exactly the same means, the same self-deception, lies, stupidity that had become so ingrained in Eichmann's mentality."[47] Two things appear in this example that immediately recall Kant's own effort to thematize reflective judgment: first, Arendt draws from a particular concept that she wants to use as a universal figure of evil; second, it is only through her interpretation that we come to see why Eichmann represents an emblematic figure of a lack of moral character. His failure to think, his ordinary clichés, and his self-deceptive character allowed Arendt to understand that he was no monstrous evil, but rather the most common of individuals. Thus she forces us to see that "despite all the efforts of the prosecution" to portray him as a monster, the only available image to describe him was that of the "clown."[48] Arendt's concept of the banality of evil would become the head figure of a paradigm of evil which has become useful for other thinkers to draw similarities and disparities with other totalitarian regimes. As a historian, Arendt provided the illustration of how "family resemblances"[49] (the Wittgensteinian term) is a device of a concrete universal.

Thus, Arendt recovers the Kantian legacy by providing the linguistic grounds on which to stress our ability to use language as the paradigm for judgment. Her theory of reflective judgment recovers stories as vehicles for collective self-reflection. The historian uses her imagination to provide us with key critical terms so we understand the nature of her judgment while debating with others. This exercise of reflective judgment in which the spectator engages becomes, then, the conscious action of choosing a moral frame within which to understand what happened—not as a way to rewind the past, but rather as a warning not to repeat it. It is a plea to prevent actions like those from ever happening again. Neither success nor naked power justifies the recovery of past actions. The effort to provide a public place in which to build a collective site for memory crystallizes only when the historian engages with witnesses in the most political of all activities—judgment. This might be the reason why Arendt chose Cato´s dictum as her prelude to her enterprise on judgment.

[illegible] not [illegible] producers. [illegible] ment in which the spectator engages [illegible]. Then there is [illegible] action of processual [illegible] with which to understand what [illegible] to find the [illegible] not [illegible] to preempt accounts like these [illegible] putting [illegible] questions. The effort to provide [illegible] to build a [illegible] only [illegible] exchanges with [illegible] of all activity [illegible] might be the reason why [illegible] to her enterprise on paintings.

CHAPTER 5
Learning from Catastrophes

I must confess that when I started writing about evil, in the summer of 1998, I was of the opinion that the work of Jürgen Habermas had not focused explicitly on the problem. Many critical scholars and colleagues would have agreed with that earlier opinion.[1] Since then, however, I have come to understand that Habermas has always been concerned with the problem of evil, but has done so from a strictly postmetaphysical view. It is for this reason that, in this chapter, I would like to develop my arguments on the ways Habermas's contribution has helped change my mind. Not since Hannah Arendt has anyone functioned in the role of critic as she defined it, which requires the inclusion of history in the public debate, in the way Habermas relentlessly has. In my opinion, Habermas best illustrates the exercise of reflective judgment. I would like to explain this claim by showing his important interventions in the three specific polemics that he initiated in the public sphere: the first is his intervention in the *Historikerstreit* ("historians' dispute") of July 1986; the second is his intervention, ten years later, in Daniel Goldhagen's polemical book, *Hitler's Willing Executioners*; the third is his defense of Victor Farías's research on Heidegger's complicity with the Nazi party. These three examples by no means represent the only times Habermas has responded to the problem of evil in the public sphere. Nonetheless, his significant contribution to the idea of learning from catastrophes deserves special attention because of the way he exemplifies this concept in these three examples. In essence, he provides the critical elements needed for reflection and judgment. I wish to show how Habermas's examples of "learning from catastrophes" imply the idea of reflective judgment. First, he connects the moral critical intervention of an intellectual to the public sphere, then he leads the debate about a historical catastrophe, and finally he provides critical arguments in order to reach an agreement about what should be done to prevent future catastrophes. It is in this sense that the core of all his ideas about ethics and politics is related to his notion of "learning from catastrophes" as a new way of recovering the concepts of moral and political judgments. The first stage is the moral collective recognition of wrongdoing; the second step is a collective agreement regarding the means by which to implement laws to prevent future catastrophes. I will begin, however, by showing that Habermas has allowed us to reframe the problem of evil according to his postmetaphysical view.

Defining the Concept of Learning from Catastrophes

In a very important essay entitled "Learning from Catastrophes: A Look Back at the Short Twentieth Century," Habermas analyzes three different historical versions of the twentieth century that focused on different understandings of the events that took place and which gave rise to unintended consequences.[2] The three perspectives Habermas cites are based on different ways of relating structural problems to terrible outcomes, and therefore, they articulate an explanatory dialectic of "light and shadow" (44), which situated the twentieth century as one that has made "the phenomena of violence and barbarism" the "signature" of our age (45). Critical diagnoses of the past century are also embedded in this negative view. Habermas does not question the dark episodes of the century; rather, he asks why the accounts that exist only deal with the crimes and atrocities committed. For Habermas, the twentieth century also represents a "turning point" (45) that not only had economic and political consequences but also paved the way for a new normative agenda for our time. For the first time, the appearance of an institutional basis for international law was set in place to deal with crimes against humanity and to deal with the horrors committed by human cruelty. What seems most interesting about Habermas's account, given that he has revised three different historical interpretations tied to structural elements, is that this basic change has also transformed the cultural and intellectual climate of our times. It opened a new horizon for what was to come in our century after the atrocities of the Holocaust were judged in Nuremberg in 1945. What happened? If we first connect those catastrophes to the collective agreements of international law, then examine the way we arrived at a consensus among democratic nations, we can see that new transformations were made possible by a psychological shift that allowed us to develop three important contributions that are somewhat related to this breakpoint. Habermas tells us that the three main historical events were (1) the Cold War entente, (2) the decolonization process, and (3) the establishment of the social welfare state. With the arrival of nuclear power and its potential for greater mass destruction came the opportunity to reach agreements to avoid such disasters. The process of decolonization was not simple or straightforward, yet many countries under colonial rule were inspired by democratic ideals to initiate their own journeys toward independence. Eventually, even a regime as terrible as the apartheid in South Africa was overturned, at least partially as a result of international sanctions. The third historical point—the emergence of the welfare state—made it possible for some developed countries to put into effect basic social rights by means of a carefully planned organization of their state policies. These three significant positive turns of our last century have been underestimated by the narratives of negative events, making Habermas question our very sense of what it entails to learn from past historical catastrophes (49). It is at this point in his argument that he first mentions the concept of "learning from catastrophes." He gives it, however, no further explanation in the essay. Thus, we need to reconstruct the meaning of his ideas and search elsewhere for a full understanding of what he attempts to communicate with this concept.

I have already explained my own definition of "learning from catastrophes" in the previous chapters as defining the material sources societies have in reconstructing past catastrophes as ways of understanding the past. Critical debates and deliberations of what went wrong should configure the normative proposals that societies envision when building up social institutions. In order to strengthen my view, in this chapter I will trace some important insights from Habermas's ideas through a careful interpretation of his interventions in the three historical episodes he used to begin a new debate about past historical atrocities. When analyzing the three different and pessimistic views of the century given by historians, Habermas stresses that because of the breakthrough of the constitution of international law, something other than genocide—a normative order—also emerged. Habermas highlights that this entails a dialectic of light and shadow, or contrasting the dark episodes with our moral understanding of them so we can change the future. It is this turning point that should be the basis of our understanding that the events that took place in the past must not only be condemned, those responsible should also be punished in order to make a transition from the moral to the legal paradigms of international justice. It is by differentiating these two realms—the moral and the legal—that we can rescue the normative notions of individual responsibility and accountability. Persons must be held accountable for their crimes and face this responsibility at their trials. Law—particularly international law—should help us translate our social notions of moral wrongdoing. Our own understanding of catastrophes depends on a careful self-examination that is visible at two different levels—on the one hand, through an open discussion that attempts to understand what happened, and on the other, through the implementation of moral and political judgments leading to initiatives that give us the legal tools needed to fight against moral wrongdoing. Moral and political judgments represent two different levels of critically assessing our past. Nonetheless, together they provide the tool that leads to the only possible solution: the law. Thus our knowledge of moral wrongdoing can and must be translated into typified crimes—crimes that are committed by humans against other humans.

Habermas will argue that in order to exercise proper judgments about our past legacies, we need (1) intellectuals, understood in their enlightened sense, (2) historical information—provided by scholars—which can give us different perspectives of what happened in the past, and (3) an open and critical debate in the public sphere.

Searching for a Concept of the Role of the Intellectual

The first premise we must examine is Habermas's concept of the intellectual as moral guide. Let's begin with his understanding of the role of the intellectual. We can find a proper assessment in his essay "Heinrich Heine and the Role of the Intellectual in Germany."[3] Habermas traces the origin of the concept of the intellectual to the role played by Émile Zola in France after he published his open letter—"J'accuse!"—to the president of the French Republic. The letter contained strong accusations against the military and legal system in their handling of the Dreyfus Affair. It stirred public opinion and many important intellectuals expressed their support, provoking what could now be called a "manifesto of intellectuals."[4] Habermas considers this historic event a perfect example of an intellectual intervention in the public sphere. He believes Zola exemplified someone who bears a public responsibility without "official jurisdiction."[5] Habermas focuses on the Dreyfus Affair because of the implications it had in a more general political culture. It was a turning point for a historical concept because, after this, the moral role of the intellectual was perceived as a duty to stir nations to debate publicly how democratic institutions should work. "When intellectuals, using arguments sharpened by rhetoric, intervene on behalf of rights that have been violated and truths that have been suppressed, reforms that are overdue and progress that has been delayed," Habermas explains, "they address themselves to a public sphere that is capable of response, alert and informed." Furthermore, Habermas insists, only then does the concept of "intellectual" in its normative context become apparent. The world of intellectuals represents an important cultural and political contribution to democracy because they rely on the articulation of justice through the institutions of a real constitutional state. Consequently, critical intellectuals are prepared to question political actions when they are not backed by the principles of democratic institutions. This is the reason Habermas chooses France as an example of the historical emergence of the moral role of the intellectual. After all, there is a continuity between what Zola stood for and the way other French intellectuals responded to this challenge in their own times. Habermas argues that this was not the case in Germany. Germans had a very different idea of the role of the intellectual. The country had to transform itself before allowing intellectuals to exert influence and help shape the historical judgments of their times. Habermas sees the emergence of a critical era with the example of intellectuals like Heinrich Böll.[6] Before Böll, Germans dismissed the idea of intellectuals because of prejudices and misguided notions of their roles and duties. Because Habermas tries to rescue his own tradition, he chooses the emblematic figure of Heine to trace the origins of real enlightened intellectuals who understand that it is their duty to employ their abilities as poets and critics in their struggles against injustice. They are only able to fill this important role by understanding their independence from state authority and by detaching themselves from German and Jewish historical traditions. It was only after 1945 that "Heine's intellectual self-understanding as a figure helped stimulate a critical tradition in Germany." Habermas tells us this was possible because "the mentalities characteristic of the educated German bourgeoisie" had to "be visibly corrupted to a great extent by the Nazi regime before Heine's painful and profound distantiation from his own identity and his cultural tradition could find a place in Germany."[7] Indeed, Habermas writes, "only the revelations of the Nazi crimes have opened our eyes to the monstrous and sinister things that Heine saw brooding even within our best, our most cherished traditions"; thus it was "only after 1945" that Germans were able to distance themselves from Heine and, by recovering his legacy, these intellectuals entered "into a reflexively disrupted relationship to the traditions and intellectual forms that have shaped our identity."[8]

It is not Habermas's intention to state that the political culture is able to solve all internal contradictions stemming from past legacies. Rather, he writes that "the revelation of a moral catastrophe" made it possible to search for a way in which constitutional institutions could lead to constitutional practices stimulated by a critical political culture. Habermas asserts that only critical feedback from intellectuals such as Heine can reinstate the importance of moral guidance in the debate for public judgments. These public judgments remain open to further questioning; they are always fallible and plural, in principle. Such qualities become relevant for a political culture because a critical examination of all traditions, including our very own, becomes possible. Habermas is able to connect between moral guidance and critical reflective judgment only, as we have seen, after moral catastrophes are available to open scrutiny by the public. Once there was a consensus that something horrendous had happened and that the political culture could no longer establish continuity with traditions, Germans finally became open to this kind of active leadership.

Leading Moral Judgment to Initiate a Debate in the Public Sphere

The second premise I wish to develop is that Habermas openly debates the role of historians and their possible contributions to develop a method to exercise collective judgment. This was achieved through his intervention in the *Historikerstreit* of July 1986. Habermas published an article in the weekly *Die Zeit*, against the "apologetic tendencies in the writing of German contemporary history" where he focuses concretely on the works of three historians: Ernst Nolte, Andreas Hillgruber, and Michael Stürmer.

As I stated at the beginning of this chapter, Habermas exemplifies a role that Arendt felt was important. We must not forget Arendt's insistence that after Auschwitz we could no longer rely on given traditions. These needed to be questioned. First, Habermas replies to this challenge by giving weight to the idea that a moral catastrophe like "Auschwitz made it definitely impossible to carry on with continuities" within traditions. If Auschwitz marks a rupture with our traditions, we can only relate to the past "with a reflexive attitude."[9] Second, the only traditions we can now appropriate are those that bear universalist value orientations. We know them only because "they were violated in such an unprecedented way at that time,"[10] which means that we are able to assess their positive normative content only because we have seen what was at stake when they were violated. Third, because we now have a "conflicting pluralism of readings of our history," and because one of its effects is a decentered historical consciousness, we need the input of critical intellectuals whose moral function is to critically examine the historical narratives that exist in the public sphere.[11]

With his intervention into the *Historikerstreit*, Habermas fulfills the role of the intellectual[12] by adding to the public debate important arguments that disclose the ideological connections between the historians' narratives and their political objectives. Habermas questions the very idea that the work of historians should be conceived only as scientific interpretation. Rather, he argues, they are narratives with ideological motives that provide reasons for a political system's need for legitimation. Noticing important inputs from critical debates, Habermas's view allows me to define those moments as the "memory wars." When we have open public spheres, we have the possibility of hearing many different points of view and can contrast them. We can see the ideological motives that propel the possibilities of giving more weight to one narrative than the other. Key in these processes is the critical role of the intellectual. Habermas is well aware that these narratives appropriate "positive pasts"[13] for political purposes. He describes Nolte's, Hillgruber's, and Stürmer's historical reconstructions as providing this kind of positive image of Germany's past.[14] Habermas's critical contribution acknowledges the inevitable pluralism provided by different readings of a historical episode. It is for this reason that these interventions should be questioned and closely monitored, for they can also provide "an opportunity to clarify one's own identity-forming traditions in their ambivalences." Thus, the "development of historical consciousness" comes only with the collective exercise of reflective judgment.[15] Collective judgment cannot be exerted with closed images of the past. It needs the constant stirring up of a critical view in the public debate because one needs to be alert to all possible pitfalls presented by close apologetic narratives. We must therefore be aware of the existence of the struggles for memories—the memory wars.

In his essay "On the Public Use of History,"[16] Habermas claims that in order to deal with public historical consciousness, we need to promote an effort to "historicize" (229) the events reconstructed critically in the public debate. By "historical consciousness" Habermas means not only the idea of our responsible assessment of past wrongs but also our full engagement in the idea of self-transformation as a result of collective judgment. Habermas wants to rescue not only the *anamnetic* powers of solidarity (Walter Benjamin's legacy) but also the political implications of critical reconstructions. These efforts imply that we develop a critical scrutiny as "a gaze educated by moral catastrophe" (234). This critical reassessment might lead us to read such intellectuals as Heidegger, Schmitt, and Ernst Jünger in a different light. If it is clear that scholarly work is mediated in the public sphere, it is through critical comparisons and debates that we assess our critical perspectives. The historians' debate was, according to Habermas, a "watershed in the political culture and self-understanding of the Federal Republic" (238). In response to pessimistic and optimistic views of past catastrophes, Habermas argues for a balance that can only be maintained if we understand what the concept of "learning from catastrophes" can teach us. The strength of this critical self-consciousness comes from a "critical appropriation, educated by Auschwitz, of [all] our traditions."[17] By revisiting history in the public debate, Habermas articulates that the concept of "learning from catastrophes" relates itself to the historical reassessments of past atrocities and can only then lead to self-transformation. This reflexive process cannot be regarded only as part of an exercise of collective formation and the creation of meaning. Rather, it is the only responsible way to understand the meaning of discontinuity with regard to our historical traditions, for "the debate on this rages all the more intensely the less we can rely on a triumphal national history, on the unbroken normality of what has come to prevail, and the more clearly we become conscious of the ambivalence in every tradition."[18] This statement fully exemplifies the dynamic view of revising the past in light of a proper goal to transform the future.

Ian Kershaw, in his book *The Nazi Dictatorship: Problems and Perspectives of Interpretation*, clearly understands the relevance of Habermas's intervention when he concludes that "it has demonstrated the political as well as historical alertness which has combated and triumphed over the variants of neo-conservative revisionism" (187). By the same token, Hans-Ulrich Wehler concludes that the *Historikerstreit* was successful "by the vigilance and critical judgment of liberal public opinion and committed historians," and "it is really [the] liberal political culture that has here proved its mettle—a political culture whose demise has often been foretold, but which showed its strength in the defense against revisionism."[19]

Coining the Idea That We Must Learn from Catastrophes

Unlike the case of the *Historikerstreit,* where Habermas was immediately backed by important historians such as Hans Mommsen and Eberhard Jäckel, among others, his intervention on the Goldhagen debate was seen as endorsing a very criticized piece of academic work. Daniel Goldhagen's *Hitler's Willing Executioners* stirred up a widespread polemic in the public sphere because a great number of academics despised it, while the larger public accepted it as a very important way to reflect on the historical problems of Germany and the Holocaust. Goldhagen's book claims that the main perpetrators of the Holocaust were ordinary Germans and their overriding reason to act as they did was their fierce anti-Semitism. Many theorists argued[20] that Goldhagen's information was not original, that he had simplified many factors and levels of complexity into a single causal historical interpretation, that his Manichean way of presenting data made it impossible to see his work as a serious academic contribution, and that the way in which he portrayed Germans was diabolical and very much against Arendt's own idea about the nature of evil, which was opposed to the notion that evil can be exemplified by demonic beings.[21] In his introduction to *The Germans, the Holocaust, and Collective Guilt: The Goldhagen Debate,* Dominick LaCapra argues that Habermas never searches for simple answers or naïvely argues against all the charges made against Goldhagen's historical research. Rather, as LaCapra is well aware, Habermas's important contribution to this debate (his essay "Goldhagen and the Public Use of History: Why Is the Democracy Prize for Daniel Goldhagen?")[22] is that he used it to reinstate some important political and moral issues with regard to responsibility and judgment. This is why Habermas's intervention in the debate should be seen as a different strategy from the approach he took toward the *Historikerstreit*. LaCapra asserts that Habermas's contribution must be understood in relation to his insistence on the importance of building public memory, and the need to use the public sphere to initiate a critical debate. On the other hand, Federico Finchelstein argues that both the *Historikerstreit* and the Goldhagen debates relate to the idea of the critical use of history in the public sphere. This is an important argument to consider when speaking of the memory wars. We need to consider that both of Habermas's interventions deal with distorted representations of the past and that his interventions stimulated important critical arguments. The debates allowed theorists to assess their critical and methodological consequences with much more depth. These critical perspectives focus on the way historical narratives can respect historical truthfulness and, at the same time, how they provide important information about historical events to the general public.[23] What interests me most about Finchelstein's view, however, is that he goes further in his interpretation of Habermas's own intentions while endorsing Goldhagen's book. As Finchelstein argues, one can accept the simplest explanation about Habermas's intervention. It could be understood as another effort to promote public and critical debate about the public use of history. We have already seen how Habermas perceived this type of participation from intellectuals in the public sphere and why it was important to provide critical views of certain historical narratives. As Finchelstein also points out, however, Habermas's analysis of Goldhagen's historical tools is the least interesting aspect of his essay. In a way, he does not confront some of the most important critical views of the book. Instead, Habermas clearly focuses on the importance of the public reaction from the Germans and on the way Goldhagen's book was avidly read, and thus, it allows us to understand that the memory wars are spaces of critical revision that change as we simultaneously change ourselves. Habermas has a thorough knowledge of history. He proves this by situating Goldhagen's thesis on the same level as Christopher Browning's book.[24] Browning is an important historian who had analyzed the problem of evil by focusing on ordinary people and their choices to participate in the murdering of Jews. Habermas's effort situates both historians—Browning and Goldhagen—at the same level, which illustrates why he is more interested in building his theory of educating through catastrophes[25] than in discussing the novelty of Goldhagen's thesis. Indeed, it is the debate itself that Habermas is interested in developing for the sake of educating the German public. It was his way of keeping the world from forgetting, and protecting the moral framework that has been established to create a space for collective memory. It is within this intervention that we can fully comprehend the concept of "learning from catastrophes" because of the relevance of the ideological struggles that take place in the public sphere. From this perspective, Habermas understands that a book like Goldhagen's can re-create the need to continue revising the past as something not mastered, as something that can still present important lessons through critical examination. The education gained from catastrophes makes it possible to learn to make sound judgments that lead to a consensus about what should be done legally to impede future catastrophes. The effort of self-transformation demands that we fully understand the magnitude and content of the normative principles of justice and democracy.

In his defense of Goldhagen's book in this same essay ("Goldhagen and the Public Use of History"), Habermas offers important clues to help us understand his idea of reflective judgment. When discussing the relevance of historians' interpretations, he contrasts them with our own moral and political assessments of historical episodes. By combining historical consciousness with the exercise of our political judgments, we begin to delimit and understand normative notions of responsibility and choice. In the case of younger generations, certain problems arise when they face the past and decide how to judge what our parents and grandparents did or did not do. This is the relevant question Habermas endorses in supporting the Goldhagen book. Such a book, he tells us, can help situate the idea that all traditions can and must be submitted to critical and collective scrutiny. Traditions can be transformed when we examine them in light of the empirical evidence of past catastrophes. It is only by starting off from critical examination, Habermas argues, that we can build a coherent moral consciousness of the meaning of collective responsibility. Furthermore, he insists, a very important aspect of his defense of Goldhagen's book is that it shows people's moral capacity or incapacity to perpetrate crimes against other humans. Habermas believes that Goldhagen has shown that cultural traditions had become so ingrained in the minds of ordinary Germans—in their daily lives—that their choices were the result of unquestioned prejudices supported by those racist beliefs. Thus, the core of the critical argument is that Goldhagen shows that ordinary Germans were able to make decisions for themselves and did so according to ideas rooted in unquestioned German traditions based on ethnic beliefs. Their choice to commit evil acts should nonetheless alert us to the fact that, even under extreme circumstances, we are always capable of choosing *not* to do evil. This idea of freedom is also shared by Kant and Arendt. Habermas mentions that one important reason why he cares about these kinds of historical narratives is because they offer material for societies' critical ways of self-examination.

It is for this reason that Habermas ends his essay by citing Klaus Günther's notions of the public uses of history and criminal responsibility. Günther highlights the connections between our ways of understanding facts and the hermeneutical horizon with which we judge those data. Indeed, claims Günther, we are capable of accepting responsibility only if we are aware that we have notions already informing us about the kind of societies we are or wish to be. It is through Günther's ideas that Habermas stresses that the only hermeneutic capacity we can acquire comes from an acknowledgement of responsibility that is tied to our notion of freedom. *Freedom* can be defined as the ability and willingness to ascribe responsibility to our actions as moral and political beings. While endorsing Goldhagen's cultural criticism based on German traditions, Habermas concludes, we once more envision the only possible way out of an uncritical reconstruction of our traditions. We must regard those traditions critically and this can happen only when we use catastrophes to educate ourselves.[26]

Who Are We in the Context of Our Traditions?

In 1988, Habermas wrote the essay "Work and Weltanschauung: The Heidegger Controversy from a German Perspective," due to be published as a foreword in Victor Farías's *Heidegger and Nazism* (1989). From the very first lines of the essay, and even from its title, we become aware that Habermas recognizes the importance of Heidegger's work and yet is also capable of separating the importance of his philosophical work from his political behavior. It is no coincidence, however, that Habermas wants us to consider the case of a major philosopher and to see the flaws in his political judgment. Like Arendt, Habermas is well aware that Heidegger's case presents a good example of poor judgment. Habermas chooses to endorse Farías's research because he believes that Farías can give an impartial view of a historical biography that reunites Heidegger's approach to philosophy with his behavior as a human being.[27] He also recognizes that by appealing to the public's "moral judgment" we can begin to review the political steps that led Heidegger to behave as he did. Because Habermas is aware of Heidegger's wide influence, he believes Heidegger exemplifies "the state of mind that persistently characterized the history of the Federal Republic until well into the [1960s]";[28] thus, with the critical examination of his case, we might understand that his lack of moral responsibility is also a trait shared by Germans who chose to keep silent, repressed their past connections with the Nazi regime, and never fully acknowledged the meaning of their actions. As such, Heidegger represents the negative exemplar of what Habermas considers as lack of judgment.[29]

In this essay, Habermas recovered new data provided by scholars who had worked closely with Heidegger. Habermas refers particularly to Otto Pöggeler, who was Heidegger's student and who presents Heidegger's work in consonance with his life and persona.[30] In his analysis, Habermas focuses on an important point: he tells us that Heidegger's refusal to articulate a historical understanding of his times led him to "rigidly maintain . . . the abstraction of historicity (as the condition of historical existence itself) from actual historical processes" (146). We can see here how Heidegger is presented as incapable of making moral or political judgments. As we have seen before, Habermas is very interested in showing us the need to fully comprehend the historicity of our times. On a second level, Habermas is also aware of the need to demonstrate how this lack of judgment happens if we focus on all the ideological elements that arise from Heidegger's works, which "belong [to] an elitist self-understanding of academics, a fetishizing of *Geist*, [an] idolatry for the mother tongue, [a] contempt for everything social, [a] complete absence of sociological approaches long developed in France and the United States, a polarization between natural science and *Geistwissenschafften*, [and] all these themes are unreflectively perpetuated by Heidegger" (147). Thus, Heidegger was an intellectual who represented an important tradition that Habermas now wishes to examine publicly.[31] This tradition is personified by a group known as "the young conservatives," which included people like Oswald Spengler, the Jünger brothers, and Carl Schmitt.[32] Habermas believes it is possible to trace Heidegger's political ideas to his scholarly work, particularly if we see it through his philosophical failures: (1) Heidegger's *Dasein* "cuts off the road from historicity to real history," (2) Habermas gives a derivative status to *Mitsein* (Being with others), and this prevents Heidegger's philosophy from addressing or considering categories such as socialization and intersubjectivity as important sources of Being, and (3) his solipsism prevents him from taking or considering moral obligations seriously.[33] Furthermore, Habermas adds, "Heidegger's thought exhibits a conflation of philosophical theory with ideological motives."[34]

Habermas's use of Heidegger as a negative examplar of someone who lacks the capacity to exercise judgment becomes apparent when he points out that Heidegger shared the "widespread anti-Western sentiments of his intellectual environment and held metaphysical thinking to be more primordial than the vapid universalism of enlightenment" (148). The terrible results of this type of thinking led him to view history as "mere ontical happening, [and] social contexts of life" as dimensions of the inauthentic, the ideas of truth as prepositional phenomena, and morality as "expressing reified values" (148).

Understanding the spirit of Heidegger's times also means visualizing the themes and authors that became a part of his tradition. After 1929, Hölderlin and Nietzsche were to be the most highly regarded authors of the following decade. This paved the road for Heidegger's "neopagan turn (*Kehre*)" (148),[51] which made the idea of mythologizing the past a privileged means to unleash the narratives of his work. Heidegger's idea of his role as philosopher also changed. First, he dismissed Goethe and German Idealism. Then he broke away from Husserl (his teacher), and later on he distanced himself from academic philosophy in order to challenge the future of universities and pave the way for the political role into which he planned to insert himself (as exemplified by his *Rektoradrede* in 1933). And last, he opened himself to the influence of the young conservatives. The most interesting fact in Habermas's account is that Heidegger deified history and put metaphysics above real history. Philosophy was seen as the only ruler. In his philosophy, however, Heidegger liquidated the moral core of the idea of the authenticity standard and all the critical moments that his work *Being and Time*[35] provided by the individualistic heritage of existential philosophy, which were then transformed into the idea of a collective fate. As Habermas says, "Now [it] is the 'people' and no longer the individual, which exists."[36] Heidegger's judgment led him to explain that whatever happened in Germany was the unfolding idea that the great leaders have put truth to work, so one can see that it was a "specifically German deformation *profesionelle* that gave" Heidegger the idea of believing that he could become the leader of the leader (i.e., Hitler). Habermas demonstrates through this analysis that Heidegger lacked a capacity for moral and political judgments. Habermas argues that Heidegger's "trajectory between 1935 and 1945 shows itself to be a process of working through a series of disappointments," but no real questioning came from the philosopher; instead, he continued with his project until he introduced the "'turn' (*Kehre*) with the texts of 1930–31" (153). Habermas focuses on three important instances in which Heidegger's lack of critical reassessment became apparent: (1) Heidegger's critique of reason through the history of metaphysics remained untouched; (2) the nationalistic estimation of the Germans came to be seen as the "heart of peoples"; and (3) his position with regard to National Socialism was never made clear nor did he ever express any critical view of what happened during the Nazi era.

More important is that Habermas views Heidegger's ideological motives translated as important features of his philosophical thinking—as, for example, when seeing that his history of metaphysics regarded technology as "the expression of the will to will, which in practice makes itself felt in the phenomena of positivistic science, technological development, industrial labor, the bureaucratized state, mechanized warfare, the management of culture, the dictatorship of public opinion, and generally mass civilization" (154). Furthermore, even after all the disappointments, Heidegger "remains convinced of the world-historical importance and of the metaphysical meaning of Nazism to the bitter end" (155). If Heidegger became increasingly disappointed, Habermas argues, it was only in the final phase of his "working through his disillusionment" that the concept of the history of Being finally took a "fatalistic form" (158).

In the end, Heidegger remained convinced that the true successors to the Greeks were the Germans, even if this was expressed only in terms of language. The leaders were now sublimated into poets and thinkers, and even the idea of political adherence was then seen as obedience to the destiny of Being. Thus, Habermas concludes, "with the help of an operation that we might call 'abstraction via essentialization' the history of Being is disconnected from political and historical events" (159).

Habermas's analysis leaves no doubt as to why he endorses the investigations of Hugo Ott and Victor Farías. Neither Heidegger's actions nor the data his defenders have provided change the fact that he never explained the Nazi crimes. In this work we can more readily trace the role of the intellectual when critically questioning the available data that can lead to good judgment. In Heidegger's case, we see that Habermas stirs up public opinion in order not to disclose the ideological relationship between his life and his work because much of it was already being provided by many of the authors on whom he himself based his own approach. Rather, Habermas proposes that Heidegger's nonapologetic conduct after the war must remain a problem to his contemporaries because "we have a right to call one another to account" (164). Judgment here relies on our capacity to understand accountability for our sense of responsibility. Habermas believes Heidegger acted no differently than many others of his time, and that his behavior represents the typical outcome of someone who refuses to take any responsibility for his deeds. To judge negative cases of silence and forgetfulness it is also necessary to come to terms with the need to resituate ourselves in a different era from Nazi Germany. Learning from catastrophes relates to the idea that accountability and responsibility are two important aspects of the moral and legal dimensions. It is our duty to understand that Heidegger and others are still a part of the German tradition even today. We must also reconsider the place, influence, and recognition we will allow such men to have in history.

Heidegger's case might lead us to an even more provocative conclusion: Habermas believes that Heidegger represents an example of someone without a guilty conscience. He had no sense of moral wrongdoing or a true understanding of what happened. This moral failure was based on his lack of judgment, which is the only conclusion one can have after reading Habermas's essay. In a way, Heidegger's case offers another instance of illustrating the figure of the "banality of evil" which led Arendt to the belief that real perpetrators of evil seldom acknowledge what they did. Only this time, the banality is not exemplified by an ordinary perpetrator because of his lack of imagination and the uses of clichés, but by an intellectual, a philosopher whose lack of judgment made him Hitler's accomplice. And his refusal to take responsibility is a result of this lack of his capacity to be an honest intellectual of his times.

PART II

The Judgments

CHAPTER 6

What Remains? Language Remains

Levi the Jew—ebreo di ritorno—acquired the ability to narrate directly from the hell of Auschwitz, and, once he had returned to life, the ability to purify his mouth of that contagion using the gift of the story, an inheritance which, like all divine or magic gifts, soon proved to be a double-edge sword.

—*Marco Belpoliti*[1]

Building a Model for Moral Judgment

In this chapter, I will use my model of reflective judgment to show that is it possible to connect the work and stories of Primo Levi to this moral type of judgment. I will then show the two different ways in which judgment is used—first, the reflective, then the determinant—the former in Levi's work, and the latter in Giorgio Agamben's *Remnants of Auschwitz: The Witness and the Archive.* The reason to focus on Levi's and Agamben's work is to show what makes a judgment a reflective one, out of specific contexts and situations, whereas the determinant judgment in Agamben's work helps clarify how easily one can turn the disclosiveness of a judgment into a generalization of a determinant perspective, which blurs the final outcome of the work of judgment. I will argue that it is the connection between these two authors—the concrete conceptualizations of Levi's experience and then the way in which his categories are turned out to be the basis of a generalization—that allows me to better explore what really constitutes the hard work of reflective judgment as a way of understanding past catastrophes.

By testifying about his experience at Auschwitz, valid essentially in and of itself, Levi uses important conceptual constructions to provide us with clues to make sense of the kind of evil he describes.[2] With those conceptual elements in hand, Agamben first develops his own judgment by using the two most important and striking categories from Levi's narratives (the concept of the "gray zones" and the concept of the *Muselmann*) and then he transforms them into a new schema to understand modern politics. By critically examining Agamben's case, I wish to provide clues into what makes reflective judgment an important tool to understand evil, but when it is used as a general theory of the political, its moral scope is obscured. In the account Agamben gives of Auschwitz, a bloody reality emerges out of the idea of the *homo sacer and the camp* and it is transformed into the biopolitical paradigm of modern politics.[3]

I have insisted since the first chapter that stories are good vehicles that can lead to the construction of reflective judgments. In previous chapters, I have dealt with historical narratives and theoretical works derived from historians' accounts as good examples that triggered reflective judgments. Until now, we have not seen the way narratives affect readers and public opinion or the impact they have on other people's ideas and judgments. Clearly, the dimension of spectators and of public opinion relates to the public sphere, but I need to clarify that what we are dealing with in this chapter is the *literary* public sphere. In Habermas's early work, he focused on the way the literary public sphere turned into a political one when the problems and debates became a question of collective efforts at an institutional level. Habermas realized the importance of the literary public sphere not only because it entailed the disclosure of individual lives and stories but also because he was aware that the literary public sphere offers an important filter through which to introduce themes, critical issues, and important disclosive angles of social problems that attract the attention of the public in order to initiate a debate about the stories' validity. By focusing on the historic emergence of the literary public sphere, Habermas was able to demonstrate how an associational way of life began to take place. Habermas also recognizes the potential power that lies at the heart of this dimension of the public sphere because of its focus on communication. The literary public sphere provides the foil that makes understandable the importance of opinion-shaping associations and debates, which occupy a prominent place in civil societies. This is why the public sphere (in both its literary and political dimensions) in totalitarian regimes is subject to the control of the secret police and the state.[4]

Hannah Arendt was also interested in the dimension of the literary public sphere and its relation to the formation of political opinion. She produced a special concept—"mastering the past"—related to this dimension of the public sphere, which involved the dynamics between stories and readers, between meanings and the significance of these in history. Arendt explains that "insofar as any 'mastering' of the past is possible, it consists in relating what has happened; but such narration, too, which shapes history, solves no problems and assuages no suffering; it does not master anything once and for all."[5] She clarifies that as long as the meaning of the events persist, mastering the past takes the form of "an ever recurring narration."[6] Stories gain their permanence in people's minds because they allow us to understand what took place, its significance; and it is through our judgment—the judgment produced by spectators in their continuous debates—that the story can take its place in history. Seen in this light, stories might not liberate us from our past, but they certainly can allow us to understand what happened. Arendt believes that the key to this understanding is the idea that the critical effort at "mastering the past" produces collective judgments.

We are about to enter the most contested area in which these kinds of narratives, which are inextricably linked to evil, become the precious material—the testimony of witnesses—in order to understand historical atrocities. It is important here to recall that Walter Benjamin, in his work on Nikolai Leskov, listed the reasons he thematized about the importance of narratives and why he believed they captured experience and memory.[7] Here we see why Walter Benjamin thought of narratives as providing the means for making experience the dominating expression that captures the concrete features of human life and why they are also important vehicles of memory.[8] Mastering the past means also providing a public space where we can recover the memories of those long gone. We need those stories as elements of our own critical appraisal of what happened.

The idea of testimonies and of witnesses has been much discussed among theorists of the Holocaust.[9] Going beyond their valuable arguments, I contend that Primo Levi has contributed significantly more than anyone else to our understanding of narratives about evil and its complexities.[10] His narratives about his own experience at the *Lager* (the German word for "concentration camp") are unique because they illuminate the empirical work through his own judgment. We, the readers, experience his process of reflective judgment through the ever-recurring narration of what happened in the *Lagers*. One may consider his works to be somewhat different from many of the narratives of other witnesses and of other writers precisely because of the different attempts, in his autobiographical stories, to tell about the experience he lived through. It has been argued that his narrations do not display anger or resentment, as is usually the case with those who have suffered the injuries of evil actions.[11] Rather, Levi's narratives possess the calm restraint of someone who has come to understand that his moral duty as a witness is to use his voice to draw upon new images that describe and disclose the hidden angles or suppressed views from the realities of those who suffered them and have disappeared from the earth. We still think of their experiences as the kinds one would consider unimaginable, conceptually speaking. Levi's narratives avoid the simplistic strategy of forming judgmental views about the moral collapse he witnessed. Instead, I wish to argue, his narratives offer us the vital elements that, when brought together, make it possible for us to form our own judgments. I want to show that Levi's narratives are exceptional in that they allow us to configure reflective judgments because he uses new concepts to describe the negative aspects of evil. He does so by creating conceptual images that allow us to see things critically and reveal hidden angles that we were incapable of seeing before. The most interesting example of Levi's narratives is the masterpiece he wrote with the poetic title of *The Drowned and the Saved*.[12] His reflective judgment is its product.

From the beginning of this narration, Levi realizes that it is impossible to separate the perpetrator from the victim. As we have seen, this is an important conceptual condition that I enlisted before, when insisting that narratives allow us to understand this linkage as an important connection to evil acts. The action that ties them together produces a moral fracture. This moral dimension illuminates how this fracture robs the victim of moral choices. Levi explains why this is possible, given that in thematizing evil actions, "We are dealing with a paradoxical analogy between victim and oppressor . . . but, it is the oppressor, and he alone, who has prepared it and activated it. . . . The oppressor remains what he is, and so does the victim . . . but both, faced by the indecency of the irrevocable act, need refuge and protection, and instinctively search for them" (24–25). The connection between offender and sufferer is thus a specific interrelation owing to evil actions, whose consequences are felt in the identities of both the agent and the victim.

Levi also seeks to recover the idea of memory as one important element of his narratives. He is aware of this need because he believes that the entire history of the Third Reich can be read as a "war against memory" (25). Thus, the Nazi regime's strategy involved erasing the evil actions of an era. Levi, however, does not believe that memory simply involves recovering historical data. Rather, his account tends to illuminate why the constructions of our human memories depend on the depth of our moral gaze and on the possibility of exploring them through the creation and use of disclosive language. This is the third element of his view that fits into my model of reflective judgment. Levi's idea is that we need a specific schema in which our experience can be grasped and offered to the public. Levi says, "We are compelled to reduce the knowable to a schema: with this purpose in view we have built for ourselves admirable tools in the course of evolution, tools which are the specific property of the human species—language and conceptual thought" (36). This schema is not simplistic. Rather, as Levi shows, it must avoid the dangers of binary definitions of perpetrators against their victims. Instead, Levi chooses to exemplify his own experience as a field of reflection, a texture that illuminates what Arendt had already defined as the most important characteristic of totalitarianism, one in which persons lose the basic conditions for what it means to be human. "The enemy was all around," explains Levi, "but also inside, the 'we' lost its limits, the contenders were not two, one could not discern a single frontier but many confused, perhaps innumerable frontiers" (38). Because of the victims' inability to resist, the moral breakup was complete, and with it, the loss of the human world. Not only did the loss of humanity become the first basic condition of this moral collapse; Habermas has also suggested that something more horrible happened:[13] The Nazis erased the human capacity of solidarity "among the oppressed," and this condition became even more unbearable than any of the previous crimes.[14] Levi offers us this kind of moral understanding through the idea that the *Lagers* could not be described in terms of absolute good apart from absolute evil. He searched for a metaphor and found the idea of "gray zones" to describe places where it was no longer possible to define the good against the bad. Everyone is corrupt because totalitarian regimes need to strip away the humanity from its most cherished attribute—namely, moral identity. The existence of the gray zones depends on a particular set of circumstances: (1) it is where the sphere of power is so restricted that one needs external auxiliaries (the victims); (2) the gray zones have complicated internal structures since they blur boundaries between perpetrator and victim; (3) they seek the corruption of victims by compromising them as much as possible, burdening them with guilt; (4) the greater the oppression the more willing the oppressed are to collaborate; and, finally, (5) the lucid calculation aimed to elude imposed orders is the gray zone's trademark.

Gray zones had the ultimate goal of erasing the concept of justice from its own normative foundation. Moral choices were reduced to zero because, with the loss of humanity, there was only the burden of the most imperious needs to be fulfilled. Levi explains that "the deprivation to which they were subjected led them to a condition of pure survival, a daily struggle against hunger, cold, fatigue and blows in which the room for choices (especially moral choices) were reduced to zero."[15] Moral identity crumbled because the Nazis reduced their victims' only remaining recourse, that of feeling oneself to be innocent before the perpetrator. The only possible moral conclusion of this chapter is to understand that, at times like this, it is impossible to know "one's place"; thus, Levi claims, "judgment must be suspended" (60). Levi asks us not to readily submit our judgment to a rushed conclusion. Indeed, the more we see the basic strategies leading to the destruction of the victims, the more we are capable of understanding what the goals of the Nazis were. Levi compels us to understand that "one is never in another's place. Each individual is so complex that there is no point in trying to foresee his behavior—all the more so in extreme situations. Nor is it possible to foresee one's own behavior. Therefore I ask that we mediate on the story of 'the crematorium ravens' with pity and rigor, but that judgment of them be suspended" (60). What he offers us, instead, are illuminating examples found in concrete stories such as that of Chaim Rumkowski, a failed industrialist who came to be the president of a ghetto (62). Levi is aware of Rumkowski's shortcomings. Nevertheless, he explains that "his identification with the oppressor alternates, or goes hand in hand, with an identification with the oppressed, because as Thomas Mann says, man is a mixed-up creature" (64). What we must not forget, as Levi goes on to tell us, is that "there was only one fate for Jews in German hands, whether they were cowards or heroes, humble and proud. Neither the letter nor the special carriage were able to save Chaim Rumkowski, the king of Jews, from the gas chamber" (66). What possible conclusion can be reached from this story? Levi warns us that the story is not self-contained, "it is pregnant, full of significance, asks more questions than answers, sums up in itself the entire theme of the gray zone and leaves one dangling" (66–67). Can we ask: Who was Rumkowski? To which Levi replies: "Not a monster, nor a common man." We must be aware that "his story" is "an exemplary form" that shows how the "almost physical necessity with which political coercion gives birth to that ill-defined sphere of ambiguity and compromise" corrupts the moral character of those who are oppressed (67). The corruption of power intoxicates humans and extinguishes the individual will. There is no possible absolution of Rumkowski's deeds on moral grounds, but there is one possible interesting nuance: "There are extenuating circumstances: an infernal order such as National Socialism exercises a frightful power of corruption, against which it is difficult to guard oneself" (68). Our concern now is: Where can one draw the moral lesson of the story in order to build up some kind of moral judgment? Levi replies that we need to remember that "we are all mirrored in Rumkowski, his ambiguity is ours, it is our second nature, we hybrids molded from clay and spirit" (69). This is the space where the story creates the possibility of self-reflection, of understanding, of seeing the example as a way of mirroring ourselves into our own corrupted shape. The description of degradation leads Levi to conclude that "the sole usefulness of useless violence" is the key to understanding how shame and guilt are the features of those degraded by a program that aimed at burdening them all with guilt, so no one turned out to remain innocent.

The second stage of this program of moral degradation leads Levi to ponder the feelings of survivors. Understanding the urge to bring back some moral dimensions to our fragility makes Levi focus on the idea of moral shame. Coming out of the *Lager* forced people to face their own shame.[16] People had been reduced to an animal condition. Their actions were aimed at fulfilling the urges of pure necessity. This is the reason it caused a deprivation of one's sense of humanity. Once released from this horrendous situation, however, one was reminded how much one had lost, and this presented "painful moments precisely because they gave us the opportunity to measure our diminishment from the outside."[17] Shame then becomes associated with guilt, because people had done little or nothing to prevent coming out of the dark stages of such a life, which meant being aware of the failed resistance to the *Lagers'* corruption. Those who were "saved" from the corruption at the *Lager* "were not [necessarily] the best, those predestined to do good, the bearers of the message... . Preferably the worst survived, the selfish, the violent, the insensitive, the collaborators of the 'gray zones'" (82). Survival, explains Levi, was more a matter of luck than of being a better person than others. He then goes on to explain why the idea of witnesses becomes a complex one. There are people who did not return. They perished in silence. Thus, there needs to be a conceptual space in which to think about them. In Levi's view, the concept of the "Muslims" helps him describe the people "who return mute" to his mind. They are the only complete witnesses. They needed to be rescued because they were the drowned. Where does this concept of the "drowned" come from? Levi replies that we can focus now on language because "where violence is inflicted on man it is also inflicted on language" (97). To understand this violence one must recover the very same words coined by the evil regime to describe the daily lives of horror. "Common to all *Lagers* was the term *Musselmann*," says Levi. This term that in ordinary language would literally refer to someone who belongs to a specific religion is now being resemanticized to produce a semantic shock. Since Levi is well aware about this semantic violence, he explains that there is a connection of this term with others like the Russian *dokodjaga*, which literally means "come to an end" or "concluded"(same page p.98). He also clarifies how in the Ravensbrück *Lager* (the only one exclusively for women) "the same concept was expressed . . . by the two specular substantives *Schmutzück* and *Schmuckück*, respectively, "garbage" and "jewel" almost homophonous, one the parody of the other"(p.98). The term acquires a violent image that is meant to shock when it is supposed to described how these persons were seen at the *Lager*, how they submitted themselves to the senseless orders of death and destruction. Losing our sense of being human makes persons accept everything without resistance. The *Muselmänner* accepted their fate with "definitive indifference" (101). Notice, however, that Levi uses the expression of the *Muselmänner* as a way of recovering a violent and charged political description first used by the Nazis themselves. In his narrative he transforms the expression into one that adds new meaning because he aims to explore the moral idea about the lack of freedom as a method of stripping away their humanity, a capacity to react against their own fate of destruction.

The Drowned and the Saved is a book of many exemplary stories. Some of these have become, as we have seen, important vehicles for conceptual moral understanding. Furthermore, they are all meant to allow us to understand the complexities of humankind. Rescuing people who are long gone is another important result of tying memory to the historical span that these stories portray. In this sense, Levi rescues the lives of many people at the *Lager*. He even attempts to rescue the story of his own colleague, Jean Améry (whose real name was Hans Mayer), to show how Améry represented a different way of coping with terror. In a way, he was Levi's alter ego. Through an analysis of Améry's struggles about his life as an intellectual, Levi shows us how his sufferings seemed to destroy him as well in spite of his resistance. He does not judge Améry's reactions to evil deeds. Rather, he compares these reactions and illuminates the idea of moral wrong by expanding the scope of it through other people's reactions. Being a Jew, for example, was for Améry, a "[condition] simultaneously impossible and obligatory" (129). He cultivated anger to endure the hellish experience of the *Lagers*. His reaction to this humiliation was reinforced by the idea of "returning the blow" (129). Améry's descriptions of the *Lager* were confined to the experiences of Auschwitz (though he had also been in Buchenwald and Bergen-Belsen). Levi, by contrast, thinks about his duty to remember by revisiting the dark corners of his memory. He shows how Améry, as an intellectual, endured even another kind of violence because he could not stop thinking about the techniques that were designed to break his sense of self forever. Améry "explored the limits of the spirit, the nonimaginable" (131), and his experience illustrates what Levi understood as the core of defining evil actions—the task of destroying one's own sense of identity. Levi shows us how Améry's identity is mutilated: he was a German native speaker. The loss of his native language—his love of it—made him mourn and relearn that German was now a violent weapon used by his perpetrators. He could not separate his love for his mother tongue from the violent experience of being subjected to listen to his beloved language in the voices of his torturers. As a result, he became an orphan. How can we understand that in losing his language, Améry lost what he loved most? Perhaps the only possible answer to this question was given by another prisoner, Paul Celan, who also endured the torture of being stripped of his own language but who made new use of this tragic knowledge in order to initiate the most radical revolution of all—creative poetry. Celan found an accurate and dark description of the expressions of hell on earth through the creation of poetic crystallizations. His "Death Fugue" became the emblematic poem of Auschwitz. This poem is chosen by Levi in his personal anthology called *The Search for Roots*[18] to define the new use of poetry after Auschwitz. What remains is language.

The Transition from Moral Judgment into a Generalized Radical Conclusion

In mastering the past, as I have explained before, we see the emergence of new stories that remake earlier ones. This is what happened when Giorgio Agamben wrote *Remnants of Auschwitz: The Witness and the Archive* to recover Levi's most important conceptualizations of his reflective judgment into a new stage of narration. In my model, this transition from the narrative to its conceptual recovery exemplifies the idea of the impact of knowledge gained from one narrative into another. Though Agamben further extends Primo Levi's reflective judgment in a moral sense with his commentaries, he then transforms this judgment into a political conclusion that generalizes the whole historical period of Auschwitz as an example of modernity, which thus loosens the grip of the judgment previously made by Levi. It is interesting to focus on this development, for political judgments are never simply derived by causes (which would then be determinate judgments in a Kantian sense).

Agamben's work is another expression of the idea of the sublime considered as horror, but this time he connects his view about the atrocities of Auschwitz as an example of the modern age derived from an up-to-date combination of sovereignty with pure power (or, as Agamben puts it, "bare life"). Agamben's goal is to show how unlimited power leads to the destruction of the human being. The concentration camp interests Agamben not as a historical fact, but as a hidden matrix of the political. Humanity is conceived here as being "stripped off" its moral resources and as a condition of the ultimate abjection. As we can see, this conception bears resemblances to those that we have already examined when discussing the aporetic views of the sublime portrayed in the works of Julia Kristeva, Jean François Lyotard, and Slavoj Žižek. Like many pessimistic views about the Holocaust, Agamben's thesis makes the general claim that modernity's idea of sovereign power is embodied in the historical example of Auschwitz. Only this time, the example of the *Muselmann*—taken from Levi's work—is seen as the realization of the ultimate abjection of "bare life." I claim that while Agamben correctly recovers Primo Levi's two particular categories about the atrocities in Auschwitz, he then generalizes them out of this historical episode into a political conclusion that relates to the modern concept of sovereignty. With this move, Agamben turns from reflective judgment to determinant judgment. This way of conceiving things is influenced by Carl Schmitt's notion of the state of exception (which Schmitt conceives as a state of emergency),[19] where the exception becomes the rule and the preexisting normative and legal categories are left behind.[20] I argue that with his conclusion, Agamben lessens the importance of what he had recovered from Levi, and uses the notion of abjection as a way to criticize modernity as a whole.[21]

Agamben is well aware that certain kinds of atrocities demand further exploration because we need a relationship between historical knowledge and truth—between verification and comprehension. Agamben sees this as a way of exploring the aporetic angles of the kinds of actions we usually call "atrocities." Here, we can see how Agamben situates his criticism in the territory of another version of the sublime. Only this time, the sacred version of the sublime is now translated into a secular one. Like Lyotard, Agamben insists on the paradox as its privileged figure and develops his arguments toward the necessity of working out new formulations to respond to aporetical views that can never reach total closure. Stories like the ones Levi offers, says Agamben, can help one go into this perpetual stage of "commentary on testimony,"[22] and draw from them a conceptual schema in which to locate these aporetic spaces of the unsayable. There is something in Levi's testimony that Agamben thinks he can point out as a "lacuna"[23] of silence and disclose a hidden view of human tragedies. Contrary to Levi's conception, Agamben's view of humanity is expressed as the absolute bankruptcy of morality and makes no use of history to provide the needed mediations in order to understand the specificity of Auschwitz. His aporetical way of developing the paradox of Auschwitz leaves us with no ability to ascribe historical responsibilities and agency in what happened. This totalistic, agentless history is concerned with politics and its eclipse, and, paradoxically, it becomes very unpolitical.[24]

First, he prevents himself from using the typical words we have commonly used to refer to the historical disaster of the genocide of the Jews in the German extermination camps—namely, the concept of the Holocaust or even the Hebrew concept of Shoah. When he refuses to use these terms, he wants to highlight not only a historical rupture but to highlight an entire era as a postapocalyptic view of sovereign power. Agamben transforms the geographical site of horror—*Auschwitz*—and generalizes the term as covering more than just one historical episode. This is why Agamben's initial exercise of reflective judgment is ultimately flawed.[25] In spite of his own recognized inspiration (taken from Foucault's works, and from Hannah Arendt's legacy), Agamben is closer to Heidegger than to these other sources.[26] This is because Foucault invented a way to articulate *concrete* historical practices as genealogical developments that led him to find out about the ways in which certain disciplinary practices make subjects. Foucault, then, was always situated within the limits of the concreteness of historical practices, and never dared to draw generalized conclusions about them. We could say that, in a way, Foucault understood what is at stake when making reflective judgments. Agamben, on the other hand, relies only on the power of concepts and on their linguistic roots to disclose a political argument (his method resembles that used by Heidegger himself).[27] Even if he shares Arendt's idea that when something like Auschwitz happens we need to refuse to rely on tradition and leave behind the perspective of moral theories that come with modernity, Arendt would not dare to conclude that we could simply get rid of all its legacy. By the same token, Arendt did not conclude that the Holocaust was the logical consequence of modernity,[28] but rather an unprecedented moment requiring all our attention in order to begin anew.

Agamben's theory claims that certain ambiguities in naming historical periods can be corrected if we go back to their original meanings. Then we must revise their incorrect usage by previous judgments in order to understand why language is the basic new element of this reordering of our moral comprehension. Agamben claims that words like *Holocaust* literally mean a "supreme sacrifice."[29] Even the Hebrew term *so'ah*—meaning devastation or catastrophe—is wrong, because it implies the idea of divine punishment. This discussion sheds light on Agamben's view about the nature of his postmetaphysical ideas. His conclusion is that we need to avoid euphemisms in order to address the historical period of crematoria and senseless death by using its proper name: Auschwitz. This term provides a concrete example of the *Lagers* in the Nazi regime. However, the camp becomes his paradigm and, paradoxically, with this categorical use of the term to define a whole era he *extinguishes all differences*. The state of exception becomes the norm, and the norm becomes the state of exception. It also becomes the political illustration of his more general view of politics. Agamben therefore rescues the geographical site of horror and gives it a new political meaning through the recovery of two of its most concrete features—categories—with which he exemplifies the whole history of politics in modern times.[30] In blurring all political differences, Agamben dismisses the problem between the law and the non-law, between democratic law and authoritarian law, and between modernity and totalitarianism. It is for this reason that his conclusion leads to an excessively one-sided understanding of perpetrators and victims as representing mere "bare life."[31] In this view, Auschwitz and the *Muselmann* will illustrate the apocalyptic conditions of our contemporary existence[32]—they are the remnants of modernity's idea of sovereign power.[33]

Agamben argues that he needs to explain the lacuna between the idea of testimony and that of the survivor. This lacuna will be exemplified by the metaphorical figures that Levi provided us with—i.e., the "Muslims," or the "drowned."[34] When focusing on Levi's account as one of a survivor, Agamben, for example, reminds us that the Greek word for witness is *martis* (martyr) (26). He then goes on to argue that "the concepts of 'witnessing and martyrdom' can be linked in two ways: The first is derived from the meaning of the verb 'to remember,' thus, the vocation of the survivor is to remember." The second, says Agamben, is even more instructive: martyrdom "justifies the scandal of meaningless death" (27). He has chosen Levi's account of the "Muslims" because he seems to be aware of the paradoxical nature of Levi's task—that of opening up a silent space where the witnesses can be brought back to direct our moral gaze with a new "meaning in an unexpected area" (34). We learn to understand Agamben's aporetical view when he interprets that Levi thought of the Muslims as the only true witnesses because they had no story; thus, they represent "the sublime witness whose testimony would be truly valuable, but who cannot bear witness."[35] The *Muselmänner* are all gone, claims Agamben, yet one has to learn to listen to their silence in order to articulate something relevant. Agamben submits them to become the subjects of multiple readings: "Levi had already attempted to listen to and to interpret an inarticulate babble, something like a non-language or dark and maimed language"[36] from people like Hurbinek.[37] Using the recovery of Hurbinek's babble, Levi "bears witness through these words"[38] that Agamben calls the new language. Thus, Levi fills the lacuna with words, and words give place to Agamben's aporetic conceptual thinking. Language here transposes itself into the dark areas where silence once reigned, not to illuminate our understanding but to obscure it.

When thinking about past catastrophes, we are faced with the challenge of rethinking our moral categories because we cannot use them as we did before. Recall Hannah Arendt's realization that what happened in Auschwitz could not allow us to continue using the same terms from our moral tradition. We need to be aware that we have several important conceptual problems: the first is that there is a bridge between the legal terminology that addresses the responsibility of crimes and the true depth of a moral deed.[39] In my theory of reflective judgments we need to establish mediations between these two different spaces. For Agamben, instead, the only important issue is that there exists "a non-juridical element of truth" such "that the *quaestio facti* can never be reduced to the *quaestio iuris.*"[40] Arendt was also aware of this gap between the juridical and the moral spheres, and her awareness was explicated in her narrative when she attended Eichmann's trial. On the other hand, Agamben claims that all moral and religious categories are "contaminated by law,"[41] and law can be directed solely to legal judgments. He argues that legal judgments are developed independently from truth and justice, while recent studies have shown that law and justice can be reconnected in a constructive critical fashion. Judgment can be self-referential in that it becomes a form of punishment. Law does not exhaust the meaning of evil actions, but it helps in designing the processes of transition where justice is redefined.[42] Furthermore, just as it is impossible to place the responsibility for evil actions on God (theodicies), it is also absurd to believe that law can exhaust the problem of moral atrocities. This is why it is necessary to have a paradigm of evil that is related to the paradigm of justice once we begin a critical period of revising our past.

One important issue for Agamben is that we need a model—a paradigm—that allows for conscious moments of self-disclosure. Instead of showing us how to do this, Agamben ends up conceiving this paradigm as the sublime—that is, as the territory of the unsayable, or the unimaginable. Agamben makes use of Levi's concept of the gray zones. Levi, on the other hand, used the idea of the color gray to illustrate how the borders between black and white were blurred and judgment became the most difficult task to accomplish. Levi's notion illuminates how the borders between victim and perpetrator were fused by an evil regime. What Levi saw as a historical way in which humanity lost its basic moral sense of having the freedom to decide between doing evil or not, Agamben sees it as a generalization of a state of exception that in modern politics has become customary. Thus, Agamben loses the moral dilemma of doing evil in terms of the Kantian idea of freedom; evil becomes the threshold of indistinction and of brute power.

We can see now how Agamben's conceptual schema for his paradigm of Auschwitz is flawed, despite its initial useful tools taken from Levi's stories. In his determinant judgment, Agamben concludes that the stories are the general features of a specific way of conceiving power in modernity. Auschwitz can be called the aporetic model of Agamben's vision of modern politics. Reflective judgments are never causal (otherwise, they would be determinant judgments in a Kantian sense), and this feature should help us clarify what is wrong with Agamben's conclusion. He derives his causal explanation on how politics are configured through the idea of sovereign power. Clearly, this is a theory of sovereign power stripped off from its normative basis.

In spite of these shortcomings, some of Agamben's ideas are able to grasp the disclosive view that made Levi such an original narrator of evil. For example, when Agamben describes the *Muselmann* in stages of deterioration as the prototype of humanity, we could interpret this view as the accomplishment of a redescription about how humanity was lost. First, he shows the *Muselmann* as exemplifying two contradictions—being human and becoming inhuman. He portrays the "Muslim" as having the symptoms of malnutrition. The ways in which the stages of malnutrition come to resemble the appearance of these people as ghastly corpses leads Agamben to capture the *violent* metaphor of the word—Muslim—as describing someone who seems to be blindly obeying his own fate. One must recall that the literal meaning of the word *Muslim* is "the one who submits unconditionally to the will of God."[43] "While the Muslim's resignation consists in the conviction that the will of Allah is at work every moment and in even the smallest events," Agamben explains, "the *Muselmann* of Auschwitz is instead defined by a loss of all will and consciousness" (45). This example allows me to show how the meaning of the word *Muslim* in Auschwitz differs from its meaning in ordinary language. This new concept seeks to create a space of disclosure for the moral use of the word *Muselmann*. He is seen as an example of the only "complete witness," the only one that illustrates the paradox of what "makes it forever impossible to distinguish between man and non-man" (47). Consider that, through this example, Agamben is able to give us a wider understanding of what Hannah Arendt had referred to before as "being stripped off humanity." "Like the pile of corpses," adds Agamben, "the *Muselmänner* document the total triumph of power over the human being" (48). The concept of the *Muselmänner* is one of the most successful metaphors for comprehending an idea that allows us to refer both to humanity versus non-humanity, to vegetative existence versus biological needs, to physiology and to ethics, to medicine and politics, and to life and death simultaneously as two contradictory components of the same term.[44] "This is why," concludes Agamben, "the *Muselmann's* 'third realm' is the perfect cipher of the camp, the non-place in which all disciplinary barriers are destroyed and all embankments flooded."[45] What we begin to understand with this view of Auschwitz is that moral concepts such as dignity and even humanity lose their meaning when confronted by extreme situations. "The *Muselmann*" has moved "into a zone of the human where not only help but also dignity and self-respect become useless" (63). Agamben concludes that "the atrocious news that the survivors [like Levi] carry from the camp to the land of human beings is precisely that it is possible to lose dignity and decency beyond imagination, that there is still life in the most *extreme* degradation" (69; emphasis added). The problem here is not the description itself, as we have seen. It is an interesting way for Agamben to give us another disclosive version of what Arendt meant with the idea of humanity being "stripped off" its very textures. Rather, the problem of Agamben's view lies in how he makes the *Muselmann the example of humanity in past and present times.* The result is that Agamben claims this knowledge will be our "touchstone by which to judge and measure all morality and all dignity" (69). This extreme situation, which in Levi's narrative was the paradigm of the daily life of Nazi *Lagers*, is now presented as a general concept of a modern view of power and politics. As with other versions of the sublime, this view arrives at the paradoxical conclusion of granting the final victory to the Nazis.

Thus, Agamben's work oscillates between further disclosing Levi's reflective judgments and then stretching those judgments into large generalizations that lose the powerful dimensions he was able to achieve when he stayed closer to Levi. It is Agamben's own way of working out the paradox and the aporetic through determinant judgments that lead him to these contradictory views. To understand Auschwitz necessarily means that we realize that we have entered the realm of a historical moment. For Agamben, on the contrary, it is the site of the aporetic where we understand that the term *man* has been applied to the human condition of a *non-man* and that this paradox is best captured by the concept of the "Muslim." He then presents it not as an exemplar of the historical atrocity of Auschwitz, but as a determinate exemplar of all politics since the horrific emergence of the concentration camp in the twentieth century was prefigured in the incipient political tradition of modernity. What was blurred now is fused.

On the other hand, we come to understand that even the most inhuman site of humanity allows us to say that something "always *remains*," and that someone is "the witness." Levi is a survivor who has saved this "*remnant*" (134) from oblivion. Herein lies the contradictory connection between what Agamben develops and concludes and what Levi wrote. We can see now that it is only through the testimony—Levi's own written narrative—that one can locate "the central threshold through which pass currents of the human and the inhuman, subjectification and desubjectification, the living being's becoming speaking and the logos' becoming living" (135) as the remains of a catastrophe. For Agamben, testimony becomes the paradoxical location of desubjectification where we encounter the archives. The potentiality of speech meets the silence of the archives. Testimony is the act of an author who renarrates the story as its coauthor. Here, the authority of a survivor like Levi, says Agamben, lies in "*his capacity to speak solely in the name of his incapacity to speak*" (158; emphasis added). Levi will always be related to the concept of the *Muselmann* because his own tale—about withstanding survival through the silence of the witness—has made such a big impact on us, his readers. Language is used here to provoke the reader, albeit in a different fashion than Arendt would do it. Though Agamben shares Arendt's views on the idea that no judgment is final, and he warns us that Levi´s account can have no end, he seems to betray this perspective with his political conclusion. Agamben focused on Levi's story not only as the "remnant" of what happened but also as an example of the perversion of the political. In spite of the fact that Agamben recovers Levi's narrative because "the poetic word is the one that is always situated in the position of a remnant and can, therefore, bear witness" (161), he ends up silencing Levi's true moral legacy. Here too, Agamben ignores Arendt's own heritage. If we could transform the question presented by Günter Gauss to Arendt about "What remains?"—when she replied that language remains—[46]and ask this question to readers, the reply would have to be something like this: What remains from Levi's account of horrors is the power of his language's disclosure, and his use of language is successful because of its moral frame .

Finally, contrary to Agamben's political judgment, it is not with anger and indignation that we come to master our past. We cannot master the past once and for all, but we have ways in which we can attach a moral meaning to what has happened. This comes with the significance of a story that provides us with the clues to understanding that the concrete disclosive features (concepts) of such a story should help us situate what happened into the meaningful realm of our moral understanding. Then, as Arendt says, "the narrative has been given its place in the world, where it will survive us."[47] Agamben sought a way to describe the fact that Levi left us with a story that has forever taken its place in our moral understanding, that of realizing that there are, after all, the "remnants of Auschwitz." If Agamben had stayed within the close limits of Levi's judgment, his conclusions about the apocalyptic view of the human as pure potentiality would have no place in his recovery of Levi's legacy. Furthermore, the idea that a limited experience—such as the one lived in Auschwitz—could become the rule, makes this atrocity emerge as if it were the *one* transhistorical example of all modern politics. Learning from catastrophes, on the other hand, means the very opposite of this view—namely, that we can always have a chance to learn something from those atrocities. This knowledge will not necessarily prevent us from confronting new ones, but it might be possible to seek important ways to understand the new meanings of moral wrongdoing. If we do so, then there exists at least the potential for creating institutional protections by which material justice can take place. Stories can provide us with representations about perpetrators' and victims' status and actions. With them, we reconstruct the prior representations of wrongdoing. What happened under previous rule can be represented then as categories of *violence*. Historical transformations are possible only because we search collectively for explicit representations involving the justification of the predecessors' political violence and then by exposing them publicly with a critical view. Material justice is not sublime. Rather, as Ruti Teitel claims, "it implies a historical accountability of past wrongs enabled by principles of documentation, representation, and entrenchment of a successor account."[48] This theory of evil claims that learning from catastrophes means *producing truths* through a workable past in order to change our future. This is the meaning of "mastering the past." What remains, then, is the need to highlight that critical reconstructions become *performative ways of redefining moral wrongs*, and they can help us to protect ourselves from repeating past wrongs.

CHAPTER 7

Hearts of Darkness

{Political Judgment}

Judging is one, if not the most, important activity in which sharing-the-world-with-others comes to pass.

—Hannah Arendt[1]

In previous chapters I have developed the idea of reflective judgment and used it to describe important tasks in the public sphere. I have been arguing, so far, only about moral judgments and their relationship to political and legal judgments. We must now focus on the specificity of political judgements, because of their connection to the creation of a model of reflective judgment.

Hannah Arendt often spoke of beginning anew. This poetic way of saying that certain transformations are required in society refers to the need to understand what happened in the past. There is no doubt that she was alluding to the horrendous events of the concentration camps in the Nazi era. She often questions, in many of her texts, whether it is possible to master the past in light of this grim reality. She believed, however, that it is necessary to focus on those historical atrocities if we ever want to begin something different—to enter a stage in which we could, somehow, not reconcile with what happened, but reconcile with our human world and the fact that we must do whatever it takes to make room for something entirely different. Key to any possible transformation of a society is the effort to understand that what happened needs a collective effort to critically reconstruct it with the goal of envisioning how a society needs to be transformed. The first stage of this critical effort is to begin by opening up the public space as a place for a wide and plural discussion. Once we leave behind the realm of the literary public sphere, in order to situate ourselves in the public debate, we can then say that we have entered the realm of the political public sphere. In this stage, the poet or the historian has moved the process of narration into the public sphere and we are now capable of grasping its impact when it unsettles our previous views of what happened. Once the narration of "history has achieved [its] permanence and persistence,"[2] we have reached the stage where political judgment should be built up. Understanding is the first step to political judgment,[3] and this results from the presentation of different proposals about how institutions of justice should work and how societal transformations allow for a collective exercise of building up memory. Political judgments can be accomplished once we learn to share them with others, when we share the space of public deliberations with others in the public sphere. Arendt calls this process of sharing the world with others the political realm. We must focus on how that common world can be possible in the process of debating with others. I argue that we do so when we come to share a critical view of what happened, once we accept that there is something that we need to understand. Arendt thought of narrations as ways to explore why actions have significance and how these perspectives allow us to find shared views that might reach some kind of consensus. This idea has already been explored in regard to how she made a negative exemplar of reflective judgment in her narrative about Eichmann's trial. Indeed, as Leora Bilsky describes it, "by criticizing the Eichmann trial and its tendency to become a 'show trial' in the hands of the prosecutor, Arendt contributed to making it a real *political trial* for her readers. Her counternarrative forces us to contemplate the most serious jurisprudential, moral, and historical dilemmas that we have raised by the trial but [were] often hidden from the public eye."[4] When we deliberate about such a way of looking at things, we can begin to see how her model—or, narrative—guides us to focus on certain particularities of actions that show us how they were possible at all. This process presupposes that we see an internal connection between moral and political judgments. This connection offers a critical normative dimension that needs to be developed by clarifying how a negative exemplar becomes a political model of how things were.

Political judgment is configured through the interplay of important interventions from different viewpoints, from critical discussions among public intellectuals, and in how public opinion begins to take shape because of these critical debates. I have spoken before about the memory wars, and the best illustration of these wars is precisely how one critical view can start to question other stories and lead the discussion into furthering the perspective of what went wrong. In the chapter where I analyzed Habermas's intervention in the *Historikerstreit,* I explored how the memory wars are helpful processes in shaping public opinion. Habermas's example became an important intervention in changing German historians' revisionist views of what had happened during the Nazi regime. The memory wars are enacted by critical efforts within societies that allow other stories to emerge in the public debates. These provide the alternative elements that allow us to construct public opinion. Political and legal trials reflect the dynamics of groups' conflicts in pluralist societies, at the same time that they allow for the redefinition of justice and make manifest the rupture with previous authoritarian regimes. Leora Bilsky, for example, has focused on how political trials show important connections between enacting certain values to transform societies, and at the same time prosecute the perpetrators while disclosing stories about their victims in order to allow for a new beginning.[5] This is clearly where the idea of political judgment acquires its substance. Bilsky is also clear that when we need to use new categories and new ways of addressing certain problems between humans, we need the help of reflective judgments.

In this chapter, Arendt's narrative interventions will be seen as empirical examples of how political judgments are constructed and how they do interrelate with other efforts from societies' critical self-examinations in order to connect the paradigm of evil with the paradigm of justice. By leaving behind Arendt's complex separations between the actor and the spectator in terms of judging, we should regard Arendt's interventions through her personal contributions in the political public sphere and conceive her approach as a way of participating in the public debate. This is why the concept of action must be understood in much broader terms. Action must be conceived as a performative tool. It can be seen as emerging from the realm of social interactions and as producing illocutionary effects.[6] Narratives and good theoretical initiatives are part and parcel of social interaction. This is the reason we might see that moral interactions presuppose effects on social and political interactions. There is no possible way to find a better connection between moral judgment and political judgment than through the idea that actions envision a perspective in which language and the world are reunited by their disclosive critical dimensions, which focus on articulating what is critical about past actions.

We have seen that stories provide us with precious material to construct moral judgments. We need now to focus on the way those stories have helped others create negative political models of a reflective kind in order to understand what happened. Let us turn again to

Hannah Arendt's model of totalitarianism, because this is an interesting first model of reflective judgment which has allowed others to build their own, based on some of her basic insights. When developing her reflective judgments, Arendt does not make use of analogies but of distinctions. She built this model as an effort to cope with the problems of her time, but her political judgment there has also helped other important initiatives to capture some universal characteristics of what she called "totalitarian regimes," along with particular concrete determinations of the specific historical atrocities of her times. She used the universalistic frame of the paradigm of evil to conceptualize the word *totalitarianism* as a general political concept that defines a specific kind of regime, the way power is developed under totalitarian rule, and the particular characteristics of two historical episodes—the Nazi and the Stalinist periods. Her model entails the use of one concrete historical concept—totalitarianism—which by itself can disclose important features of concrete particularities. This is why I have called this a model of reflective judgment. The successful use of the concept of totalitarianism lies in the possibilities it presents other scholars to frame other important historical regimes, and in the way they have further developed particular and concrete dimensions of those historical regimes. These kinds of comparative works have fruitfully proved that Arendt's model is an important guide for historical studies and for social and political theories about historical atrocities.

Drawing the Modern Literary Exemplar of Political Evil

Kirstie M. McClure has called our attention to what she calls "Arendt's double movement" in her concept of exemplarity. McClure means by this that Arendt uses "Kant's notion of 'publicity' [in its] exemplary status" along "with the 'freedom to speak and write' "[7] in public as a way of building up political judgment. Speaking publicly, communicating her own mind, going "from example to example, through comparison, qualification, distinction, and elaboration,"[8] allows Arendt to draw her exemplary cases and to exert a condition of being with others, for she leaves her examples as "vulnerable to the elements of living contestation"[9] in order not to shut down the dialogue with others. This fallibilism suits the way we think of normative validity nowadays.[10] Arendt could not have imagined that her own work would be used as an important tool for criticism and for further developing some of her greatest insights.[11] Indeed, *The Origins of Totalitarianism* unfolds as a narration in which themes reach multiple variations, disclosing dimensions of reality coined by the way she uses words (differing from so-called tradition), and by the way she develops her own logic—her own judgments—through "premises, derivations, and corollaries."[12] Judging, to Arendt, meant reasoning in community with others and learning to do it without the banisters of tradition and of general rules.[13]

This is the reason, argues Arendt, that "comprehension does not mean denying the outrageous, deducing the unprecedented from precedents, or explaining phenomena by such analogies and generalities that impact the reality and the shock of experience." It means, rather, that by "examining and bearing consciously the burden that the events have placed upon us," we arrive at a stage at which "comprehension" allows one to learn in the company of others. In other words, we become aware of "the unpremeditated, attentive facing up to, and resisting of, reality—whatever it may be or might have been,"[14] in order to draw a model for comparing our views with those of others, in light of the task of producing a disclosive view, and in order to produce a critical political judgment. Arendt gave the concept of political judgment its normative criteria by this critical disclosive connection between political and moral judgments. Seyla Benhabib, for example, has mentioned that Arendt's model for understanding totalitarian regimes has some particular elements that highlight its relation to the moral sphere, because the "imagination of history gathered together in the present," as crystallized tropes, "reveal[s] an altogether different meaning than what they had stood for in the original context,"[15] but only after understanding this internal connection between moral and political questions. Benhabib argues that Arendt found critical normative elements that allowed her to describe how this form of domination was possible. It entailed (1) the death of juridical persons, (2) the death of the moral person, and (3) the death of the individual (and the loss of the moral identity).[16] She used history, sociology, and culture rather than resorting to abstract metaphysical descriptions of evildoing. Benhabib's analysis of Arendt's own model shows us how important it was for Arendt to stress the need to consider that totalitarian regimes are antidemocratic models of power whose main target is the suppression of the individual and the destruction of plurality. Totalitarian regimes facilitate the total domination of people and the destruction and corruption of the most basic elements of humanity. This is the critical connection between a moral argument and political judgment. It is also the reason Arendt grasped the metaphorical meaning of Joseph Conrad's *Heart of Darkness* and used it as a disclosive tool to explain the way humans can submit themselves to their darkest impulses. The immersion into the heart of darkness begins by descending into the unmaking of the human world. The totalitarian motto—"everything is possible"—becomes emblematic of evil in the twentieth century because of the ways humanity has been destroyed.

Seyla Benhabib is correct to point out that "what interests Arendt, and what proves to be such a powerful guide for the exploration of Conrad, is this mixture of attraction and repulsion, kinship and antagonism that the European soldiers of fortune who dug into Africa in search of gold and riches, as well as the Boers settlers, felt for the natives."[17] Conrad's story helps Arendt use this metaphor as a disclosive mechanism with which she describes the way one can submerge into the unmaking of everything that culture has brought to our human world.[18] Without the pride of "Western and European institutions," and "outside all social restraint and hypocrisy," the tunnel of darkness appears as "the impact of a world of infinite possibilities for crimes committed in the spirit of the play, for the combination of horror and laughter, that is for the full realization of their own phantom-like existence."[19] It is this process of the unmaking of the human world, as captured by Conrad's metaphor and from which Arendt drew the "crystalline structures" of her own disclosive method, that we see the emergence of a model of totalitarian regimes that are embodied in certain political actions in order to facilitate evildoing. We can begin to explore the meanings of darkness through several models of understanding totalitarian regimes based on Arendt's insights. The "heart of darkness" offers a metaphor that reveals how easy it is to cross the line between good and evil when we begin to unravel social and political mechanisms in which evil has become the norm. For Arendt, the figure of Kurtz is used to explore the idea of how political evil is constructed through the generalization of cruelty, with the complicity of others, and through the acceptance of the opposite of lawful law, by turning the political world upside down. Some people might argue that when Arendt chose Kurtz she was thinking about him as the man of talent described in part in Conrad's novel. In my opinion this is not so. If we pay attention to what she has to say when she first refers to Kurtz in *The Origins of Totalitarianism*, she explains that, "like Mr. Kurtz in Conrad's 'Heart of Darkness,' they [the Boers] were "hollow to the core."[20] Recall that it is also hollowness that she spots in Eichmann's character. This profound insight is developed further when Arendt connects evil to an ordinary person in *Eichmann in Jerusalem: A Report on the Banality of Evil.* In choosing to explore the literary figure of Kurtz as a metaphor, however, Arendt wanted to highlight that men like him, "gifted or not,"[21] were all ready to learn how to become willful murderers when they believed that no moral consequences would derive from their actions. One interesting way of interpreting Conrad's cryptic ending is to return to the scene where Kurtz's life is about to end as he gains some conscience about his deeds and utters his final words—"the horror, the horror." A possible interpretation of the meaning of this ambiguous expression could be that Kurtz finally realizes how easily one can cross the line between avoiding evil and willingly embracing it. Indeed, most totalitarian regimes from the twentieth century do exhibit the conditions that Arendt outlines in her narrative of those two totalitarian regimes (the Nazi and the Stalinist eras), and the literary figure of Kurtz appears to be the key metaphor by which she discloses the contemporary tragedy of genocidal totalitarian states.

Understanding Totalitarian Regimes

One important result of the ability of a thinker to provide us with a reflective judgment is that it can help others to draw on larger distinctions based on the same model. This is what has obviously happened with Arendt's view of totalitarian regimes, and with her conclusion that evil is mostly perpetrated by ordinary people. Tzvetan Todorov, for example, warns us that "the concept of monstrousness is of limited utility in helping us to understand evil, [and by] positing some reversion to bestial or primitive instincts [which] takes us no further,"[22] we tend to shrink the space of moral choice. Thus, if we interpret Arendt's connection to Conrad's metaphor, as Benhabib correctly does, we realize that the most significant dimension of the metaphor is not the obvious one of Kurtz's geographical journey into the "Dark Continent of Africa," but, rather, the way in which Kurtz "regresses into ever deeper recesses of his psyche, into the night of memory."[23] This night of memory is not a place for psychoanalytical debate. Rather, it is a description of the dissolution of all moral constraints in light of new experiences triggered by otherness or alienation. The way to arrive at this kind of loss is made possible by relating everyone else to the corruption of the moral character, where no democratic institutions or moral standards can survive. In light of these considerations, Todorov assumes that Arendt was right when she later thought of Eichmann as an example of evil—an ordinary man rather than a monster—for, "to call this evil banal is not to trivialize it: precisely what made this evil so dangerous was that it was so easy, that no exceptional human qualities were required for it to come into being. The wind had only to blow in the right direction, and the evil spread like wildfire."[24] We must thus understand that the paradoxical nature of the concept of evil that Arendt was looking for, and which she later found with her idea of Eichmann as an ordinary example, was somehow connected to Kurtz's voyage—his descent into the heart of darkness—because "evil can be extreme without being radically different from its virulent forms." Evil is "at once ordinary and exceptional."[25] In Arendt's theory, then, actions can be labeled as extraordinarily evil, but humans are ordinary beings.[26]

We have seen that Levi provided us with stories that illustrate this view, with the exemplarity of concrete stories of human beings caught up in the Nazi *Lagers*. Christopher Browning, on the other hand, has focused on the historical side of ordinary men to further strengthen this view that ordinary Germans committed extraordinary crimes.[27] Arendt, no doubt, connected her idea of moral judgments to the idea of political judgment in *The Origins of Totalitarianism*, yet we can only understand her transition from the political concept of evil to the moral definition of an agent of evil by reinterpreting Conrad's metaphor. Moral and political spaces were already critically connected in *The Origins of Totalitarianism* by her descriptions of the loss of the juridical figure, the loss of the moral figure, and the loss of identity suffered by persons in totalitarian regimes. In *The Origins of Totalitarianism*, Arendt located the kind of political model that was used to destroy the basic elements of humanity. The interesting connection here is that we can relate moral judgments to political judgments when we point out the loss of humanity in totalitarian regimes and the consequences of this loss.

Arendt's descriptions have stimulated other models such as the one developed by Tzvetan Todorov, particularly when he points out that totalitarian regimes exert a certain influence on moral behavior. Todorov's connection of the moral to the political sphere begins by stating the following:

1. Evil is constructed when a state invokes the principle of evil as personified by otherness. "The enemy," warns Todorov, is usually an internal one. Todorov explains that "totalitarian doctrines always divide humanity into two groups of people" and the state maintains that "inferior beings must be punished or annihilated."[28] One can conclude that totalitarian regimes are never universal in character.
2. Totalitarian states, because of their repudiation of universality, become the "custodian of society's ultimate aims" (127). The loss of individuality is paired with the loss of plurality.
3. Totalitarian states aspire to control the totality of every individual's existence. There is "no refuge, no escaping [the] state's control" (128). Private and public spaces dissolve and humans become tools for domination.

Todorov argues that this is the way social schizophrenia becomes the biggest weapon of such a regime, for subjects start their degradation by first becoming accomplices to many of the state's crimes. We have already seen that this is illustrated in Primo Levi's narratives. Todorov has Arendt's model in mind, for he notes that Arendt repeatedly warns us not to interpret that, when we say ordinary people create evil, we mean "that there is a little Eichmann in each of us and therefore we are all the same" (137). If we fall into this trap, suggests Todorov, we forget Arendt's major accomplishment with regard to the idea of freedom (based on Kant), namely, that the capacity to act speaks to our ways of resisting evil, and that the relevance of the category of action lies in the fact that it is the only place where we can grasp the internal connection between the doer and the sufferer. If "crimes" seem inhuman, "criminals are not" (138). What we see here is that crimes can be committed by ordinary people. Nevertheless, their actions can be conceptualized as "extraordinary" cases of evil deeds (138). This is the reason Kurtz's descent is the best illustration of the fact that ordinary men and extraordinary crimes can be linked through the disclosive concept of "the heart of darkness." In a way, this was a means to recovering Kant's most profound insight—that humans possess the paradoxical nature of a wicked heart.[29] This is why Arendt saw Conrad's metaphor as an important disclosive expression of evil described in totalitarian regimes.

It is in the last part of *The Origins of Totalitarianism* that Arendt reveals the most interesting political features of the unraveling of human darkness. The title of her chapter is "Ideology and Terror: A Novel Form of Government." Here she explains what it is that distinguishes the idea of totalitarian power from previous ideas of power. In the heart of darkness, we lose the distinctions between "lawful and lawless government, between arbitrary and legitimate power" (461). The destruction of institutions, of cultural interactions, and of spaces of deliberation where agreements between people are possible, makes way for a new logic. The laws become "the laws of movement," Arendt says, and this movement allows history and nature to melt into one force that does not need mediation by humanity (463). Terror is the essence of totalitarian domination. People begin this descent into their dark stages of corruption "by pressing men against each other, [where] total terror destroys the space between them" (465). When humans lose the ability to move, argues Arendt, they lose the space that makes freedom conceivable.[30] Spontaneity is impossible. Nothing remains that is not controlled by the state. Ideologies become their religion. The concept of ideology, warns Arendt, is "quite literally what its name indicates: it is the logic of an idea."[31] As such, ideologues pretend to know all the mysteries of the historical process, past, present, and future. All ideologies possess totalitarian elements, "but only in totalitarian regimes do they become fully developed" (470). It is then that the logic of a "total explanation promises to explain all historical happenings" (470). History and nature now become the two strands of an inseparable logic because "nature serves merely to explain historical matters and reduce them to matters of nature" (470). This is why Margaret Canovan sees Arendt's concept of ideology as original, for what she "has in mind [is] something much more serious." Ideologies are "aspiration[s] to omnipotence, the price of which must necessarily be human plurality and spontaneity, and therefore human nature itself." The leaders of totalitarian regimes see themselves as the "servants of the inhuman laws that govern the universe."[32] The expansion of power becomes the most relevant goal because, in the pursuit of total domination, people lose their humanity.

With Arendt's description of totalitarian regimes we find a new way of conceptualizing a political system. If terror is its essence, ideology becomes its principle of action. Just as she saw that the suppression of freedom results in the loss of space between humans (as, for example, in the concentration camps), she saw that "loneliness" is the trademark of the masses under totalitarian rule. "Isolated men are powerless by definition," she explains.[33] It is the result of the inability to act. It is this experience of not belonging to the world at all, where finally all cultural and political achievements of the human world are lost.

Here Kurtz's example becomes relevant: as a figure of extraordinary talent and of decisive leadership, he is transformed into an ordinary criminal—a butcher. His crimes surpass the crimes of those who represent another culture, one with alien traditions and beliefs. When confronting these crimes at last, Kurtz begins to realize that he has become an evil perpetrator, perhaps even overshadowing all others. With this disclosive view of Conrad's story, Arendt's model has paved the road to understanding what happens in the heart of darkness. In these kinds of totalitarian experiences, the reality of the loss of humanity is fully captured by such a metaphor. As Arendt argues,

> Like Mr. Kurtz in Conrad's *Heart of Darkness*, [these men] were "hollow to the core," "reckless without hardihood, greedy without audacity and cruel without courage." They believed in nothing and "could get (themselves) to believe anything—anything." Expelled from a world with accepted social values, they had been thrown back upon themselves and still had nothing to fall back upon except, here and there, a streak of talent which made them as dangerous as Kurtz if they were ever allowed to return to their homelands. For their only talent that could possibly burgeon in their hollow souls was the gift of fascination which makes a "splendid leader of an extreme party."[34]

Constructing the Enemy

Todorov argues that "totalitarian crimes are crimes of a new species altogether . . . there is nothing either extrahuman or subhuman about these crimes . . . their cause resides neither in individuals nor in nations but in the political regime under which they are committed."[35] These political regimes begin to lose their solidarity, as Arendt has clearly shown in *The Origins of Totalitarianism*. Following Arendt's idea of the loss of space and the isolation of individuals, Mark J. Osiel explains that "such movements provide a quick-fix cure for loneliness and anomie, but only by subjecting their unwitting victims to a still-deeper alienation."[36] Totalitarian regimes need, then, to mobilize public support. They attempt to do so through the radicalization of their ideologies or, as Osiel rephrases Arendt's view, as a "transvaluation of values" in order "to convince the public that acts long considered profoundly immoral have suddenly become morally obligatory" (83). The epitome of this transvaluation can be exemplified by the public endorsement of genocide, as has been demonstrated in Rwanda, Cambodia, Argentina, and the former Yugoslavian Republic, as well as many other historical examples. The idea of turning against others as targets of destruction requires public mass mobilization to produce "moral disorientation." This effect of building up, or constructing an enemy, and requiring the complicity of the public produces a loss of the "capacity for sound judgment." The masses that become involved in committing crimes have no sense of moral responsibility (84). This corruption of moral character translates itself into a condition of complicity in regard to the murderous tasks of state genocide. In mobilizing large groups of people, totalitarian regimes ensure that those enforcing such actions will not be held legally accountable in the future, for everyone has, in one way or another, participated in the mass murders. The Nazi regime itself also became a model to be copied by totalitarian regimes that came after. All proved that the "Nazis' use of collective responsibility as a preemptive self-defense was not lost upon" others (86). Here again, the best metaphor to describe the process of becoming the accomplice of perpetrators is this journey into the heart of darkness.[37]

Key to this loss of the human world is the cultural construction of "the other" as an evil being. The procedure for locating the enmity of others is accomplished through a fictitious conspiracy. It is under these conditions that ideologies are transformed into real weapons. The new use of ideologies in totalitarian regimes ensures that such ideas become "the logical process" by which the destruction of others reinforces their premise. It is important here to focus again on language as the vehicle that can accomplish this cultural construction of so-called evil opponents. The cultural construction of the other is done through the moral loss of the idea of person—that is, the process of dehumanization. Language becomes its powerful political tool. As Herbert Hirsch argues, "when political leaders seek to target a population for abuse, they will produce negative characterizations that can usually be found linguistically in deprecating nouns such as 'kike,' 'wop,' 'spick,' 'bohunk,' 'Jap,' 'Chink,' or 'dago.' "[38] Ideologies of hate and racism function to dehumanize people and to prepare the way for oppression and extermination.[39] As Waller has noted, dehumanization involves categorizing groups of people as inhuman by using "subhuman categories (that is, animals) or by using categories of negative evaluation of unhuman creatures (such as demons or monsters)."[40] Dehumanization often categorizes the other through some connection to a difference in racial, ethnic, religious, sexual, or political characteristics. These "others" are stigmatized as alien and are always portrayed by the dominant group as an immediate and personal threat to the majority. Dehumanization, however, as a cultural process, is a complex undertaking that is connected to the idea of first depriving victims of their moral identity "by defining them entirely by a category to which they belong" (245). The second exclusion is political: this group—these "others"—must be cast out from any idea of community and excluded from the human family, from the country, and from political recognition, etc. Exclusion from the moral universe is produced almost immediately. And when victims lose their connection to the moral universe, then of course, "compassionate treatment removes normal moral restraints against aggression" (245). The cultural process of dehumanization thus concludes that even the bodies of victims possess no "meaning" at all; they are seen as "waste" and their "removal is [only] a matter of sanitation" (245).

Language, in addition, becomes key in redefining victims. As Waller argues, "The moral disengagement of the perpetrators is completed by a barbarity of language that dehumanizes the victims" (246). Stories of genocide, mass killings, rape, and "ethnic cleansing" are full of examples of the linguistic dehumanization of victims. Waller reminds us that the Nazis called the Jews "bacilli, parasites, vermin, demons, syphilis, cancer, excrement, filth, tuberculosis and plague" (246). The Nazi state also used specific words such as *Figuren* (type or kind) to describe human corpses. The extraordinary performative tools of language exemplify the way perpetrators dehumanize their victims by using words that become part of the very identities of victims by substituting earlier perceptions and representations of "human beings" (246). Once the process is complete, victims are reduced to pure data and mere statistics. The process of dehumanizing victims is highly ritualistic. By degrading them in every possible way, the last stage of the loss of moral identity is completed through starvation, deprivation, filth, helplessness, torture, and other forms of humiliation.

Dehumanization as a cultural process is translated into a reinforced propaganda that becomes a powerful tool for completing the transformations of norms and the needed support for the institutionalization of crimes. Language is also an important vehicle of the institutionalization of crimes, and it is always important to recall how words and phrases are utilized by totalitarian regimes. As Norman Naimark argues, "New concepts are consistently being invented to describe, classify, and arrange events of the past in order to understand them in the present."[41] Ethnic cleansing, for example, was "used with increasing frequency after May 1992," and it is a useful term for "understanding the war in former Yugoslavia" (3). Naimark argues that the goal of ethnic-cleansing strategies is "to get rid of the 'alien' nationality, ethnic, or religious group and to seize control of the territory they had formerly inhabited" (3). More interestingly, the words and phrases coined by regimes become real distinctions, conceptually speaking. Naimark essentially proves this point by showing that when we reference the concept of "ethnic cleansing," we associate the term with other historical and geographical meanings such as the Slavic word *chishchenie* (Russian) or *ciscenja* (Serbo-Croatian), both of which refer to political elimination or the purging of enemies. The term used in the Soviet Union became *chistki*, while the term used in German was *Saüberung*, also associated with racial "science" in Nazi ideology. Moreover, as Naimark suggests, the Germans created the term "völkische Flurbereiningung," deriving the metaphor from agriculture. It is a highly illustrative term that "indicate[s] the cleansing, in this case, of alien ethnic elements from the soil" (4). Thus, the concepts coined by totalitarian regimes often create and use terms that have a specific historical context, and it is only through our understanding of their historicity and their context that we learn to find their critical disclosive meanings. Naimark suggests, for example, that the term "ethnic cleansing" is not limited to a technique particular to the twentieth century, but "its occurrences are highly dependent on the particular characteristics of state, society, and ideology during the period itself" (6). Therefore, he concludes, "ethnic cleansing as experienced in the former Yugoslavia" is "a profoundly modern experience" (6). Furthermore, "ethnic cleansing in the twentieth century is a product of the most advanced stage in the development of the modern state,"[42] because only in the modern state can there be found an organized census, surveys, measures, weights—all categories that seek to "homogenize" a community under one single political entity.[43]

The stories of Nazi Germany, the Stalinist Soviet Union, Cambodia, and the former Yugoslavia, as well as the tragedy of Rwanda, show that those who are first depicted as enemies almost invariably become targets of mobilization and annihilation, creating a bridge between strategies that began as "forced deportation" and then became "genocidal."[44] Thus, the socially constructed categories of the enemy are always culturally built according to their negative characteristics. They become reified in those totalitarian regimes because it is always the goal of such regimes to produce their own enemies. Signs of the appearance of a constructed enemy allow for a reversal of norms. Violations of all types of ethical norms become the new rules of totalitarian regimes. These are the kinds of examples provided by new studies inspired and based on Arendt's work. They show us that tools for killing were different in each of the historical atrocities of the twentieth century. For example, rape was used as a weapon of war between the different ethnic groups of the former Yugoslavia, and they found this particular weapon to be a horrendous action with a significant meaning immersed in its very cultural roots. The Rwandan genocide could not have happened on such a large scale without the use of the radio as a massive tool to stimulate the participation of the Hutus in killing the Tutsis.

The answer to the question "What makes political judgment sound?" is best illustrated by calling upon Arendt's model of Eichmann: she reached her mature idea of evil by using Eichmann as an example of an ordinary human being. I do not wish to reconsider the copious amounts of literature written on this subject. The debate itself, it seems to me, is relevant enough to have changed the way we discuss the subject of evil—an undertaking that requires an in-depth analysis of Arendt's work. She thus produced an illocutionary effect even though she was not prepared to argue the issue with the conceptual clarity she needed.[45] I would only like to suggest that her model of Eichmann can be considered a negative example of evil because it has helped us realize that many other historical examples can be accommodated into such a model. With her novel use of the concept of ordinary men who commit extraordinary evil deeds, Arendt departs completely from the prevailing tradition of thought—in literature, in the theological tradition, and in the philosophical tradition as well. Hers was a postmetaphysical definition of evil because it was not a description of the nature of evil, but rather a description of the moral code of a man who committed evil. As an example of an ordinary man, Eichmann became a negative exemplary figure, one who illustrated that a normal human being—indeed, a mere bureaucrat—was often a shallow character who could disfigure the higher moral framework in order to accommodate his behavior to that of the Nazi worldview. His deeds showed how a regime can make a person rationalize one's own actions in order to serve the larger purposes of the state's politics of genocide. Inserted into the social hierarchy of the Nazi regime, Eichmann proved that it becomes entirely possible to commit an extraordinary crime by following the new rules designed by a totalitarian regime. Arendt's view of evil as personified by Eichmann thus departed forever from our previous notions of conceptualizing evildoing as the product of strong passions (e.g., ambition, hatred, pride, or envy) and made us aware that descending into the heart of darkness is a turn anyone can take at any corner of our complicated historical crossroads when we need to exercise moral judgment.

CHAPTER 8
Death and the Maiden

Throughout previous chapters, I have insisted on the idea that narratives—that is, stories about evil—presumably provide the best illustrations or descriptions of the problems of evil. I have not yet defined why this connection is conceptually so important. I would like to argue in this chapter that moral wrongdoing is best described in actions wherein the characters are revealed in the complexity of their interactions, which are crystallized in plots. I have argued before that moral wrongdoing is one of the basic conditions for understanding evil because the perpetrator of evil actions causes permanent damage—that is, moral harm—to the identity of the sufferer. For this reason, evil actions forever link the destiny of the doer with that of the sufferer. Previous theories about evil always focus either on the sufferer[1] or on the perpetrator[2] in order to thematize evil actions. This theory, in contrast, asserts that evil deeds must concentrate on actions and their interactive effects on people because together these constitute an important dimension of the way we can recognize evil deeds when they are performed. By focusing only on one side, we weaken the possibility of understanding the interaction between perpetrator and sufferer, and the specific meaning that these kinds of actions bring to us when assessing the permanent moral harm done to the lives of people.

I will argue in this chapter that literature, specifically contemporary literature, has captured this idea through a reelaboration of moral wrongdoing by creating a literary story that involves an aesthetic reflective judgment. Again, we will not focus on this problem through the lens of psychoanalysis, but rather, on the idea that moral harm—in relation to moral wrongdoing—has been thoroughly described in the full range of its complexity by many stories, and that this is the reason literature has played a leading role in understanding evil. Just as we saw in previous chapters that Arendt's model helped other theorists build their own theories of evil based on historical and particular accounts of evil deeds, we will see the way reflective judgment is articulated throughout the construction of a plot, where the idea of moral wrongdoing is the main concept that becomes transformed into a literary device (or metaphor). I have thus given this chapter the same title that Schubert gave to one of his most famous masterpieces: "Death and the Maiden" (the String Quartet in D Minor). This theme was later developed as a play by the Chilean writer, Ariel Dorfman.[3] Dorfman's story develops the concept of moral wrongdoing as exemplified through torture and its effect, or moral harm, on the life of a woman. Dorfman's powerful account of the broken identity of a human being was later made into a movie by Roman Polanski, in which Sigourney Weaver plays the main character and Ben Kingsley her torturer. This chapter analyzes this example in detail.

Moral Wrongdoing as Reflective Judgment

Plays have been partly replaced by film in our society. This is not because people have stopped attending the theater. Rather, it is because theater has a limited audience whereas movies reach many more people. Indeed, one could say today that the greatest source of our moral imagination comes from films (and of course television). They are often key to our understanding of the most important historical catastrophes of our century.[4] Furthermore, many of the great plays that were first presented to limited audiences have in due course also been made into movies. For example, most of Shakespeare's plays have been made into films. There have been many good film versions of tragedies such as *Macbeth, Othello,* or *King Lear.* Greek theater has also been adapted for film, making available what was once limited in time and space, and even on economic grounds. The best dramas of our times have been made into movies because of the development of a suitable cinematic language. It is now possible to know about various historical catastrophes because of the ways in which Holocaust dramas, modern wars, the weapon of widespread rapes and ethnic cleansings have been portrayed by great filmmakers and artists. For this reason, I have chosen to explore Dorfman's dramatic play and its film adaptation to concretize my conception of moral wrongdoing through a specific story of torture and its aftermath. It is my claim that both the author of the drama and the filmmaker have successfully captured this idea through an aesthetic-moral reflective judgment. Furthermore, because it is well developed, the idea of permanent moral harm is explored by illuminating or disclosing hidden dimensions of the interrelationship between sufferer and perpetrator. This reflective judgment is also depicted by the metaphor provided through the title of Schubert's piece (as we will see at the end of this chapter).

When Ariel Dorfmann wrote his play, he never imagined that the very same person who made *Macbeth* (1971) would direct a film version of *Death and the Maiden* (1994). But perhaps this is not entirely the coincidence it seems, for in his films Roman Polanski has always been obsessed with the problem of evil.[5] In any case, his version of Dorfman's play raises the key points to be discussed in this chapter—namely, that an evil act has a permanent effect on both the sufferer and the perpetrator, and that their destinies are forever dramatically linked. Dorfman found a literary way to illuminate this reality: in his play he presents an encounter between two persons who, after many years, accidentally meet for a second time. The historical context for this drama is the reality that, in most Latin American countries, after their dictatorships had ended, the new leaders had to grant amnesty to the perpetrators (usually the Military) in order to make the transition to democracy smoother and to avoid the threat of a future coup.[6] These terrible compromises raised the possibility that one could encounter one's torturers at any moment. Dorfman illustrates this tragedy through Dr. Miranda's random encounter with one of the persons he tortured. The doctor learns that the man whom he has helped on the highway is in fact the husband of a person he had tortured in the past, and that the man is also the appointed lawyer who will head the commission investigating his and others' responsibility in the many cases of torture during Pinochet's regime. (The film itself never names Pinochet or Chile directly: an opening intertitle sets the action in "A country in South America ... after the fall of the dictatorship.") The drama evolves from the way the three characters confront each other with this terrible burden from the past.[7]

In the film, the theater itself is both source and narrative center.[8] It is in the interplay of theater and reality that the drama comes to life and unravels before us. The action begins after the demise of the (Pinochet) dictatorship. There are three characters: Paulina Escobar—maiden name Lorca in the film, quite possibly an allusion to the great Spanish poet—(played by Sigourney Weaver), her husband Gerardo Escobar (Stuart Wilson), and Dr. Roberto Miranda (played by Ben Kingsley). In the opening framing scene we see Paulina and her husband at a concert hall as the musicians begin to play Schubert's title piece. She is searching the crowd for someone she knows must be there. Her husband, understanding her state of mind, holds her hand supportively. The next scene begins the long flashback sequence that will make up most of the film, and here we see Paulina again, alone and nervously preparing dinner at home during a long thunderstorm. As the rain pours down, she takes her food and eats it alone in a closet while reading the newspaper. Soon after, we learn that the person she has been waiting for is her husband. He has arrived late because his car had a flat tire and he had desperately stopped a passing motorist (Dr. Miranda) on the highway to help him. After realizing that the spare tire is also useless, Dr. Miranda offers him a ride home. On the way to the Escobar house, Gerardo reveals that he is a lawyer and that he has been appointed by the (Chilean) president to head a commission to investigate the deaths and torture of persons during the (Pinochet) dictatorship. The doctor drops Gerardo off at the front entrance to his house. When Gerardo enters, Paulina, afraid of being seen, is hiding. As Gerardo begins to eat the dinner Paulina has prepared, he explains to her why he is late, then proceeds to tell her about his appointment by the nation's president, though she already knows this, having heard it on the news. They argue over the fact that Gerardo thinks he can successfully complete his new job, whereas she doubts that justice is possible as long as the militaries and their accomplices still hold a degree of power. We also learn that in the past she, too, has suffered from torture at the hands of the regime and, as a result, is in a frail state of mind. Gerardo gently tries to console her and they end up making love. In the next scene, Gerardo wakes up in the middle of the night, hears a noise outside, and goes to the door. The doctor had forgotten to return the spare tire in his trunk and now offers to help fix the car. He is invited into the house, and they stay up late talking about Gerardo's appointment. When they hear the doctor's car engine start up and see the car start to pull away, Gerardo realizes that it is Paulina who has taken it. He thinks she is leaving him because of his decision to accept the appointment. Both Gerardo and the doctor stay up late, drinking heavily and discussing Paulina's fragile condition. At last the men decide they must get some sleep, and as the doctor stretches out on the couch, he assures Gerardo that Paulina will return in the morning. In the next scene, near dawn, Paulina quietly enters the house, finds some plastic cord and duct tape, and awakens the doctor at the point of a gun. She has recovered a cassette that Dr. Miranda had in his car: it is Schubert's "Death and the Maiden." When the doctor resists, she viciously knocks him unconscious with the gun and ties him upright in a chair. As he comes to, she tells him that she recognized his voice as soon as she heard it, and that she is going to do to him what she has experienced herself. As the Schubert music plays on a small tape deck/recorder, she stuffs her underwear in his mouth as a gag and tightens his bonds; she describes how she was tortured by him. All this while, however, the audience cannot be sure if the doctor is indeed the person she thinks he is. The play uses this ambiguity to illuminate the moral wrong done to her and the moral harm she suffers because of it. From thc beginning, we have been aware of Paulina's extreme and eccentric behavior. She throws out her husband's meal as a sign of her rejection of his ideas about justice, for example, and she moves tensely and nervously around the house, clearly giving the impression that she has no peace in her soul. This information becomes necessary for us to understand the story, because the husband doesn't immediately react to what she tells him about the torturer. He doubts her. He is not entirely sure if she is capable of remembering accurately—merely by hearing his voice—the man who harmed her. She offers him further proof by saying that she has also recognized his smell, and the way he talks and expresses himself. The discussion between husband and wife helps us learn more about her broken sense of self as a result of the torture and the multiple rapes she has endured (the details of which she has kept from her husband until now). The urgency of the drama is increased because we, the audience, also doubt her sanity. We become aware that she is especially sensitive to any signs that might reveal the true identity of the torturer. She remembers, for example, that he used to talk about Nietzsche and music—which echoes an earlier conversation between Gerardo and the doctor. Such signs indicate that he is indeed the torturer, and soon Gerardo is himself beset by doubts. Yet he also keeps reminding us that Paulina is incapable of leading a normal life. Nonetheless, she seems convinced that justice will not be served by the commission, nor will there ever be a way out of her suffering. Paulina wants to interrogate the doctor and seeks her husband's help in obtaining a confession from her torturer. From the conversation between husband and wife, we learn all the excruciating details of her terrible experience and about their troubled life in the aftermath. The couple has had to move out of the city in order to lead a quieter life because Paulina is haunted by ghosts from the past. She experiences terror on a regular basis. Even the routine of daily life presents extraordinary challenges, as we can see in the scenes showing Paulina's growing frustration and rage in the face of her husband's doubts. Paulina begs her husband to help her get revenge, and tells him that she will set the doctor free if he confesses. With the doctor still bound, Gerardo questions him using the tape recorder. At this point, he believes the doctor might yet be saved if he will only confess to what Paulina wants. Again, she promises Gerardo that she will release Dr. Miranda if he does what they ask of him. Gerardo fears he will have to resign his appointment because of the way this situation will impact their future lives. By the time they both agree to this private trial, however, he knows he cannot avoid what she has asked for.

Films have the potential to tell us about the past through flashbacks and by opening up the dramatic action of the play (as when Paulina pushes the doctor's car over the cliff to the rocks below). We hear how Paulina had been tortured by Dr. Miranda. Then we hear Dr. Miranda's version, which at first is an elaborate lie, as coached by Gerardo. The drama reaches its peak when Paulina and her husband, after threatening to throw Dr. Miranda over the cliff and into the abyss, get his final confession. He admits that he is the person who tortured her, that he sadistically raped her and others, that he exhilarated in this power and, finally, that he even wished to experience this power over others again. This harrowing scene leaves no doubt as to what truly happened. Devastated and spent, Paulina and Gerardo just walk away from the doctor, leaving him free to go. The movie ends where it started, at the concert: as Paulina and Gerardo listen to the famous Schubert piece that is the title (and metaphor) for the drama, her searching eyes finally find those of her torturer, who is also at the concert with his family. This visual encounter confirms one last secret: it is no coincidence that both are at the concert. The perpetrator loved this piece of music and played it while torturing her. It becomes horrendously clear that, in spite of anything she might do to free herself from the damage she has endured, her torturer will always be a permanent presence in her life. The music contains this terrifying memory of their past, and it is therefore more vivid than anything else she could ever experience in the future.

Only a story like this can provide us with such a powerfully illuminating vision of human complexity. We learn that once a moral wrong is done, there is no way out for the sufferer. We also learn that the perpetrator cannot erase his deed. He, too, must remember their past through the music and cannot forget what he has done. In this case, Dorfman's literary achievement is reflected through his representation of the woman displaying her madness/sanity before us. As a victim, she knows this vivid image of her past experience is the defining moment of her life. But when revenge becomes an option, she realizes the impossibility of finding any real punishment for what she has suffered. This bitter acknowledgment allows her to set her torturer free. She learns, however, that the greatest tragedy is the inability to forgive. We also experience fear from the standpoint of the torturer. At first, we doubt his identity when he is questioned. He claims he is not the torturer, and with him we experience the fear of a possibly pointless death, dying for something he did not do. This empathy leaves us once he is himself again. When we learn who he really is, we recall his sudden interest in Gerardo's newly appointed job, and we realize that he was so interested because he knew he could be called to justice. This is the reason that betrays him and makes him go back to the Escobar house. He knows that he cannot be forgiven and that his escape from death was only a matter of chance, but this happenstance only strengthens his power. The drama illustrates this assurance with their last exchange of looks during the concert. Whatever might have happened between them, the doctor remains defiant. As the music plays, Schubert's piece becomes translated as the sounding notes of this terrifying memory. Now revealed is the metaphor of the drama: it becomes the reflective judgment that captures the concrete dimensions of the meaning of permanent moral harm to the sufferer. The doer is empowered by this knowledge. When we see the torturer and the tortured at the concert, the metaphor finally makes sense. The title reveals a disclosive interpretation: the sufferer is the maiden, who confronts her own death while not being able to forget her torturer and his deeds. The music and its title give way to this metaphorical interrelationship, which has profound disclosive dimensions for both the perpetrator and sufferer. We are left to arrive at judgments that allow us to grasp the depth of the moral dimension which makes this story disclose its awful truth.

Coda: Memory Wars—Bringing Material Processes of Collective Examination to the Forefront

The tragedy of Paulina's story is one similar to that which many people lived in the aftermath of Pinochet's dictatorship and in other Latin American countries. The story also illustrates the need to deliberate on what happened once stories like this move into the public sphere and make a big impact. This story allows me to demonstrate that the operation of memory is vitally connected to these kinds of stories and to show how memory makes urgent the need for open discussion so that societies may understand the meaning of state terror and violence.

One important aspect of what we have been discussing is how making moral judgments can lead to further developments in the public sphere and the impact these have between the paradigm of evil and the paradigm of justice. The mediating link between these two paradigms, as I have argued, is in fact the public sphere and public deliberations in regard to past actions. Because it is in the public sphere that memory struggles to release its dynamics about *what really happened*, the making of collective memory becomes an intensely political process. But memory possesses *moral* and *existential dimensions as well as a political one*. Further, it is in the terrifying and often divisive times of trauma, rupture, and historical catastrophe that societies struggle to generate these efforts to shape collective memory as a part of their new beginning. In the era of Pinochet, Chileans found themselves moved or shattered when confronted with the atrocities of his regime. The wider cultural sensitization to human rights was enforced not only by activists for human rights but also from narratives of memory provided by different actors. Many survivors, friends and relatives of victims, and others who were there to see these horrors considered themselves morally obligated to assume the role of public witness. As we've seen, Dorfman's story focuses on the specific moment that the truth commission began to reshape the memories of Chileans, which allowed him to see that his representation of the fictitious kidnapping and trial of a perpetrator was taking place in the collective moral imagination, even though Chileans were still living under the boot of the dictator. Yet in the political space that was opening for a transition to democracy, "many Chileans were grappling with the hidden traumas of what had been done to them while other Chileans wondered if their crimes would now be revealed."[9] The impact of stories like this was wide—not only inside Chilean society but also outside, in the international public sphere. It is no coincidence, in my view, that many of the trials and prosecutions of militaries within Chile found support and fortification from cases in which European governments also decided to prosecute Chilean (and Argentinian) militaries for crimes committed against Europeans living in Chile during Pinochet's dictatorship.[10] The worldwide news of Pinochet's indictment in London, led by Spanish judge Baltasar Garzón, became a hallmark for the possibility of applying the role of international justice to countries making the transition to democracy.[11]

More recent new studies have focused on the way distinct social actors dispute "the official story" in various countries and provide different accounts of what happened in the past and how these processes have shaped their transitions toward more democratic orders.[12] Indeed, as Steve Stern has argued, "the history of 'memory' enables us to see an additional aspect of Chilean life that is subtle, yet central: the making and unmaking of political and cultural legitimacy, notwithstanding violent rule and terror. In the struggle for the hearts and minds in Chile, *the memory question became strategic*—politically, morally, existentially—both during and after dictatorship.".[13] The uses of memory provide a site for struggles in the public sphere. This dynamic appears to be the focus of many studies now because we have come to realize how they played a pivotal role in shaping the future of societies undergoing democratic transition. For nations like Chile during the 1970s and 1980s, the only source of reflection about what happened was the presence of stories like Dorfman's.[14] Since memory is the *meaning* we attach to our experiences, stories like the one represented in *Death and the Maiden* were helpful in *opening* the struggles against oblivion in Pinochet's era. Steve Stern has called these kinds of memories the "memories of unresolved rupture," because they portray "the trauma of sorrow, fear, uncertainty"[15] and cause many individuals to lose their sense of self. A metaphoric story like this one is therefore helpful in developing the disclosure of truth that needs to be constructed. This truth, argues Stern, began clarifying that by denying the truth of torture, disappearance, and execution for years, by holding back key aspects *of this truth*—especially the specific detailed fate of individual victims—once total denial was no longer an option, and by engineering an amnesty that impeded full truth-seeking linked to justice, General Pinochet and other military rulers blocked the possibility of inner peace or transcendence for the families of victims. They imposed, as a consequence, an ongoing moral bankruptcy on the nation. (109)

Death and the Maiden became an emblematic story about memory because it captured *this* essential truth about the collective experience of society. The story was not only something that happened to Paulina but to many people, and this idea represented a specific truth. The story proved helpful in providing a mirror image that had an echo effect in the public cultural domain, "one that realizes that others have come to a similar understanding of collective memory, experience, and truth" (113). The potential for finding an echo into the wider Chilean society was also helped by different practices of documentation against torture from groups involved in the defense of human rights and in truth commissions of different kinds at various historical times. Collective memory, however, is a complex process in which many stories gain resonance, strength, and recognition, while others are lost. Stern speaks of "emblematic memories" as those that help reshape the future of one country and make the political process of democratic transition an important public process of convincing others while establishing the meanings of the experiences of rupture. For this reason, Stern argues that "the meaning frameworks we have called memory, although a human creation and inherently selective, are not arbitrary" (119); rather, they have an echo effect on emblematic memory because they possess historicity, authenticity, truth, projection into the public space, embodiment in a culturally convincing social referent, and support from other people. These memory struggles, which are represented by stories like *Death and the Maiden*, proved key to the political process that unraveled during the 1990s. Struggles over Chile's military past were cultural battles that aimed to clear up the present and reshape the future of Chile as a democratic country. Since memory is always narrated, those stories most effectively mobilized the hearts and minds of people. The efforts to construct emblematic memories to transform societies like those of the Chileans have the goal of restricting and reshaping state power while legitimizing the new democratic order. The public sphere is where these efforts articulate the possibility of displaying arguments to shape values, provide new understandings of reality, and echo the voices of influential social actors whose voices become moral guidelines. Social actors struggle to define what is true and what matters in regard to the experience of atrocities. Learning to attach moral meanings to past atrocities is thus a never-ending process of reshaping the critical stance of memories. The formation of collective memory is the constructed *bridge* between the paradigm of evil and the paradigm of justice. The cycle of material justice begins when there are enough stories to disclose historical truths about moral wrongs, which can allow societies to strengthen their cases for the prosecution of criminals and perpetrators. With this example, I have tried to show how a story helps to bridge a connection between the paradigm of evil and the paradigm of justice. The collective exercise of memory in the reconstruction of moral wrongs helps societies to find a possibility for real transition from a totalitarian regime into a new democratic order.

CHAPTER 9

The Place of the "Angelus Novus"

[Between Catastrophes]

"Learning from Catastrophes" Revisited

Adorno claimed that, after Auschwitz, the moral imperative for the twentieth century was "never again." It was through the use of a historical understanding of his experience that he arrived at this reflective judgment of what it meant to be alive after Auschwitz. His assessment pointed to a historical rupture between our traditions and modernity itself. Instead of founding the normative basis for morality on the positive use of reason, as Kant had done before, Adorno sought to recover the negative aspect of the categorical imperative through the notion that our experience of evil is the most significant historical knowledge of the twentieth century. Much has already been written about this and about Adorno's categorical imperative.[1] Adorno's judgment, however, should now be taken only as a point of departure to help us question whether any such judgment can ever be considered complete without further critical revision. This chapter presents an attempt to further develop this insight. The primary goal here is to provide a meaningful account of the historical rupture that took place after Adorno's judgment of Auschwitz—something which must still be thematized in order to avoid turning the Holocaust into what Andreas Huyssen has called a "cipher."[2]

Auschwitz has today become the common paradigm of evil as the term is used to conceptualize various ideas. Many intellectuals who lived through the historical moment of the paradigmatic atrocities illustrated by Auschwitz and its aftermath became concerned with the best way to cope with this enormous historical rupture, and the roles that memory and accountability play in our understanding of these significant events.[3] While it is true that the resonance of the traumatic events of Auschwitz has made way for a "Holocaust discourse" and for important developments within the discipline of history, as well as for newly founded places to conduct academic research in universities, we nonetheless face the possibility that we still lack a link between Adorno's judgment and the true meaning of "learning from catastrophes."[4]

The collective exercise of memory has played an important part in our sense of this rupture with modernity, albeit in an ambiguous way. For this reason, Andreas Huyssen believes that the ways we assess the problematic events of the Holocaust have led it to function as a global paradox.[5] This paradox situates the Holocaust as "the paradigm of evil," but if this is true, it is turned from a reflective judgment into a determinant one. Instead of using it to develop deeper understandings through newer *distinctions found* from other catastrophes, however, we have turned the Holocaust into an easy touchstone without having to further elaborate on other historical atrocities. It thus becomes a determinant judgment. I suggest that we should challenge the two different theoretical positions that render paradoxical the notion that the Holocaust is a paradigm of evil: at one extreme, we find those thinkers who sacralize the Holocaust[6] and use the concept as synonymous with such terms as "ineffable," "unknowable," or "incomprehensible." These scholars envision evil as something inscrutable and deny the possibility of gaining knowledge about evil actions. The paradox here, consequently, lies in the way evil then collapses into an overwhelming event, one that impedes further understanding of the Holocaust or of any other atrocity. Every specific historical event needs multiple comparisons and distinctions in order to bring new insights about its moral wrongs. Sacralizing the idea of the Holocaust is related to the prohibition of images, as Tzvetan Todorov argues.[7] Yet when we think about the Holocaust as the *sole* paradigm of evil, we end up concluding that it is ineffable and we run the risk of reducing the past to nothing more than an empty screen on which to view the present. Such a view therefore prevents us from finding ways to come to terms with what really happened. On the other hand, we find those who have caused what Todorov has called the "banalization" of the word *Holocaust*.[8] Those who use the Holocaust as a synonym for any crime thus erase all historical specificities and forfeit the historical meaning of moral wrongs, which consequently become assimilated into those of a specific past. Here too, it is evident that what comes out is a determinant judgment instead of the reflective one that I have been defending throughout this book. The tragedy is that Adorno's judgment becomes nothing more than a rhetorical device. It is this paradox that best reflects the difficulties that exist when envisioning what moral learning entails. One cannot say that we can draw lessons from our past in a linear or causal way. Nor are we able to exorcise future evils by a mere act of will. The refusal to say something meaningful about evil and the collapse of all specificities into a single historical episode are ultimately two sides of the same coin. No real knowledge can come from either extreme. Moral learning can only occur when we are subject to a public dialogue through open debate, where our judgments are permanently challenged and revised. It is through these public deliberations that we realize that every historical atrocity always brings something new that needs to be understood about the ways we inflict human cruelty.

The dangers of sacralizing or banalizing the Holocaust by turning it into the paradigm of evil lead to several possible outcomes. Politicians, for example, are reluctant to use the legal terms that were created in 1945, after the Holocaust, to describe crimes against humanity. They understand all too well that when they refer to a historical (or, for that matter, contemporary) atrocity as being a genocide or ethnic cleansing, it means that they must take action against it.[9] As Samantha Powers has argued, the problematic paradox of our historical judgments ought to be confronted with our need to be proactive.[10] Our understanding of the meaning of "learning from catastrophes" will only be possible if we see the material outcomes of such knowledge translated into legal action.

We need to understand how the concept of "learning from catastrophes" can help us avoid conceptualizing our historical traumas such that they become empty ciphers and impede the development of new reflective judgments. When thinking about the twentieth century's histories of destruction, Andreas Huyssen draws attention to the significant role that memory has acquired in "re-presenting" the past. As he says, "The seduction of the archive and its trove of stories of human achievement and suffering has never been greater."[11] We owe this success to the importance of the concept of trauma, which has acquired a deeply significant place in our understanding of what has happened from the atrocities of Auschwitz.[12] One important dimension of the way the idea of trauma has articulated our concerns with memory was precisely what led Adorno to formulate the categorical imperative of "never again." The meaning Adorno attributed to his categorical imperative was that we should find enough fortitude to look back at our historical traumas and find resources with which to create material ways to prevent them from being repeated. Furthermore, he understood that the past also requires us to situate ourselves in a different present. We need to challenge the conceptual positions that sacralize or banalize the experiences of the Holocaust by grouping them into a determinant judgment as the paradigm of evil. We can begin to do so by highlighting important questions of what we need to consider here. We need to find ways to thematize evil and take into account two important parts of our experiences: one relates to our ideas about conceptualizing an atrocity and our ways of discovering that moral wrongs were committed in specific contextual situations. The second involves recognizing the moral lessons learned, and then redefining them into positive laws. The problem with these ways of coping with crimes lies in the idea that it is truly possible to change the future. Indeed, our notions of historical trauma provide important ways of making sense of the violence suffered and the cruelty perpetrated by humanity. This book has attempted to show that the world's moral vision has been historically articulated by the notion of "learning from catastrophes." Nonetheless, it is still necessary to explore one more aspect of this category—which also happens to articulate the opposing argument—namely, the dynamic connection that we must recognize when it is possible to provide a conceptual link between trauma and moral learning. Such was Habermas's original aim when he formulated the concept. Since Habermas did not develop a more systematic account of this dynamic movement (as noted earlier), it is now important to return to the stage in which this connection between the concepts of trauma and the exercise of moral learning is made apparent. I wish to argue that this connection becomes possible when the paradigm of evil links itself to the paradigm of justice. It can only do so, however, through the complex use of democratic institutional activities that help societies understand themselves. It is in this very act of self-analysis that societies become aware of the moral dimension of the critical exercise of historical knowledge. This is why we must now focus on ways of understanding moral learning and its critical historical articulation. Only by delving deeper into the dynamics of learning from catastrophes can we avoid the easy escape of believing that all we have to do is make traumatic experiences sacred to avoid human cruelty. The concept of trauma should not be the only category that helps us articulate the complexities of our historical failures when coping with human cruelty. What I would like to argue instead is that the only way our notion of learning from catastrophes can be enhanced is by constructing a strong concept of material justice, which in turn presupposes that we have an open public sphere, with multiple narratives; that we develop critical discussions that are shaped in light of different stories; and that those stories help us return to the territory of accountability, where the institution of law invites specific kinds of reflective judgments based on the disclosure of the meanings of our moral learning. We also need new ways for democratic institutions to help us shape activities (human rights activism, truth commissions, juridical proceedings, memorials, art works, public spaces of commemoration) that allow societies to actively shape themselves into moral subjects. The depth of our moral view can only be reflected in how we decide to draw these lessons from our past. In my view, when Habermas created his concept of "learning from catastrophes," he meant not only considering the dark episodes framed as historical traumas but also the way traumatic events have led us to consider those atrocities from a legal and material perspective. His dialectical approach to history, with its inherent conflicts and contradictions, is the last important element to explore here. If the notion of "learning from catastrophes" situates itself somewhere between the historical traumas of our past and our ways of creating material institutions of justice through memory and accountability, then we may find that it is possible to overcome the sense of impotence that has prevailed in the historical legacy of those theorists who felt overwhelmed by the depth of the atrocities committed during the twentieth century. Learning from catastrophes must give rise to a conscious effort to consider the collective exercise of memory in a way that is connected to a critical understanding of human actions. Consequently, we will be able to call upon institutional legal resources to help us cope with the problems found. Learning from catastrophes understands human action as a complex entanglement of "transparency and opaqueness,"[13] of the voluntary and involuntary sides of human action. This dialectic needs to be captured in its very conceptualization in order to dispel the easy ways in which we tend to blur any particularity and difference between historical episodes. This is the reason I would like to emphasize such a double structure for the meaning of "learning from catastrophes," which does not presuppose linear or causal ways of considering moral learning. Rather, we should dispel the naïve idea that human will alone can prevent future catastrophes. There must be greater effort made to understand the particularities of each case of atrocity perpetrated throughout history. Our various collective methods of shaping historical reconstructions of the past can only be helpful if we gain moral knowledge about the complexity of human souls. Nothing assures us that this is done unless we see this knowledge reflected in the material structures of democratic institutions. Habermas attempted to correct historical mistakes when he intervened in the *Historikerstreit*, for example. His efforts alerted us to the need for dealing with a complex dynamic between transparency and blindness, with remembrance and forgetting, and with the idea that memory and accountability are products of critical ways of coping with our past. Thus, our efforts to thematize stories in the public sphere, our duty to build up sites for memory, and our disclosure of the hidden and suppressed views of what has happened can become coherent judgments, but only if we understand that "mastering the past" means not expecting closure with our past deeds. Rather, by exploring the difficulties that arise in our quest for moral learning, we might become conscious of the contradictory aspects of human action and of the narratives that come after them. If, instead of believing that it is possible to erase evil actions from our human world, we allow ourselves to change the way we understand human actions, through the specificities of all historical atrocities, and point out the subtle and difficult ways humans still find new methods to cause harm to others, we might be able to dispel a maelstrom of ciphers. Such transformations, however, entail acquiring a sense of moral depth that enables us to find avenues for building material sources of justice. These efforts, if successful, can teach us to highlight how challenging it has been to widen the material structures of justice. The struggles to create international institutions of justice have already shown us the importance of expanding our collective attention toward the long and unending processes of understanding evil actions.

Memory and Accountability

The twentieth century was one of extreme cruelty, massive killing, systematic rape, ethnic cleansing, torture, and genocide in many places around the world, including Europe. These events have threatened our belief that moral and democratic institutions can exist. The effort to find links between memory and accountability aims at providing an important bridge to the comprehension of evil actions. My goal is to stress that the socially constructed understanding of the rule of international law needs to reconsider the linkages between collective memory and accountability. Ruti Teitel has already questioned the idea that we can draw a single determinant lesson from the past. This critical view, however, should alert us that, because historical understanding depends on social and political contingencies, we must try to draw a clear connection between critical processes of historical understanding and the struggles to enlarge the material sources of justice. It is not merely through law that justice materializes, but also through the ways social actors strive to give meaning to past actions. This is why the category of collective memory should help us realize that the function of social actors in public debates is to give normative meanings to our efforts to reconstruct and understand past actions. Transitional truths are socially constructed within processes of collective memory. They are instances of conscious historical production. We must realize that collective memory is a process of reconstructing representations of the past in light of the present. This type of exercise highlights the critical aspects of the nature of the cultural enterprise we call "collective memory" and provides us with an consciousness of our frameworks, of the way we use symbols, of the ways rituals provide us with moral meanings, and the ways we situate ourselves as moral subjects with the capacity to envision a different future.

Ruti Teitel's pioneering work, *Transitional Justice*, has demonstrated that the task of shaping social memory is one of the functions of the law. The procedural process of trials, the availability and display of stories, and the disclosure of truth (what really happened) provide important scenarios in which the rituals of justice can take place. These historical narratives and their reconstructions possess justificatory epistemes and allow us to define the ways our future can be shaped. The framework of law—the procedures and vocabularies of justice—plays a significant role. As Teitel argues, "The pursuit of historical truth is embedded in a framework of accountability and in the pursuit of justice";[14] thus, accounting for the past sets the stage for a distinctive view of justice.

The idea that collective memory is a site for representation can now be connected to the way representations of collective history re-create and dramatize actions. Huyssen has focused attention on the fact that our times have enhanced "the culture of memory" because of "the successful marketing of memory by the Western culture industry."[15] This culture of memory, however, is always tied to different political uses and can vary from an aggressively chauvinistic and nationalistic culture (like Serbia) to the more progressive attempts of, say, the

Argentinians to produce an accurate historical memory (accounting) that will protect their civil society from oblivion. (For an excellent example of this process, in content as well as the sheer existence of the film itself, see *The Official Story* [1985, Argentina], directed by Luis Puenzo.) These are the sites of the memory wars. We cannot deny that all the representational possibilities of memory have increased and that their impact on the public sphere through the mass media (e.g., televised court proceedings) has also infused popular culture with new expectations for an international order.

The past has no sense or value by itself. We, the social subjects, give meaning and value to our reconstructions. For this reason, all our reconstructions of the past should be subjected to open public debate. Public debates clarify for us the ways we have chosen specific strategies of representation. Huyssen has called our attention to the importance of thinking critically about the often subtle defining lines between traumatic memories and the ways in which commercial media markets have framed political issues out of such memories. A notion of reflective judgment is urgently needed here, and we must connect it to the category of learning from catastrophes. At stake, as Huyssen has well argued, is the way "modern societies" have displaced "a growing fear of the future at a time when the belief in modernity's progress is deeply shaken" (19). The problems that contemporary societies face when dealing with political transformation have much to do with the fact that the traumatic events of the twentieth century have overshadowed other social efforts which have sought to lead the way toward a different future. Huyssen also believes that we rely more and more on the past because of "a slow but palpable transformation of temporality in our lives, brought on by the complex intersections of technological change, mass media, and new patterns of consumption, work, and global mobility" (21). As a result, Huyseen argues, we have erased our expectations for a different kind of future. Indeed, Huyssen adds, the culture of memory has played an important role in how we experience our fears for the future. He is right to point out that, with our fractured notions of temporality, there is too much present living in the past. We have brought our negative experiences of the past into the present and thereby tarnished the linkages that make it possible to envision a transformative sense of the future. We must thus understand what the concept of learning from catastrophes can really mean in light of this challenge. There is yet an enabling dimension of memory that can help us articulate an idea about the social need to design new ways of envisioning a better future. However, this concept needs to be connected to a critical scrutiny of the ways we have questioned our past. We have allowed the idea of trauma to occupy the only important space in which the past could lead to our self-understanding. We need not go back to utopias. But neither should we fall to the other extreme. The obsession with recovering the dystopic sides of our historical experience cannot be meaningful if it is not contrasted with a sense of what we have learned from past events. Only by articulating the material gains of our informed visions of the past can we begin to understand the importance of the processes of the culture of memory. These efforts have led to democratization and stimulated the struggle for human rights. The power to build up public spheres that will produce wider debates about the past can, in the end, begin to produce a better articulation of our memories from different catastrophes as linked to the project of a global system of justice. Because memory is no substitute for justice, its emergence cannot be separated from the material results of democratic institutions. The best use of Huyssen's critical views on the culture of memory is to emphasize the importance of the critical task to never "forget the future" (22).

We can begin now to explore the normative possibilities of using Habermas's concept of learning from catastrophes. Our notions of responsibility have dramatically changed in the past century (though there is a long road to go in this regard). Legal and cultural developments have coincided with an increased sense of the need to debate obligations of humanitarian intervention and to raise questions about the moral and legal responsibilities for past atrocities.

We must focus on ways of shaping collective memories. The construction of such collective memories comes with different representations of state action that enable a society, through different devices of "categorization" and "emplotment," to achieve new, more democratic narratives for the successor. As Ruti Teitel has forcefully argued, "constructing past actions" requires "reporting facts" in ways that highlight relevant distinctions.[16] Narratives that represent the status of both the perpetrator and the victim and their actions constitute the material elements that societies should consider. We need to focus on the ways representational devices help us acknowledge the violence in those actions and to understand how "historical transformations occur through the explicit re-presentation involving the categorization of the facts in controversy—in particular, the nature and justification for the predecessor's political violence" (85).

I have offered as an important example of the ethical and political implications of this kind of "transitional narrative" Hannah Arendt's *Eichmann in Jerusalem: A Report on the Banality of Evil*. As we have seen in previous chapters, her report presents a relentless normative argument through the juxtaposition of Adolf Eichmann's responsibility as a perpetrator. The way narratives stir polemical discussions and critical responses gives us an idea about collective memory as the site of conflictive views. It is important to focus on this constructive space in order to show that historical accountability can only be possible through principles of documentation, representation, and successor accounts that report the nature of moral wrongdoing. Thus, collective memory and accountability are inextricably linked. Together they form the basis for the normative idea of learning from catastrophes. The narrative explorations of the negative spaces—the omissions, the exclusions, the deliberate blind spots enforced on maps of the past—are often invested with energies much oriented to shaping a different future. The strong normative thesis based on the concept of learning from catastrophes shows that the search for critical historical reconstructions can lead us to find new meanings in the sphere of the political global order.

The shaping of different futures in places where there has previously been state violence, for example, demands that the new political order be held accountable to the rule of law. Indeed, as Ruti Teitel has argued, "these are extraordinary circumstances of past injustices," which are often "state-sponsored," and for this reason "the argument from impunity takes on new meaning" (28). As a guiding concept, "learning from catastrophes" demonstrates that the critical historical reconstruction of the development of the rule of law, in the context of moral wrongdoing, has played a significant role since the Middle Ages.[17] Our historical understanding of the relationship between law and justice, however, has made a great leap forward and had a profound impact on global order as a result of the Nuremberg trials and the normative message that attempted to go beyond the idea of a defeated regime. This historical understanding focused on the examination of "violence" as "just" or "unjust."[18] The normative core of our gained assumptions about violence has been linked to a condemnation of past political violence and the desire to establish trials as the lawful setting where the meaning of state injustice can be defined. Indeed, the idea that no one can be above the law is a direct result of the long historical reappraisal of state violence that took place within legal institutions.

When facing past atrocities, it is possible to say that we have acquired a new sense of the way material institutions of justice have taken a leading role in allowing us to envision a different future. For example, we have seen past trials that have not only allowed the public condemnation of past violence but have also served as instruments for the legitimation process of the rule of law as the most significant element for the future of any democracy. Teitel's research shows us that historical context is the most important aspect of this collective task, for, as she argues, it is a transitional defining moment for a different future. Even so, we cannot say that this defining moment becomes foundational because "using criminal justice to draw the line between regimes raises profound dilemmas chiefly relating to the implied relation of law to politics."[19] Thus, we need to connect this exercise to my general concept of reflective judgment. The main dilemma, as Teitel explains, is the political context of the normative shift that should take place. Teitel argues that "this core dilemma raised by the political shift from illiberal to liberal rule is inextricably enmeshed in the problem of retroactivity in the relevant norms during the change of regime and the exercise of the successor regime's new normative rules as applied to the past regime's behavior."[20] In such contexts, we need the use of reflective judgments[21] The importance of making the material sources of the idea of justice apparent implies that those who begin by articulating their historical understanding of past atrocities in connection to the rule of law (through trials, punishment, etc.) need to keep themselves associated with the full legality of such an order. They can only conduct themselves within the most restrictive principles of justice and develop these further with an exercise of reflective judgment. Otherwise, they run the risk of falling into the most dangerous situation, namely, to send the wrong message of political justice to a broken society.[22]

The fact that an important stage of moral learning came into being after 1945 can be shown if we analyze the significance of the Nuremberg trials in their full historical and political context. Before, national trials were considered hopeless and politically doomed because of "the failure of that earlier postwar national justice is said to explain only the subsequent resurgence of German aggression; [thus] the failure of accountability is itself considered to cause the failure of liberalization."[23] The transformation of our moral legacy from this new understanding of atrocities such as the Holocaust allowed the idea of international justice to become an institutional reality. It was through the concept of accountability—which could only be possible if it remained in the hands of the Allied countries, where the jurisdiction broadened from national to international scope—that we began to envision a global order. Rather than punishing the country, as before, the aim was to ascribe individual responsibility to crimes. Though plagued with problems and paradoxes, Nuremberg's precedential significance is the result of what we have called "a successful reflective judgment" because Nuremberg "shaped the dominant scholarly understanding of successor justice with the shift in the approach, from national to international processes, as well as from the collective to the individual"; thus, "successor criminal justice—Nuremberg style—implied a wholly novel and international forum, multinational criminal procedure, as well as offenses such as the 'crime against humanity.'"[24] We can conclude that it is only after 1945 that we have a new meaning for the concept of accountability that is related to international law. With the renewed idea of accountability, international criminal law provided us with ways to conceptualize the "paradoxical" possibility of "an evil regime under the law." Through the reflective judgment built into the historical analogy of postwar justice that dominated the Nuremberg trials, the definition of justice was articulated against the offense of "waging war."[25] Because of the Nuremberg trials, we now have a different conception of accountability based on individual responsibility.[26] Teitel's conclusion allows us to envision international law as a framework of what she calls "successor justice." Meanwhile, the concept of accountability, drawn from the Nuremberg trials, provides us with the novel concept of "individual responsibility," and the Nuremberg Principles enable us through "a radical expansion of potential individual criminal liability with no clear stopping point."[27] It is now our historical responsibility to see the real dilemmas of historical experiences in light of concrete transitions and to find new ways of creating possible solutions against evil actions.

Another important material construction of our historical conception of justice is the idea of crimes against humanity. As Teitel observes, "The adjudication of this offense has acquired the force of a reigning symbol of the liberal rule of law."[28] Furthermore, the invocation of such a crime is now seen to be at the heart of the rule-of-state laws because it helps distinguish between a liberal and an illiberal regime. We find, with this concept, the greatest potential for a normative concept of transitional justice. It comprises grave offenses such as murder, deportation, torture, and so forth. It was first used at Nuremberg to describe the way states persecute and commit crimes against their own citizens. These crimes were now seen to transcend the confines of national laws and nations, and thus gave us, for the first time, an awareness of the need to create international forums of justice (e.g., tribunals). The most significant accomplishment of such a typified crime was that the offense was understood to have been perpetrated against "humankind." This allowed us to see the need to project the matter into the international arena as the larger site for justice. Teitel argues that the "adjudication of the crime against humanity has come to forge the very meaning of the contemporary response to modern persecution,"[29] and it is conceived as an offense against humanity, hence prosecutable by all nations, giving it the meaning of universality as its founding material basis. This principle of universality was first enacted when Adolf Eichmann was captured and prosecuted by the State of Israel for crimes committed during the Second World War. The importance of this historical situation was that "the trial was held decades after the events," and the crime violated neither retroactivity nor the territoriality principles. It set the first major precedent in important contemporary proceedings. More recently, because of this same understanding of universality, we have seen Spain issue a significant initiative for crimes against humanity committed under the military rulers of Chile and Argentina.

The idea of international law has been one of the most important material scenarios created during the past century. Much of the work was accomplished because of our historical understanding. Indeed, social knowledge of the past can be constructed through public processes. These processes in turn generate a democratizing truth that helps construct a sense of societal consensus. Habermas is thus correct to highlight the idea that a consensus of history is predicated upon a public display of truth from past actions and on its subsequent critical revision in the public sphere. We owe the important sources of material justice to the trials of Nuremberg and Tokyo. Because truth is not synonymous with justice, we, the political actors, must find ways to build bridges between collective memory and accountability. We must envisage that histories in the plural do advance epistemic and moral purposes associated with criminal sanctions and moral and political responsibility. Collective memory is seen as a construction of representations and the scenario in which truth can be produced through a workable "past" in order to change our future. Performative narratives of democratization are the result of attaching collective memories to strong normative ideas of memory and accountability.

By Way of Conclusion: Benjamin's "Angelus Novus"

In his "Theses of the Philosophy of History," Benjamin argues that "the tradition of the oppressed teaches us that the 'state of emergency' in which we live is not the exception but the rule."[30] Instead of interpreting this claim in regard to how modern politics makes the "state of emergency" the rule of biopolitics, as Agamben does (very much inspired by this Benjaminian thesis), I would like to suggest a different interpretation. My interpretation is that when we pay attention to those stories about the oppressed and perished, we should remind ourselves that as long as we are human, we cannot consider the task of rescuing them with simplistic characterizations or without any individualizing distinctions. Indeed, our reconstructions of stories should be critical and falsifiable. Benjamin's insight is a warning that heightens our attention and critical knowledge about past catastrophes and about the role of storytellers—in other words, who writes the stories and what they bring to our point of view. If it is true that we are condemned to live between catastrophes and that our moral duty is to be aware that no single narrative can lead us to a final truth, then we must recognize that no final judgment can be made without further exploration and by scrutinizing each narrative in comparison with other stories. Benjamin's Angelus Novus sees past atrocities through a nonlinear understanding of history and yet as "one single catastrophe which keeps piling wreckage upon wreckage and hurls it in front of his feet" (258). His Angel is not immobilized. Rather, he is forced to move on because there is a storm that "propels him into the future" (258). We need to begin to make distinctions of narratives within history in order to break this continuum of "one single catastrophe" that weighs down the whole past. Benjamin knew all too well that the connection between the past and the future was an important one, and he tried to articulate it through his own critical ideas about experience and hope. With Benjamin's critical view of "progress" we have arrived at the last normative insight into our category of learning from catastrophes. We cannot hold any messianic hope, as Benjamin once believed. Instead, our awareness of catastrophes should help us establish a link with the concept of learning from catastrophes to the historical knowledge that we gain from critically examining the past. This is the place where we can learn to make distinctions, and thus move to the territory of understanding each particular historical episode as a result of our new reflective judgments. This is also what is implied in the dialectical dynamics of our horizons of experience in conjunction with our horizons of expectations. As Reinhart Kosselleck argues, "Hope and memory, or expressed more generally, expectation and experience—for expectation comprehends more than hope, and experience goes deeper than memory—simultaneously constitute history and its cognition," and they do so by making apparent the inner *critical* relationship "between past and future."[31] With the concept of learning from catastrophes, we aim to restore the idea that, when understanding past atrocities, drawing on distinctions enables moral knowledge. Moral awareness becomes the frame where we construct a chance for a different future.

[illegible]

[illegible] Moreover these become the future [illegible]

[illegible]

Epilogue

This theory of evil has highlighted what we can learn from catastrophes. Such a statement, however, does not mean that I can claim there has been progress in history. Rather, it means, as was Habermas's main intention when he coined the concept, that there always exists the possibility of creating another side to the story of evil. This dynamic dialectic should allow us to situate ourselves beyond the paradigm of total despair (the apocalyptic), and beyond the naïve idea that modernity can still entirely hold the pure promise of enlightenment without a critical examination of past atrocities. Moral progress is possible only if we learn to see the depth and gravity of our actions through the moral filters that enable us to find new techniques that we humans use to destroy each other. In this sense, there is no possible redemption from past catastrophes. There is only the potential for finding ways to begin the difficult processes of understanding. This collective exercise of comprehension is helpful in shaping individuals and societies as they build their moral identities. This is why judgments become central in the reflexive task of looking back into our past and in designing ways for the future to be shaped and transformed.

Even if we observe setbacks and failures in the ways national and international institutions meet the challenges of confronting the perpetrators and victims of violence and hatred, it is our duty to insist that things do not have to end in those failed historical episodes. Rather, part of our moral responsibility as human beings is to insist that nothing is determined, that there are other ways to change the outcome of historical catastrophes, and that those changes need to be mediated by the collective effort of critically revising our past and understanding what happened.

Although the main goal of this book has been to demonstrate that stories can be tremendously helpful in our attempts to understand the complexities of our evil actions, this claim cannot depend merely on narrative devices to grasp those intricacies. There are plenty of ways that narratives establish links to other interpretative efforts at understanding. Historical representations of the past provide ways to transform our organization of knowledge. They certainly allow us to disclose the hidden or dark dimensions of human interaction. For this reason, historical representations of the past are informed by previous discussions. In open debates, social actors can also see the way certain accounts of our historical past are received, furnishing us with a clearer understanding of past actions—morally speaking, that is. This is the level where interpretations gain *recognition. It is for this reason that we have spoken of Wirkungsgeschichte* (Gadamer). Knowledge can be structured as a filter through which morality permits us to perceive atrocities. Because they provide us with moral knowledge, historical narratives are not arbitrary. Hannah Arendt's search for ways to meet the challenge of facing those transitional times (the dark times she always had in mind) should be a reminder that we will never erase the peril of facing other, more heinous episodes of human suffering and violence.

Arendt was also correct when she claimed that "legal and moral issues are by no means the same, but they have a certain affinity with each other because they presuppose the *power of judgment*.[1] Even if this theory asserts that we have learned more from, say, Dostoyevsky, Conrad, and Shakespeare than from any theodicy, my arguments about the need for judgment are mainly philosophical. Thus, I cannot conclude that this theory situates itself comfortably within the realm of postmodern theories of narratives that erase the boundary between philosophy and literature. This proposal provides a link, through judgment, between narratives and philosophy. It is a theory about reflective judgment. As a political measure facing times marked by human cruelty, the ultimate criterion for what is at stake in order to have moral conduct is whether we have learned how to construct a moral image of the world, on the one hand, and how to construct moral and political judgments, on the other. Arendt is also right in her assertion that "for human beings, thinking of past matters means moving in the dimension of depth, striking roots and thus stabilizing themselves, so as not to be swept away by whatever may occur—the *Zeitgeist* or History or simple temptation. The greatest evil is not radical, it has no roots, and because it has no roots it has no limitations, it can go to unthinkable extremes and sweep over the whole world" (95).

Learning from catastrophes presents a theory that insists on our need to critically revise our past because we construct our sense of self while we construct a different kind of political and moral community. We also make a moral choice when we decide with whom we wish to spend our lives, and, as Arendt knew, "this company is chosen by thinking in examples, in examples of persons dead or alive, real or fictitious, and in examples of incidents, past or present" (146). We can agree with Arendt when she concludes that the refusal to judge at all "out of the unwillingness or inability to choose one's examples and one's company, and out of the unwillingness or inability to relate to others through *judgment*, arise[s] the real *skandala*, the real stumbling blocks which human powers can't remove because they were not caused by human and humanly understandable motives. *Therein lies the horror and, at the same time, the [new] banality of evil*" (146; emphasis added).

Notes

Introduction

1. María Pía Lara, *Moral Textures: Feminist Narratives in the Public Sphere* Berkeley: U of California P, 1998).
2. Hannah Arendt, *The Life of the Mind* (New York and London: Harcourt Brace Jovanovich, 1971), 216.
3. Raul Hilberg, *The Destruction of the European Jews* (1961; rpt., New York: Holmes and Meier, 1985).
4. She later made the articles into a book. See Hannah Arendt, *Eichmann in Jerusalem: A Report on the Banality of Evil* (1963; rpt., New York: Penguin, 1994).
5. We will see more about this debate in several of the chapters in this book dealing with Hannah Arendt's work.
6. Victor Farías, *Heidegger and Nazism* (Philadelphia: Temple UP, 1989).
7. Daniel J. Goldhagen, *Hitler's Willing Executioners: Ordinary Germans and the Holocaust* (New York: Knopf, 1996).
8. W.G. Sebald, *On the Natural History of Destruction* (New York: Random House, 2003).
9. Anonymous, *A Woman in Berlin: Eight Weeks in the Conquered City* (New York: Metropolitan Books, 2005).
10. Jan Thomas Gross, *Neighbors: The Destruction of the Jewish Community in Jedwabne, Poland* (Princeton and London: Princeton UP, 2002).
11. A new movie directed by Lajos Koltai (2005), based on his book *Fateless* (1975), and his own script discloses a different angle about his experience as a survivor of the concentration camp. It is a tale about how a young man survives the harshness of the *Lager* only because someone else teaches him how to resist. Once liberated from the camp, the boy returns to his native Budapest and realizes that know one truly understands how the experience at the *Lager* redefined his whole being. He finds that the lack of understanding and solidarity to what he has become is an even harsher reality than the one endured at the concentration camp. Fateless is the metaphor for someone

like him who finds himself emotionally attached to a place that seems to has ceased to exist but that defined his whole being.

12. Determinant judgments subsume the particular under a general rule. Reflective judgments, on the other hand, derive the rule from the particular. One can understand "the universal" through the particular.
13. Raphael Lemkin, *Axis Rule in Occupied Europe* (Washington D.C.: Lawbook Exchange, 2005).
14. Primo Levi, *The Drowned and the Saved* (1986; rpt., New York: Vintage, 1989).
15. See Richard J. Bernstein, *Radical Evil: A Philosophical Interrogation* (Cambridge, Eng.: Polity Press, 2002).
16. Immanuel Kant, *Critique of Judgment* (1790; rpt., Indianapolis and Cambridge, Eng.: Hackett, 1987).
17. Giorgio Agamben, *Remnants of Auschwitz: The Witness and the Archive* (New York: Zone Books, 1999).
18. Joseph Conrad, *Heart of Darkness* (1902; rpt., New York, Penguin, 2000).

1. Why Do We Need to Create a Moral Image of the World?

1. Immanuel Kant, *Political Writings*, ed. H. S. Reiss (Cambridge: Cambridge UP, 1970), 227.

   I use this notion of the "moral image of the world" in a broad Kantian sense. It refers to a concept of the world that arises in particular contexts, and it is with regard to such contexts that we can account for the world. For more on this issue see Dieter Heinrich, *Aesthetic Judgment and the Moral Image of the World: Studies in Kant* (Stanford, Calif.: Stanford UP, 1992).
2. See Richard J. Bernstein, *Radical Evil: A Philosophical Interrogation*; Claudia Card, *The Atrocity Paradigm: A Theory of Evil* (Oxford and New York: Oxford UP, 2002); Susan Neiman, *Evil in Modern Thought: An Alternative History of Philosophy* (Princeton: Princeton UP, 2002).
3. I have appropriated this phrase from Jürgen Habermas, "Learning from Catastrophes: A Look Back at the Short Twentieth Century," *The Postnational Constellation:Political Essays*, ed. Max Pensky (Cambridge: MIT Press, 2001), 38–57. Habermas clarifies this notion by pointing out some of the characteristics of catastrophes: "They oblige us to look at the gruesome features of a century that 'invented' the gas chambers, total war, state-sponsored genocide and extermination camps, brainwashing, state security apparatuses, and the panoptic surveillance of entire populations. The twentieth century 'generated' more victims, more dead soldiers, more murdered civilians, more displaced minorities, more torture, more dead from cold, from hunger, from maltreatment, more political prisoners and refugees, than could ever have imagined. The phenomena of violence and barbarism mark the distinctive signature of the age." Habermas, "Learning from Catastrophes," 45.
4. See Jonathan Glover, *Humanity: A Moral History of the Twentieth Century* (London: Jonathan Cape, 1999).
5. Notice that our legacy of cruelty is embedded in the use of *religious terms*, such as this one. One should understand, however, that these terms can be

taken as secularized once they become widely used, as in the case of the term *Holocaust*. Nevertheless, it is important to consider that these types of terms (*Shoah* is another example) imply a religious interpretation or metaphor. In order to prevent mistakes here, we should be aware that the most difficult task for a postmetaphysical theory is to acknowledge the origin of words coined for the description of human cruelty. Ira Katznelson argues that "'Holocaust' as the most common label for the planned annihilation of Europe's Jews as a central ideological goal aiming at total erasure and succeeding in murdering most—an act for which we can find no meaning except for Nazi meaning—would have to wait for some two decades of representational incoherence to pass for what Winston Churchill had called 'a crime without a name' to secure one, eventually besting 'Shoah,' 'Churban,' 'Final Solution,' 'Judeocide,' 'War against Jews,' '*Judenvernichtung*' (annihilation of the Jews), and 'Auschwitz,' among other alternatives. 'Even though it implies a particular (a Jewish) perspective and is misnomer to its original religious meaning,' the historian of anti-Semitism Gavin Langmuir has observed, 'nonetheless, precisely because of its ambiguous religious overtones, the word suggests a cosmic overarching perspective that could embrace all the structures, events, agents, and causalties in the killing.'" Ira Katznelson, *Desolation and Enlightment: Political Knowledge After Total War, Totalitarianism, and the Holocaust* (New York and Chichester, Eng.: Columbia UP, 2003), 26–27.

6. Tim Cole, *Images of the Holocaust: The Myth of the "Shoah Business"* (London: Duckworth, 1999), 7.
7. Cole, *Images of the Holocaust*, 7.
8. Ruti G. Teitel, *Transitional Justice* (Oxford and New York: Oxford UP, 2000).
9. Cole asserts that "perhaps more than anything else, it was the capture of Adolf Eichmann by Israeli Secret Service personnel in May 1960, and his subsequent trial in Jerusalem in 1961, which first awoke popular interest in the Holocaust. From the start it was clear that the trial was not simply about Eichmann. It was a trial concerned with the Shoah, and was a self-conscious attempt to bring to awareness of the massacre of six million European Jews to both native-born Israeli youth and to the wider world." Cole, *Images of the Holocaust*, 7.
10. Habermas recalls the importance of this connection through Schelling's own idea about human freedom. In an interview with Eduardo Mendieta, he offers this explanation: "Schelling appropriated this tradition and anchored the tense relation between 'egoity' and 'love' in God himself. The rather 'dark' tendency toward finitization (Verendlichung) or contraction is intended as an explanation of God's capacity for self-limitation. This was the subject of my doctoral dissertation. . . . The problem concerns the creation—which, like the notion of Hegel's logic, took place within God's spirit—to its conclusion. In order to be able to see Himself confirmed in His own freedom. That is, He equips Adam kadmos (first Adam) with the unconditional freedom of good and evil, and thus assumes the risk that Adam may make wrong use of this gift by sinning and thereby dragging the whole idea of creation with him into the abyss. . . . Of course, this 'worst case scenario' is just what happened. The story solves the problem of theodicy, but at a tremendous cost: that first, the horrific act of freedom inaugurates a new age for the world, the age of world history. In

this second, historical stage of the world, a humbled God must himself await redemption, since humanity has taken on the burden of resurrecting fallen nature... . This myth—and it is more than just a myth—illuminates two aspects of human freedom: the intersubjective constitution of autonomy and the meaning of self-binding of the will's arbitrary freedom to unconditionally valid norms." Jürgen Habermas, *Religion and Rationality: Essays on Reason, God, and Modernity*, ed. Eduardo Mendieta (Cambridge: MIT Press, 2002), 161.

11. This is precisely the reason why I use the notion of the "moral image of the world": because the moral image could be a constitutive component of the moral perspective itself. One can say that the moral image of the world develops jointly with the constitution of our moral conscience.
12. As Martin Jay has argued, "Although there may be no progress towards some perfect truth about the past, *historical representations can learn from the discussion that preceded them and thus produced what Gadamer called a "Wirkungsgeschichte," a history of effects or receptions of history.*" Martin Jay, "When Did the Holocaust End?" in *Refractions on Violence* (New York and London: Routledge, 2003), 47–70 (57; emphasis added).
13. Hans-Georg Gadamer, *Wahrheit und Methode* (Tübingen: J. C. B. Mohr, 1975).
14. Of course the Serbs were not the only ones who used this technique of terror to destroy others. During the war between Croatians, Serbs, and Muslims, all sides used rape as a weapon of war.
15. Aryeh Neier claims that, "The *New York Times*, which a few weeks earlier had published John Burns's riveting account of the atrocities committed by Borislav Herak, including many rapes, featured the report prominently on its front page, and cited in its headline the statistic that 20,000 women had been raped." Aryeh Neier, *War Crimes: Brutality, Genocide, Terror, and the Struggle for Justice* (New York: Random House, 1998), 176.
16. To learn more about the way "rape" became considered a crime against humanity, see Larry May, "International Crime: The Case of Rape," in *Crimes Against Humanity: A Normative Account* (New York: Cambridge UP, 2005), 96–111.
17. Neier explains that, "Prior to Bosnia, there was never an issue involving women in countries that preoccupied American Women. Overnight, however, it seemed that the plight of Bosnian women had become a domestic political issue to American feminists." Within days, "*Washington Post* columnist Judy Mann reported a finding by prominent feminist law professor Catharine MacKinnon that 50,000 Muslim women had been raped in the Bosnian conflict"; later on, "MacKinnon appeared on a panel with me at a forum sponsored by the Bar Association of the City of New York and spoke of 30,000 women who had become pregnant as a consequence of rape in Bosnia." Neier, *War Crimes*, 176–78.

    Larry May also explains that "recently we have seen rape elevated into a clear strategy of war, seemingly justifying several high-profile international prosecutions for rape, and also raising again questions of why and whether rape should be seen as an international crime." Larry May, *Crimes Against Humanity*, 98.
18. See how Bernard Williams explains the differences of the concept of the divine for the Greeks in Bernard Williams, *Shame and Necessity* (Berkeley: U of California P, 1993).

19. Williams, *Shame and Necessity*, 18.
20. Martha Nussbaum, *The Fragility of Goodness: Luck and Ethics in Greek Tragedy and Philosophy* (Cambridge and New York: Cambridge UP, 1986), 379. Subsequent references to this book are cited in the text.
21. Nietzsche says that "the myth seems to wish to whisper to us that wisdom, and particularly Dionysian wisdom, is an unnatural abomination; that he who by means of his knowledge plunges nature into the abyss of destruction must also suffer the dissolution of nature in his own person." Friedrich Nietzsche, *The Birth of Tragedy* (New York: Vintage, 1967), 69.
22. Harold Bloom, *Shakespeare: The Invention of the Human* (New York: Riverhead, 1998). Where indicated, subsequent references to this book are cited in the text.
23. Kant dealt with this problem in his development of perverted ill will.
24. This point is emphasized by Hannah Arendt in what she calls "enlarged mentality."
25. Both Kant and Arendt recognized that people always find "reasons" to justify the commission of a crime. In fact, there are but few exceptions to the rule of denying the fact that they have committed evil actions.
26. Agnes Heller, *The Time Is Out of Joint: Shakespeare as Philosopher of History* (New York and Oxford: Rowman and Littlefield, 2002), 100.
27. Heller argues that "these relationships all contributed to crimes. They were conditions—among others—under which those crimes were committed. Thus, justice, law, legitimacy, morality, life, and security were annulled and subverted." Heller, *The Time Is Out of Joint*,110.
28. Ibid., 113.
29. Ibid., 147.
30. Bloom, *Shakespeare*, 507.
31. Lawrence Berns, "Transcendence and Equivocations: Some Political, Theological, and Philosophical Themes in Shakespeare," in John E. Alvis and Thomas G. West, eds., *Shakespeare as Political Thinker* (Wilmington, Del.: ISI Books, 2000), 397–406 (398).
32. Theodor Meron, *Bloody Constraint: War and Chivalry in Shakespeare* (Oxford and New York: Oxford UP, 1998), 151.
33. Meron, *Bloody Constraint*, 167.
34. Theodor Meron, *Henry's Wars and Shakespeare's Laws: Perspectives on the Law of War in the Later Middle Ages* (Oxford and New York: Oxford UP, 1993).
35. See María Pía Lara, *Moral Textures*, and María Pía Lara, ed., *Rethinking Evil: Contemporary Perspectives* (Berkeley: U of California P, 2001).
36. María Pía Lara, "Narrating Evil: A Postmetaphysical Theory of Reflective Judgment," in Lara, ed., *Rethinking Evil*, 239–50.
37. Claudia Card was the first to use this expression to describe the paradigm of evil. Card, *The Atrocity Paradigm*.
38. Dana R. Villa, *Politics, Philosophy, Terror: Essays on the Thought of Hannah Arendt*. Princeton: Princeton UP, 1999), 104.
39. This is the basic claim of Claudia Card's book on evil.
40. In the play *Death and the Maiden* by Ariel Dorfman, which was later made into a movie by Roman Polanski, the character of a woman, a victim of

torture during the dictatorship in Chile, explicitly shows how this kind of moral wrongdoing impedes the character from having a normal sense of the self. Instead, we see that she is permanently haunted by nightmares, fears, and the memory of the torture she so desperately wants to forget.

41. Neier recalls that "the word *genocide* was coined not long before the Nuremberg trials by Raphael Lemkin, a Polish-Jewish scholar working for the U.S. State Department. In a 1944 book, he argued that a new term was needed to describe what the Nazis were doing to the Jews, Gypsies, and Slavic peoples in territory that they conquered. . . . Lemkin discussed precedents, citing the extermination of the Carthaginians by the Roman legions in 146 b.c. as the first historical example of genocide." Neier, *War Crimes*, 121–22.

42. After Lemkin's effort to define these kinds of crimes, in 1948 the word became institutionalized through the Genocide Convention. The convention defined genocide as "acts committed with intent to destroy, in whole or in part, a national ethnic, racial, or religious group as such."

43. Marguerite Feilowitz, *A Lexicon of Terror: Argentina and the Legacies of Torture* (Oxford: Oxford UP, 1998).

44. Samantha Powers tells us the story of Raphael Lemkin, who fought to build up a concept like *genocide* to describe the actions that could not be described as "barbarity" or "vandalism." He then thought that he needed a word that "would bring with it 'a color of freshness and novelty' while describing something 'as shortly and as poignantly as possible.' Lemkin scribbled and circled 'THE WORD' and drew a line connecting the circle to the phrase, penned firmly, 'MORAL JUDGMENT.' His word would DO IT ALL. It would be the rare term that carried in it society's revulsion and indignation. It would be what he called an 'INDEX OF CIVILIZATION.' The Word that Lemkin settled upon was a hybrid that combined the Greek derivative geno, meaning 'race' or 'tribe,' together with the Latin derivative cide, from caedere, meaning 'killing.' 'Genocide' was short, it was novel, and it was not likely to be mispronounced. Because of the word's lasting association with Hitler's horrors, it would also send shudders down the spines of those who heard it." Samantha Powers, *A Problem from Hell: America and the Age of Genocide* (New York: Basic Books, 2001), 42.

45. See Neiman, *Evil in Modern Thought*.

46. Richard J. Bernstein, *Hannah Arendt and the Jewish Question* (Cambridge: MIT Press, 1996), 12.

47. Claudia Card also uses this expression when she says that "evil may be what Ludwig Wittgenstein called the 'family resemblance' concept." Card, *The Atrocity Paradigm*, 4.

48. I am borrowing this term from Claudia Card, who coined it.

2. Storytelling: The Disclosive Dynamics of Understanding and Judging

1. See María Pía Lara, *Moral Textures: Feminist Narratives in the Public Sphere*.
2. Lisa Jane Disch, *Hannah Arendt and the Limits of Philosophy* (Ithaca and London: Cornell UP, 1994), 4.

3. Arendt argues that "language, by lending itself to *metaphorical usage,* enables us to think, that is, to have traffic with non-sensory matters, because it permits a carrying-over, *metapherein,* of our sense experiences. There are not two worlds because *metaphor* unites them." Arendt, *The Life of the Mind,* 110 (emphasis added).
4. Disch says it is "her resistance to the abstract impartial model of critical thinking that predominates in the Western political tradition." Disch, *Hannah Arendt and the Limits of Philosophy,* 12.
5. Hannah Arendt, *Men in Dark Times* (1955; rpt., New York and London: Harcourt Brace, 1968), ix.
6. Arendt says, "The tragic impact of this repetition in lamentation affects one of the key elements of all action; it establishes its meanings and the permanent significance which then enters into history. . . . Insofar as any 'mastering' of the past is possible, it consists in relating what has happened; but such narration, too, which shapes history, solves no problems and assuages no suffering; it does not master anything once and for all. Rather, as long as the meaning of the events remains alive—and this meaning can persist for very long periods of time-- 'mastering of the past' can take the form of ever-recurrent narration. The poet in a very general sense and the historian in a very special sense have the task of setting this process of narration in motion and of involving us in it." Arendt, *Men in Dark Times,* 21.
7. Arendt, *Men in Dark Times,* 21–22.
8. Ibid., 105.
9. Disch says that storytelling "makes visible the fact that experience never just *is.*" Disch, *Hannah Arendt and the Limits of Philosophy,* 8.
10. Arendt says, "What counted in the French Revolution, what made it a world-historical event, a phenomenon not to be forgotten, were not the deeds and misdeeds of the actors but the opinions, the enthusiastic approbation, of spectators, of persons who themselves were not involved." Hannah Arendt, *Lectures on Kant's Political Philosophy,* ed. Ronald Beiner (Chicago: U of Chicago P, 1982), 65.
11. Arendt clarifies that "judgment . . . always reflects upon others and their taste, takes their possible judgments into account. This is necessary because I am human and cannot live outside the company of men. *I judge as a member of this community and not as a member of a supersensible world.*" Arendt, *Lectures on Kant's Political Philosophy,* 67 (emphasis added).
12. Lisa Disch observes that "storytelling, then, makes visible the fact that experience never just *is,* but is always narrated, thereby directing attention to the discourses by which 'experience' is produced, and to the processes of *transcription* by which it is constituted as evidence"; thus, "stories make a powerful vehicle for marginal critical theory." Disch, *Hannah Arendt and the Limits of Philosophy,* 8–9 (emphasis added).
13. "To think with enlarged mentality"—says Arendt—"means that one trains one's imagination to go visiting." Arendt, *Lectures on Kant's Political Philosophy,* 43.
14. Lisa Disch devotes some of her chapters to Arendt's use of narratives, Robert Pirro writes more systematically about the different uses Arendt gives to

narratives, and Seyla Benhabib deals with them as well to prove that Arendt had a closer connection to Kant than many scholars have accepted. See Disch, *Hannah Arendt and the Limits of Philosophy*; Robert C. Pirro, *Hannah Arendt and the Politics of Tragedy* (De Kalb: Northern Illinois UP, 2001); Seyla Benhabib, *The Reluctant Modernism of Hannah Arendt* (Thousand Oaks, Calif., and London: Sage, 1996).

15. Arendt, *Lectures on Kant's Political Philosophy*, 58.
16. Judith Shklar says that "Hannah Arendt was what [Nietzsche] called a monumental historian. At its best, monumental history is addressed to political actors, to remind them that greater deeds were performed by notable men and that what was once feasible is at least possible again." Judith N. Shklar, "Rethinking the Past," in Shklar, *Political Thought and Political Thinkers*, ed. Stanley Hoffmann (Chicago: U of Chicago P, 1998) 353–61 (353).
17. Pirro, *Hannah Arendt and the Politics of Tragedy*, 12–27.
18. "This happens," says Arendt, "by reflecting not on an object but on its representation . . . and this is what Kant calls 'the operation of reflection.' [again]" Arendt, *Lectures on Kant's Political Philosophy*, 65.
19. Judith Shklar argues that "politics ought to be an expression of the faculty of judgment. As such it is the appeal of the disinterested spectator to all others who strive to be impartial. Their enlightened common sense must be assumed to yield *universally* acceptable standards, and it is in terms of these that we judge and try to persuade each other." Shklar, "Rethinking the Past," 360 (emphasis added).
20. Pirro, *Hannah Arendt and the Politics of Tragedy*, 14.
21. Arendt argues that Kant is important to her theory of the political because, when dealing with taste, Kant understood that "in taste egoism is overcome; we must consider the original meaning of the word. We must overcome our special subjective conditions for the sake of others. In other words, the nonsubjective element in the nonobjective sense is *intersubjectivity*. (You must be alone in order to think; *you need company to enjoy a meal*.)" Arendt, *Lectures on Kant's Political Philosophy*, 67 (emphasis added).
22. Judith Shklar agrees with this claim when she says that "we have taste when we willingly join the best judgment of our peers, and we are free when we engage in unbroken political argument with them." Shklar, "Rethinking the Past," 360.
23. Arendt clarifies that "the chief problem of the *Critique of Judgment* therefore became the question of how the propositions of judgment could possibly claim, as they indeed do, general agreement." Arendt, *The Life of the Mind*, 111.
24. Arendt argues that "judgment, finally, in terms of discovery the late-comer of our mental abilities, draws, as Kant knew so well, its *metaphorical* language from the sense of *taste*." Arendt, *The Life of the Mind*, 111 (emphasis added).
25. The reference I can offer here for what I say is that Arendt cited Cicero's *On the Orator*: "much more judging the rhythms and pronunciations of words, since these are rooted (*infixa*) in common sense, and of such things nature has willed that no one should be altogether unable to sense and experience them (*expertus*)." Arendt, *Lectures on Kant's Political Philosophy*, 63.

26. Judith N. Shklar, *Ordinary Vices* (Cambridge: Harvard UP, 1984), 229.
27. Disch, *Hannah Arendt and the Limits of Philosophy*, 160.
28. Ibid., 155.
29. Hannah Arendt, *Rahel Varnhagen: The Life of a Jewess*, ed. Liliane Weissberg (Baltimore and London: Johns Hopkins UP, 1997).
30. Benhabib, *The Reluctant Modernism of Hannah Arendt*, esp. ch. 1, "The Pariah and Her Shadow: Hannah Arendt's Biography of Rahel Varnhagen," 1–34.
31. Hannah Arendt, *The Origins of Totalitarianism* (1951; rpt., New York: Harcourt Brace Jovanovich, 1975).
32. Arendt, *Eichmann in Jerusalem*.
33. Arendt, *Men in Dark Times*. Of particular interest are the stories of Isak Dinesen, Rosa Luxembourg, and Walter Benjamin that she offers there.
34. Arendt created stories about authority and beginnings in *Between Past and Future* and in *On Revolution*. See Hannah Arendt, *Between Past and Future: Eight Exercises in Political Thought* (New York: Penguin, 1968), and Hannah Arendt, *On Revolution* (New York: Penguin, 1977).
35. See Hannah Arendt, *The Human Condition* (Chicago: U of Chicago P, 1958).
36. See Dana R. Villa, "Theatricality and the Public Realm," in *Politics, Philosophy, Terror*, 128–54.
37. Pirro, *Hannah Arendt and the Politics of Tragedy*, 48.
38. Hannah Arendt, "Humanity in Dark Times: Thoughts About Lessing," in *Men in Dark Times*, 3–31 (6).
39. Arendt, *Men in Dark Times*, 6.
40. Arendt clarifies the relation of language to the ineffable by saying that "as I mentioned before that language, the only medium in which *the invisible can become manifest in a world of appearances*, is by no means as adequate for that function as our senses are for their business of coping with the perceptible world, and I suggested that *the metaphor in its own way can cure the defect*. . . ." Arendt, *The Life of the Mind*, 112 (emphasis added).
41. Pirro clarifies that Arendt found the connected etymology between the words *theatron* and *theorein*, both coming from the root *theos*. Pirro, *Hannah Arendt and the Politics of Tragedy*, 127.
42. Villa, *Politics, Philosophy, and Terror*, 90.
43. See Leora Y. Bilsky, "When Actor and Spectator Meet in the Courtroom: Reflections on Hannah Arendt's Concept of Judgment," in Ronald Beiner and Jennifer Nedelsky, eds., *Judgment, Imagination, and Politics: Themes from Kant and Arendt* (New York and Oxford: Rowman and Littlefield, 2001), 257–85.
44. Arendt begins by saying, "Whoever planned this auditorium in the newly built *Beth Ha'am*, the House of People, had a *theater* in mind, complete with orchestra and gallery, with proscenium and stage, and with side doors for the actors' entrance." Arendt, *Eichmann in Jerusalem*, 4 (emphasis in original).
45. Arendt writes, "Yet no matter how consistently the judges shunned the limelight, there they were, seated at the top of the raised platform, facing the audience as from the *stage in a play*." Arendt, *Eichmann in Jerusalem*, 6 (emphasis added).
46. Arendt says, "They were to *watch a spectacle as sensational as the Nuremberg Trials*." Arendt, *Eichmann in Jerusalem*, 6 (emphasis added).

47. Bilsky argues that "political acting, just like theater performance, depends on an audience of spectators for its completion. The actors and spectators reciprocate each other in the public realm: actors rely on a community of spectators who endow their actions with *meaning*; spectators reenact '*exemplary actions*' that affirm their communal identity. The theater metaphor captures the reciprocity and *illuminates* the constitutive nature of *actor-spectator* bond for their continual existence of a public realm." Bilsky, "When Actor and Spectator Meet in the Courtroom," 260 (emphasis added).
48. Bilsky, "When Actor and Spectator Meet in the Courtroom," 259.
49. See Lara, *Moral Textures.*
50. Arendt argues that "the importance of the occurrence (*Begebenheit*) is for him [the actor] exclusively in the eye of the beholder, in the opinion of the onlookers who proclaim their attitude in public. Their reaction to the event proves the 'moral character' of mankind. Without this sympathetic participation, the 'meaning' of the occurrence would be altogether different or simply nonexistent. For it is this sympathy that inspires hope." Arendt, *Lectures on Kant's Political Philosophy*, 46.
51. Arendt, *Eichmann in Jerusalem*, 5.
52. Ibid., 9.
53. Bilsky, "When Actor and Spectator Meet in the Courtroom," 261.
54. Ruti Teitel argues that "the principle of universality as it relates to crimes against humanity is epitomized by the prosecution of Adolf Eichmann for crimes committed in Europe during the World War II. Though the trial was held decades after the events in the state of Israel, it violated neither retroactivity nor territoriality principles." Teitel, *Transitional Justice*, 61.
55. According to Kant, determinant judgment is the exercise of subsuming the particular under a general rule. See Kant, *Critique of Judgment.*
56. Kant refers to the exercise of reflective judgments as "deriving" the rule from the particular.
57. Teitel explains that "the ethical and political implications of this sort of transitional narrative are exemplified in Hannah Arendt's 'Report' of the major Nazi trial in Israel. Arendt's so-called trial report is an instance of relentless *normative argument through juxtaposition*, most saliently, of Adolf Eichmann's responsibility as perpetrator against that of his victims. Indeed, it is this juxtaposition within the same account, of Eichmann's bureaucratic role against that of his victims that is thought supportive of Arendt's central claim of the 'banality' of evil." Teitel, *Transitional Justice*, 87 (emphasis in original).
58. See María Pía Lara, "Introduction," in Lara, ed., *Rethinking Evil*, 1–14.
59. Bilsky, "When Actor and Spectator Meet in the Courtroom," 265.
60. Think, for example, of all the arguments used by the militaries in Argentina when they were on trial, and how much these resemble Eichmann's arguments about due obedience to authorities. For an excellent narrative about the Argentinian trials, see Carlos Santiago Nino, *Radical Evil on Trial* (New Haven and London: Yale UP, 1996).
61. Bilsky, "When Actor and Spectator Meet in the Courtroom," 272.
62. It is permanent because those who survive always feel guilty about the condition of surviving their peers (i.e., the now well-known concept of "survivor

guilt"). See, for example, Primo Levi's accounts about this in *The Drowned and the Saved.*

63. Bilsky, "When Actor and Spectator Meet in the Courtroom," 272.
64. Ibid.
65. This is why so many of the Arendtian scholars have accepted Ronald Beiner's interpretation. See Ronald Beiner, "Interpretative Essay," in Arendt, *Lectures on Kant's Political Philosophy*, 89–156.
66. Lara, "Introduction."
67. In a letter written to Gershom Scholem, Arendt writes that "you are completely right that I have changed my mind and now no longer speak of radical evil. . . . It's unclear to me why you characterize the phrase 'banality of evil' as a slogan. So far as I know, no one has ever used it before. But this isn't important. The fact is that today I think that evil in every instance is only extreme, never radical: it has no depth, and therefore has nothing demonic about it. Evil can lay waste the entire world, like a fungus growing rampant on the surface. Only the good is always deep and radical." Anthony Skinner, ed., *Gershom Scholem: A Life in Letters, 1914–1982* (Cambridge and London: Harvard UP, 2002), 400.

3. Reflective Judgment and the Moral Imagination

1. Scholars from the field of Holocaust studies have written extensively on the subject of the impossibility of representing the ineffable. See Arad Ne'eman, ed., *History and Memory. Passing into History: Nazism and the Holocaust Beyond Memory* (Bloomington: Indiana UP, 1997); Cathy Caruth, ed., *Trauma: Explorations in Memory* (Baltimore and London: John Hopkins UP, 1995); James E. Young, *Writing and Rewriting the Holocaust: Narrative Consequences of Interpretation* (Bloomington: Indiana UP, 1988); Shoshana Felman, *The Juridical Unconscious: Trials and Traumas in the Twentieth Century* (Cambridge and London: Harvard UP, 2002); Dominick LaCapra, *History and Memory After Auschwitz* (Ithaca and London: Cornell UP, 1998).
2. Albrecht Wellmer, "The Myth. Of God Who Suffers and Becomes: Questions Addressed to Hans Jonas (1992)," in *Endgames* (Cambridge: MIT Press, 1998), 263–68 (265).
3. Hannah Arendt clarifies that "language is entirely metaphorical and whose conceptual framework depends entirely on the gift of metaphor, which bridges the gulf between *the visible and the invisible.*" Arendt, *The Life of the Mind*, 123 (emphasis in original).
4. Arendt, *The Life of the Mind*, 196.
5. Coming from a totally different point of view, Paul Guyer, for example, has argued that "Kant develops a model of judgment that an object is beautiful as the outcome of a complex process involving both the production of pleasure by the faculty of reflective judgment and the estimation of the intersubjective validity of such pleasure by the same faculty." Paul Guyer, *Kant and the Claims of Taste* (Cambridge: Cambridge UP, 1997), 61.
6. Guyer, *Kant and the Claims of Taste*, 60.
7. Henry Allison, *Kant's Theory of Taste: A Reading of the Critique of Aesthetic Judgment* (Cambridge: Cambridge University Press, 2001), 257.

8. Allison, *Kant's Theory of Taste*, 264–65.
9. Ibid., 265.
10. Richard Kearney, *The Wake of the Imagination* (London: Routledge, 1994), 155.
11. "It becomes instead the *sine qua non* of all genuine knowledge." Kearney, *The Wake of Imagination*, 169.
12. Ibid., 173.
13. The best argument to strengthen my point is found in Peter Strawson's discussion of Kant's concept of imagination in his essay "Imagination and Perception." See P. F. Strawson, *Freedom and Resentment and Other Essays* (London and New York: Methuen, 1974), 45–65.
14. Strawson argues that Kant, influenced by David Hume, took the role of imagination as a connecting or uniting power which operates in two dimensions: "a) it connects perceptions of different objects of the same kind; in the other dimension, b), it connects different perceptions of the same object of a given kind." Strawson, "Imagination and Perception," 47.
15. Strawson, "Imagination and Perception," 47.
16. Strawson again argues that this combination is what is called synthesis or "the kind of exercise of the imagination (in Kant's extended sense) which is involved in perception of objects as objects, is empirical in one aspect and transcendental in another: it is empirical (that is non-necessary) in so far as it happens to consist in the application of this or that particular empirical concept (elephant or ink bottle); transcendental (that is necessary) in so far as the application of such concepts represents, though in a form which is quite contingent, the utterly general requirements of a possible experience." Strawson, "Imagination and Perception," 47.
17. See Dulce Maria Granja, "El juicio reflexivo en la Etica kantiana [Reflective judgment in Kantian ethics]," *Dianoia* 42 (1996): 125–44.
18. Guyer, *Kant and the Claims of Taste*, 113.
19. Mary Warnock argues that "the idea embodied in the sublime object is beyond representation or complete explanation, but *yet it can be apprehended and recognized by the human mind.* According to Kant, the man of genius, as distinct from the man of ordinary imaginative powers, will be the one who, in poetry or painting or music, comes closest to expressing these great ideas of reason which cannot be exactly expressed. *The imagination,* Kant says, *is a powerful agent 'for creating as it were a second nature out of the materials supplied to it by the first nature.'*" Mary Warnock, *Imagination and Time* (Oxford and Cambridge: Blackwell, 1994), 30 (emphasis added).
20. Immanuel Kant, *Observations on the Feeling of the Beautiful and the Sublime* (Berkeley: U of California P, 1960).
21. Kant, *Critique of Judgment*, 106. Subsequent references to this book are cited in the text.
22. Warnock argues that "the works of genius, which body forth these ideas are 'exemplary.'" Warnock, *Imagination and Time*, 30.
23. Strawson, "Imagination and Perception," 55.
24. Young, *Writing and Rewriting the Holocaust*, 99.
25. Guyer, *Kant and the Claims of Taste*, 30.

26. Rudolf A. Makkreel, *Imagination and Interpretation in Kant: The Hermeneutical Import of the Critique of Judgment* (Chicago and London: U of Chicago P, 1990), 3. Subsequent references to this book are cited in the text.
27. Young, *Writing and Rewriting the Holocaust*, 107.
28. It is important to discuss here the idea behind many theorists from the Holocaust, namely, that there are certain experiences which cannot be represented. My theory emphasizes that all experience captured through disclosive representations offer some light about the moral truths involved in such experiences.
29. Northop Frye, *Anatomy of Criticism: Four Essays* (Princeton: Princeton UP, 1971), 102.
30. In philosophy, Martha Nussbaum and Bernard Williams, among others, have focused on Greek literature because of their archetypes; in literature, Northrop Frye has extensively dealt with the issues of archetypes; and, in psychology Freud, and especially Jung, have used the concept of archetypes because of the links between collective moral imagination and disclosive symbolic meanings. See C. G. Jung, *Encountering Jung on Evil*, selected and introduced by Murray Stein (Princeton: Princeton UP, 1995). See also Nussbaum, *The Fragility of Goodness*; Williams, *Shame and Necessity*; and Frye, *The Anatomy of Criticism*.
31. Frye, *Anatomy of Criticism*, 84.
32. Young, *Writing and Rewriting the Holocaust*, 109.
33. Richard Kearney, *The Poetics of Imagining: Modern and Postmodern* (New York: Fordham UP, 1998), 142.
34. Mark Johnson argues that "it appears that the *chief imaginative dimension of moral understanding is metaphor*, ... the *metaphorical character of morality has radical implications for our moral understanding*." Mark Johnson, *Moral Imagination: Implications of Cognitive Science for Ethics* (Chicago: U of Chicago P, 1993), 193 (emphasis added).
35. Paul Ricoeur, *The Symbolism of Evil* (Boston: Beacon Press, 1967).
36. Kearney, *The Poetics of Imagining*, 151.
37. Ricoeur, *The Symbolism of Evil*, 165.
38. Ricoeur, *The Symbolism of Evil*, 166.
39. Ibid., 37.
40. Ibid., 89.
41. Paul Ricoeur, *Freud and Philosophy: An Essay on Interpretation* (New Haven and London: Yale UP, 1970).
42. Kearney, *The Poetics of Imagining*, 154.
43. Ricoeur, *Freud and Philosophy*, 306.
44. Paul Ricoeur, Time and Narrative (Chicago: University of Chicago Press, 1984)
45. See Lara, *Moral Textures*.
46. Kearney, *The Poetics of Imagining*, 159.
47. Ibid.
48. Ibid., 162.
49. See Ricoeur, *The Symbolism of Evil*.
50. See Immanuel Kant, "On the Miscarriage of All Philosophical Trials in Theodicy," in *Religion and Rational Theology* (New York: Cambridge UP, 1996), 24–39.

51. The best essay I have read on this subject is Richard J. Bernstein's "Radical Evil: Kant at War with Himself" in *Radical Evil*, 11–45.
52. See Shoshana Felman, "Introduction to Claude Lanzmann's Speech," in Caruth, ed., *Trauma: Explorations in Memory*, 200–204.
53. See Claude Lanzmann, "Lanzmann's Speech," in Caruth, ed., *Trauma*, 204–18. See also Dominick LaCapra, "Lanzmann's *Shoah*: 'Here There Is No Why,'" in *History and Memory After Auschwitz*, 95–138.
54. See Caruth, ed., *Trauma*.
55. Richard Kearney, *Strangers, Gods, and Monsters* (New York and London: Routledge, 2003), 88.
56. Kearney argues that "the impossibility of representing the Shoah, he [Peter Haidu] suggests, as well as its designation with the special status of 'exceptionality,' bears similarities to the initial stage of the notion of the 'holy' which Otto and Eliade relate back to the experience of primordial awe—the experience of the divine as *tremendum et fascinans*." Kearney, *Strangers, Gods, and Monsters*, 88.
57. There is already plenty of literature critical of this position. See Tzvetan Todorov, *Facing the Extreme: Moral Life in Concentration Camps* (New York: Metropolitan Books/Holt, 1996). See also Kearney, *Strangers, Gods, and Monsters*, 1–31.
58. To consult a very good careful examination of those authors, see Kearney, *Strangers, Gods, and Monsters*, 88–105.
59. Julia Kristeva, *Powers of Horror: An Essay on Abjection* (New York: Columbia UP, 1982).
60. Kearney, *Strangers, Gods, and Monsters*, 91.
61. Jean François Lyotard, "The Sublime and the Avant-Garde," in *The Inhuman* (Stanford, Calif.: Stanford UP, 1988), 89–90.
62. Slavoj Žižek, *The Plague of Fantasies* (London: Verso, 1997), 218–29.
63. Levi narrates this dream: "I am alone in the centre of a grey and turbid nothing, and now, I *know* what *this means*, and I also know that I have always known it; I am in the Lager once more, and nothing is true outside the Lager. All the rest was a brief pause, a deception of the senses, a dream; my family, nature in flower, my home." Primo Levi, *La Tregua* (1963; rpt., México: Océano, 1998), 186.
64. Lawrence Langer, *Preempting the Holocaust* (New Haven: Yale UP, 1998), 29.
65. Langer, *Preempting the Holocaust*, 33.
66. "Todesfuge": "Schwarze Milch der Frühe wir trinken sie abends / wir trinken sie mittags und morgens wir trinken sie nachts / wir trinken und trinken / wir schaufeln ein Grab in den Lüften da liegt man nicht eng / Ein Man wohnt im Haus der spielt mit den Schlangen der / schreibt / Der schreibt wenn dunkelt nach Deutschland dein goldenes / Haar Margarete/ er schreibt es und tritt vor das Haus und es blitzen die Sterne er / pfeit seine Rüden herbei / er pfeift seine Juden hervor lässt schaufeln ein Grab in der Erde / er befiehlt uns spielt auf nun sum Tanz."

    This is the first paragraph of "Todesfuge" by Paul Celan, published in German and English in Paul Celan, *Poems of Paul Celan* (New York: Persea, 1995), 62.

67. Shoshana Felman, "Education in Crisis, or the Vicissitudes of Teaching," in Caruth, ed., *Trauma*, 13–60 (36).
68. Kearney, *Strangers, Gods, and Monsters*, 103.

4. Hannah Arendt and Negative Exemplarity: The Moral Paradigm of History and Its Particularity

1. Michael Denneny, "The Privilege of Ourselves: Hannah Arendt on Judgment," in Melvyn A. Hill, ed., *Hannah Arendt: The Recovery of the Public World* (New York: St. Martin's, 1979), 245–74 (266).
2. This is Ronald Beiner's main thesis in the critical essay he published about Arendt's *Lectures on Kant's Political Philosophy*. Many scholars agree with him (Richard J. Bernstein, Albrecht Wellmer, Dana Villa, Seyla Benhabib, Maurizio Passerin D'Entreves, etc.). See Ronald Beiner, "Interpretative Essay," in Arendt, *Lectures on Kant's Political Philosophy*.
3. Arendt, *Lectures on Kant's Political Philosophy*, 133.
4. Arendt, *The Life of the Mind*, 216. Subsequent references to this book are cited in the text.
5. See Benhabib, *The Reluctant Modernism of Hannah Arendt*.
6. See Beiner, "Interpretative Essay."
7. In a letter written to Gershom Scholem, T. W. Adorno also notices the similarities between Heidegger's ideas on language and those of Benjamin. Adorno says, "It now strikes me that there are certain astounding, mostly linguistic, similarities between Benjamin and Heidegger, whose favorite expresión vis-à-vis Hölderlin is 'the poetized.'" Skinner, ed., *Gershom Scholem: A Life in Letters, 1914–1982*, 392.
8. Arendt, *The Life of the Mind*, 122.
9. Hannah Arendt, "The Hunchback," in *Men in Dark Times*, 153–92 (156).
10. Arendt, "The Hunchback," 157.
11. Walter Benjamin, "Theses on the Philosophy of History," in *Illuminations: Essays and Reflections*, ed. Hannah Arendt (New York: Schocken, 1968), 257.
12. Gerhard Scholem's poem is called "Gruss vom Ángelus," and it says: "My wing is ready for flight, / I would like to turn back. / If I stayed timeless time, / I would have little luck."
13. Benjamin, "Theses on the Philosophy of History," 257.
14. Ibid., 257.
15. "Er hat zwei Gegner: Der erste bedrängt ihn von hinten, vom Ursprung her. Der zweite verwehrt den Weg nach worn. Er kämpft mit beiden. Eighentlich unterstützt ihn der erste im Kampf mit dem Zweiten, denn er will ihn nach vorn drängen und ebenso unterstützt ihn der zweite im Kampf mit dem Ersten; denn er treibt ihn doch zurück. So ist es aber nur theoretisch. Denn es sind ja nicht nur die zwei Gegner da, sondern auch noch er selbst, und wer kennt eigentlich seine Absichten? Immerhin ist es sein Traum, dass er einmal in einem unbewachten Augenblick—dazu gehört allerdings eine Nacht, so finster wie noch keine war—aus der Kampflinie ausspringt und wegen seiner Kampferfahrung zum Richter über seine miteinander kämpfenden

Gegner erhoben wird." Franz Kafka, "Er," in *Aufzeichnungen aus dem Jahre* (1920, Bd. V, 287).

An English version appears in Hannah Arendt's essay, "Walter Benjamin, 1892-1940," published in *Men in Dark Times*, 192: "Everything he does appears to him extraordinarily new but also, because of the impossible abundance of the new, extraordinarily amateurish, indeed hardly tolerable, incapable of becoming historical, tearing asunder the chain of generations, breaking off for the first time the music of the world which until now could at least be divined at in all its depth. Sometimes in his conceit he is more worried about the world than about himself" (Franz Kafka, "He," from "Notes from the Year 1920").

16. Hannah Arendt and Martin Heidegger, *Briefe (1925–1975)* (Frankfurt am Main: Vittorio Klostermann, 1999), 159.
17. Arendt, "The Hunchback," 167.
18. Arendt describes Homer's role as a storyteller. He is the bard of his times and understands that stories are lost if he does not recover them. Arendt explains: "Homer himself says: the bard sings for men and gods what the Muse, Mnemosyne, who watches over Remembrance, has put into his mind. The Muse gave him good and bad: she deprived him of eyesight and gave him a sweet song." Furthermore, Arendt adds that "the meaning of what actually happens and appears while it is happening is revealed when it has disappeared; remembrance, by which you make present to your mind what actually is absent and past, reveals the meaning in the form of a story. The man who does the revealing is not involved in the appearances; he is blind, shielded against the invisible, in order to be able to 'see' the invisible. And what he sees with blind eyes and puts into words is the story, not the deed itself and not the doer, although the doer's fame will reach the high heavens." Arendt, *The Life of the Mind*, 132–33.
19. Hannah Arendt, "The Pearl Diver," in *Men in Dark Times*, 193. Subsequent references to this work are cited in the text.
20. Recall that Kant thought, as we have seen in chapter 3, that it is the originality of the saying that makes a genius's work communicable.
21. Denneny, "The Privilege of Ourselves," 265.
22. This idea is developed in Arendt's account of how totalitarian regimes see the forces of history and how they define their goals of power as if they represented material pillars of progress. See Arendt, *The Origins of Totalitarianism*.
23. Benhabib, *The Reluctant Modernism of Hannah Arendt*, 87.
24. Nussbaum, *The Fragility of Goodness*, xiii.
25. Walter Benjamin, "The Storyteller: Reflections on the Works of Nikolai Leskov," in *Illuminations*, 90. Subsequent references to this work are cited in the text.
26. Denneny, "The Privilege of Ourselves," 264.
27. This has been pointed out by Michael Denneny as well. Denneny, "The Privilege of Ourselves," 261.
28. Arendt, *The Life of the Mind*, 173.
29. Ibid., 175.
30. Villa, *Politics, Philosophy, and Terror*, 89.

31. Denneny, "The Privilege of Ourselves," 264.
32. Arendt, *The Life of the Mind*, 192.
33. Arendt, *The Human Condition*, 186.
34. Villa, *Politics, Philosophy, and Terror*, 84.
35. Villa, *Politics, Philosophy, and Terror*, 84.
36. Ibid., 85.
37. Ibid.
38. See Alessandro Ferrara, "Judgment, Identity, and Authenticity: A Reconstruction of Hannah Arendt's Interpretation of Kant," *Philosophy and Social Criticism* 24.2–3 (1998): 113–36 (122). See also Albrecht Wellmer, "Hannah Arendt on Judgment: The Unwritten Doctrine of Reason," in *Endgames*, 291–311 (298).
39. Hannah Arendt, "Understanding and Politics (The Difficulties in Understanding)," in *Essays in Understanding, 1930–1954*, ed. Jerome Kohn (New York and London: Harcourt Brace, 1994), 307–327 (309).
40. Dana R. Villa, *Arendt and Heidegger: The Fate of the Political* (Princeton: Princeton UP, 1996), 219.
41. Arendt, "Understanding and Politics," 309.
42. Seyla Benhabib, "The Politics of Memory and the Morality of Historiography," in *The Reluctant Modernism of Hannah Arendt*, 86–91 (86).
43. Benhabib, "The Politics of Memory," 88.
44. James Bohman, *Public Deliberation: Pluralism, Complexity, Democracy* (Cambridge: MIT Press, 1996), 214.
45. Arendt, "Understanding and Politics," 319. Subsequent references to this work are cited in the text.
46. Arendt, *The Origins of Totalitarianism*, 459.
47. Arendt, *Eichmann in Jerusalem*, 52.
48. Ibid., 54.
49. Ludwig Wittgenstein, Philosophische Untersuchungen, ed. G. E. M. Anscombe and R. Rhees (London: Blackwell, 1958).

5. Learning from Catastrophes

1. In his Kyoto lecture (delivered for the Kyoto Prize on November 11, 2004), Habermas mentions that he became interested in the concept of the public sphere for four different reasons. Of these, the most important to me were the third because "during my adolescence I was strongly influenced by my generation's experience of the historical caesura of the year 1945 in world politics," and the fourth because "in the course of my adult life I have been troubled by the political experience of a slow and repeatedly endangered liberalization of German post-War society and culture." See Jürgen Habermas, "Public Space and the Political Public Sphere—The Biographical Roots of Two Motifs in My Thought," Commemorative Lecture, Kyoto, November 11, 2004.
2. Habermas, "Learning from Catastrophes: A Look Back at the Short Twentieth Century," in *The Postnational Constellation: Political Essays*. Subsequent references to this work are cited in the text.

3. Jürgen Habermas, "Heinrich Heine and the Role of the Intellectual in Germany," in *The New Conservatism: Cultural Criticism and the Historian's Debate*, ed. Shierry Weber Nicholsen (Cambridge: MIT Press, 1989), 71–99.
4. Habermas, "Heinrich Heine and the Role of the Intellectual in Germany," 73.
5. Ibid.
6. In moments of intense intellectual debate in the Germany of the 1970s, Böll questioned the role of the state in creating antiterrorist laws against the group Baader-Meinhoff. He also questioned the conservative views of his times.
7. Habermas, "Heinrich Heine and the Role of the Intellectual in Germany," 91.
8. Ibid., 92.
9. Jürgen Habermas, "Remarks from the Römberg Colloquium," in *The New Conservatism*, 209–11 (210).
10. Habermas, "Remarks from the Römberg Colloquium," 210.
11. Ibid.
12. For more detailed accounts of the relevance of this polemic, see Peter Baldwin, ed., *Reworking the Past: Hitler, the Holocaust, and the Historians' Debate* (Boston: Beacon Press, 1990).
13. Jürgen Habermas, "Apologetic Tendencies," in *The New Conservatism*, 212–28 (214).
14. See Ian Kershaw, *The Nazi Dictatorship: Problems and Perspectives in Interpretation* (London and New York: Edward Arnold Editors, 1989); Richard J. Evans, *Hitler's Shadows: West German Historians and the Attempt to Escape from the Nazi Past* (New York: Pantheon, 1989).
15. Habermas, "Apologetic Tendencies," 226.
16. Jürgen Habermas, "On the Public Use of History," in *The New Conservatism*, 229–40. Subsequent references to this work are cited in the text.
17. Jürgen Habermas, "A Kind of Settling of Damages," in *The New Conservatism*, 207–248 (248).
18. Jürgen Habermas, "Historical Consciousness and Post-Traditional Identity," in *The New Conservatism*, 249–67.
19. Hans-Ulrich Wehler, "Unburdening the German Past? A Preliminary Assessment," in Baldwin, ed., *Reworking the Past*, 214–23 (222).
20. See Federico Finchelstein, ed., *The Germans, the Holocaust, and Collective Guilt: The Goldhagen Debate* (Buenos Aires: Eudeba, 1999).
21. In the second chapter of Dana Villa's *Politics, Philosophy, and Terror*, where he argues against Goldhagen's view. Villa claims that Goldhagen's book is "partly intended as a refutation to Arendt's *Eichmann in Jerusalem*." See Villa, *Politics, Philosophy, and Terror*, 39–60 (40).
22. Jürgen Habermas, "Goldhagen and the Public Use of History: Why Is the Democracy Prize for Daniel Goldhagen?," in Finchelstein, ed., *The Goldhagen Debate*, 205–16.
23. Federico Finchelstein, "The Goldhagen Debate in Context: Collective Memory and Critical Representation," in Finchelstein, ed., *The Goldhagen Debate*, 31–72 (36).
24. See Christopher R. Browning, *Ordinary Men: Reserve Police Battalion 101 and the Final Solution in Poland* (New York: HarperCollins, 1992). The debate on Goldhagen's book has shown that Christopher Browning is the person who

discovered that members of the 101st Battalion had the option not to collaborate in the murder of Jews and only a few chose not to participate. It has been pointed out that the title of Browning's book is later reframed in Goldhagen's own title (from the original "ordinary men" to "ordinary Germans").

25. Finchelstein, "The Goldhagen Debate in Context," 71.
26. Habermas, "Goldhagen and the Public Use of History," 216.
27. For a very critical review of Victor Farías's work, see Philippe Lacoue-Labarthe, "On Victor Farías's Book, *Heidegger et le Nazisme*," in *Heidegger, Art, and Politics* (Oxford: Blackwell, 1990), 123–37.
28. Jürgen Habermas, "Work and Weltanshauung: The Heidegger Controversy from a German Perspective," in *The New Conservatism*, 140–72 (144).
29. See Berel Lang, *Heidegger's Silence* (Ithaca, N.Y., and London: Cornell UP, 1996).
30. Habermas, "Work and Weltanshauung," 145. Subsequent references to this work are cited in the text.
31. See Rüdiger Safranski, *Martin Heidegger: Between Good and Evil*, trans. Ewald Osers (Cambridge and London: Harvard UP, 1998). See also George Steiner, *Martin Heidegger* (Chicago: U of Chicago P, 1987).
32. For a very interesting account of the life and influence of Carl Schmitt, see Jan-Werner Müller, *A Dangerous Mind: Carl Schmitt in Postwar European Thought* (New Haven: Yale UP, 2003). See also Ellen Kennedy, *Constitutional Failure: Carl Schmitt in Weimar* (Durham, N.C., and London: Duke UP, 2004).
33. In this sense, it is very illuminating to see how Dana Villa shows the way Arendt overcame the pitfalls of Heidegger's philosophy and used her understanding of Heidegger against him. See Villa, *Arendt and Heidegger*, 113–70.
34. Habermas, "Work and Weltanshauung," 148. Subsequent references to this work are cited in the text.
35. Martin Heidegger, *Being and Time* (New York: Harper and Row, 1962).
36. Habermas, "Work and Weltanshauung," 151. Subsequent references to this work are cited in the text.

6. What Remains? Language Remains

1. Marco Belpoliti, "I Am a Centaur," in Primo Levi, *The Voice of Memory: Primo Levi's Interviews, 1961–1987* (New York: New Press, 2001), xvii–xxv (xx).
2. Tzvetan Todorov argues that "Levi's position with regard to his experience of the camps is characterized by a double transcendence: he is beyond both hatred and resignation, which may explain, among other things, why his book came and went relatively unnoticed during a period directly following the war, a time when people preferred the security of clear-cut positions and radical solutions." Tzvetan Todorov, *Facing the Extreme: Moral Life in Concentration Camps* (New York: Holt/Metropolitan Books, 1996), 261.
3. See Giorgio Agamben, *Homo Sacer: Sovereign Power and Bare Life* , trans. Daniel Heller-Roazen (Stanford, Calif.: Stanford UP, 1998.
4. Jürgen Habermas, "Further Reflections on the Public Sphere," in Craig Calhoun, ed., *Habermas and the Public Sphere* (Cambridge: MIT Press, 1996), 421–61 (454).

5. Arendt, *Men in Dark Times*, 21.
6. Ibid.
7. Benjamin, "The Storyteller: Reflections on the Works of Nikolai Leskov," in *Illuminations*, 83–109.
8. Benjamin says: "The storyteller takes what he tells from experience—his own or that reported by others. And he in turn makes it the experience of those who are listening to his tale." Benjamin, "The Storyteller", 87.
9. See Young, *Writing and Rewriting the Holocaust*, and LaCapra, *History and Memory After Auschwitz*.
10. Here again, Todorov agrees with me when he says that "Levi's books have come from this effort to understand and to judge. Several are devoted to the camp experience, especially the first, *If This Is a Man* (Survival at Auschwitz), and the last, *The Drowned and the Saved*. By the variety of questions they raise and the quality of Levi's thought, these works represent an accomplishment unparalleled in modern literature." Todorov, *Facing the Extreme*, 262.
11. Todorov says that Levi's project "is to understand and to judge, and since the dispensation of justice in a formal sense was a task that could be left to others, to the professional judges, the major preoccupation of his final years becomes that of understanding the Germans." Todorov, *Facing the Extreme*, 268.
12. Levi, *The Drowned and the Saved*. This book was not written after he was released from the camps; it took decades to be developed and was first published in 1986. This distance allowed Levi to offer us a major narrative from which to learn. Subsequent references to this work are cited in the text.
13. Habermas, "Historical Consciousness and Post-Traditional Identity: The Federal Republic's Orientation to the West," in *The New Conservatism*, 249–67 (251).
14. Levi, *The Drowned and the Saved*, 40.
15. Levi, *The Drowned and the Saved*, 50. Subsequent references to this work are cited in the text.
16. Todorov understands Levi's model so well that he is able to capture the three kinds of shame that survivors suffered: (1) the shame of remembering , (2) the survivor's guilt, and (3) the shame of being a human being. Todorov, *Facing the Extreme*, 263–65.
17. Levi, *The Drowned and the Saved*, 75. Subsequent references to this work are cited in the text.
18. Primo Levi, *The Search for Roots: A Personal Anthology* (Chicago: Ivan R. Dee, 1981).
19. Carl Schmitt says, "Sovereign is *he who decides on the exception*." Carl Schmitt, *Political Theology: Four Chapters on the Concept of Sovereignty* (Cambridge: MIT Press, 1988), 5 (emphasis added).
20. Ellen Kennedy argues that, "By reversing the usual relationship of norm and exception, sovereignty appears as the decision about the exception, the moment outside the normal in which the political appears. The political in this sense is unpredictable; it is not specified in the state's institution, or in competition for power within the state... . Schmitt's definition of sovereignty transforms its political theory from one located in a person or institution

(Hobbes and Bodin) into a moment of existential intervention in a process over which the sovereign in that formal sense does not preside as creator and controller." Kennedy, *Constitutional Failure*, 95.

21. Andreas Kalyvas explains that, "Unfortunately, [Agamben's] *Homo Sacer* returns to a representation of time—the time of sovereignty—as uniform, one-directional, and rectilinear. It is this focus on an interrupted historical and philosophical continuity, embodied in the survival of sovereignty over a period of twenty-five centuries that also distinguishes Agamben from Foucault. Foucault's genealogical inquiries of the contingent, accidental, small, but not trivial, surprises of lost events and his notion of episteme can hardly be accommodated in Agamben's grand narrative. And they are not. Agamben explicitely rejects Foucault's thesis that political modernity represents a break with the past, marked, among other things, by the passage from the juridical model of a unitary and localizable sovereign power to diffuse, transversal, and impersonal disciplinary relations of power." Andreas Kalyvas, "The Sovereign Weaver: Beyond the Camp," in Andrew Norris, ed., *Politics, Metaphysics, and Death: Essays on Giorgio Agamben's "Homo Sacer"* (Durham, N.C., and London: Duke UP, 2005), 107–134 (111).
22. Agamben, *Remnants of Auschwitz*, 13.
23. Ibid.
24. It is again Andreas Kalyvas who best explains this paradox: "Agamben's gesture toward a coming politics presupposes a profoundly Manichean vision of the political world split between two reified entities: the state and humanity (the nonstate). It is also informed by a rejection of political power as identical to the state-form. He does not differentiate among various forms and modalities of political power and overlooks instances of mediation. By disregarding the distinct aspects of political power, politics is relegated to a single, pejorative version of sovereign power and state authority. It evokes that hostility toward political power found in many antistatist discourses, of both the libertarian and anarchist variety." Kalyvas, "The Sovereign Weaver," 115.
25. Agamben, *Remnants of Auschwitz*, 14.
26. For a more general criticism of Agamben's works, see Vanna Gessa-Kurotschka, "Lebensform, nachtes Leben, Untaetigkeit ohne Werk," *Deutsche Zeitschrift für Philosophie* 52 (2004): 929–43.
27. Indeed, as Andrew Norris concludes, "in his insistence that the history of politics must be understood first and foremost as the history of metaphysics, Agamben clearly follows his former teacher Heidegger." Andrew Norris, "The Exemplary Exception: Philosophical and Political Decisions in Giorgio Agamben's *Homo Sacer*," in Norris, ed., *Politics, Metaphysics, and Death*, 262–83 (265).
28. This is the view that Agamben develops in *Homo Sacer: Sovereign Power and Bare Life*. See esp. his introduction (1–12).
29. Agamben, *Remnants of Auschwitz*, 30.
30. LaCapra argues that, "One reason for what might be seen as a deficit of historical understanding and of immanent critique is Agamben's reliance on etymology, which tends to substitute for both historical analysis and

argument. Agamben will often provide an etymology, at times lending it greater certainty than it may warrant, or he will cite some authority who has provided such an etymology, and then proceed from the putative etymology to a conclusion, thereby omitting any analysis or argument linking etymology to the point he wants to assert. This is a feature Agamben shares with Heidegger, the philosopher who has probably had the most formative role in his thought. Etymology, however putative or even fictive, can be thought-provoking when it opens up a line of investigation or reflection." Dominick LaCapra, *History in Transit: Experience, Identity, Critical Theory* (Ithaca, N.Y., and London: Cornell UP, 2004), 168.

31. There are conceptual problems between this vision of biopower and biopolitics and the ones that Foucault developed. An interesting criticism of this perspective is offered by LaCapra. LaCapra, *History in Transit.*
32. Interestingly, Ruti Teitel has written an essay showing how George W. Bush has made use of Schmitt's notion of sovereignty, and develops her arguments as a demonstration of how this kind of view of sovereignty is related to a state that conceives itself as a police state. Teitel says, "In this world vision, the United States has sovereign power over the 'law of exception.'" Ruti G. Teitel, "Empire's Law: Foreign Relations by Presidential Fiat," in Mary L. Dudziak, ed., *September 11 in History: A Watershed Moment?* (Durham, N.C., and London: Duke UP, 2003), 194–211 (198).
33. "The state," argues Kennedy, "is the 'decisive unity' in which members are commanded to kill and be killed." Kennedy, *Constitutional Failure*, 107.
34. Agamben, *Remnants of Auschwitz*, 34. Subsequent references to this work are cited in the text.
35. LaCapra, *History in Transit*, 175.
36. Agamben, *Remnants of Auschwitz*, 37.
37. This is one of the characters that Levi refers to in *The Drowned and the Saved.*
38. Agamben, *Remnants of Auschwitz*, 38.
39. I agree with LaCapra when he says that "responsibility and guilt are concepts that are differentially shared by ethics and law, and Agamben does not provide any idea of a form of social life in which ethics would not be involved these concepts." LaCapra, *History in Transit*, 186.
40. Agamben, *Remnants of Auschwitz*, 17.
41. Ibid., 18.
42. Teitel, however, has provided us with good arguments in which law has helped restore a concept of justice through important trials. In this way, she argues, "these practices offer a way both to delegitimate the past political regime and to legitimate its successor by structuring the political opposition within the democratizing order. . . . The transitional sanction illuminates the relation between the concepts of democratic accountability and individual rights in their contribution to the construction of a liberal politics." See Teitel, *Transitional Justice*, 6–7.
43. Agamben, *Remnants of Auschwitz*, 45. Subsequent references to this work are cited in the text.
44. This view, however, has been criticized by LaCapra and not with bad arguments. He claims that "Agamben takes a potential in humanity and, rather

than examining closely its historical role in Auschwitz and comparing carefully to other situations and possibilities, actualizes it in universal terms by generalizing the *Musselmann* as the prototype or exemplar of humanity." LaCapra, *History in Transit*, 180.

45. Agamben, *Remnants of Auschwitz*, 48. Subsequent references to this work are cited in the text.
46. Hannah Arendt, "'What Remains? The Language Remains': A Conversation with Günter Gauss," in *Essays in Understanding, 1930–1954*, 1–23.
47. Arendt, "'What Remains? The Language Remains,'" 22.
48. Teitel, *Transitional Justice*, 87.

7. Hearts of Darkness: Political Judgment

1. Hannah Arendt, "The Crisis of Culture: Its Social and Its Political Significance," in Beiner and Nedelsky, eds., *Judgment, Imagination, and Politics*, 3–25.
2. Arendt, *Men in Dark Times*, 22.
3. See Robert Fine, "Understanding Evil: Arendt and the Final Solution," in Lara, ed., *Rethinking Evil*, 131–50.
4. Bilsky, *Transformative Justice: Israeli Identity on Trial* (Ann Arbor: U of Michigan P, 2004), 87.
5. Bilsky, *Transformative Justice.*
6. See my idea of action as developed in my book *Moral Textures.*
7. Kirstie M. McClure, "The Odor of Judgment: Exemplarity, Propriety, and Politics in the Company of Hannah Arendt," in Craig Calhoun and John McGowan, eds., *Hannah Arendt and the Meaning of Politics* (Minneapolis and London: U of Minnesota P, 1997), 53–84 (60).
8. McClure, "The Odor of Judgment," 61.
9. Ibid., 62.
10. Though Arendt was trying to liberate the political sphere from the constraints of truth, as McClure has well argued, she did not want the sphere of the political to be stripped off its own validity. Arendt was against the idea that the truth could be the only criteria expressing the validity of all spheres of life, and she was overly conscious of how ideologies are presented as candidates for truth. In trying to avoid this problem, Arendt thought that opinion was a better way to propose validity, and the idea of consensus would be its warrant. This position could be approached critically (in my view), but the fact of the matter is that Arendt was trying to prevent authoritarianism in the political realm, and thus, this is the reason why she wanted to extricate the territory of the political from an epistemic conception of truth as a determinant judgment (one single definition of how things are).
11. McClure explains that "the common world presupposed by both Arendt and her critics is a world that is fundamentally posttraditonal, but a world in which substantive claims of custom and tradition have been divested of authority is a world of questions, and in a world of questions the question how to think takes on a singular significance." McClure, "The Odor of Judgment," 68.

12. McClure, "The Odor of Judgment," 67.
13. And, as McClure argues, "it appears as a sort of mental practice, a mode of intellectual discipline or self-formation that enables one to assess the particulars of the world and deeds, its events great and small, without subsuming them under general rules." McClure, "The Odor of Judgment," 74.
14. Arendt, *The Origins of Totalitarianism*, xiv.
15. Benhabib, *The Reluctant Modernism of Hannah Arendt*, 64.
16. Ibid., 65.
17. Ibid.,, 84.
18. Benhabib argues that "Arendt's brilliant insight was that experiences in the Dark Continent and the heart of darkness in Europe were profoundly related." Ibid., 86.
19. Arendt, *The Origins of Totalitarianism*, 190.
20. Ibid., 189.
21. Ibid.
22. Todorov, *Facing the Extreme*, 123.
23. Benhabib, *The Reluctant Modernism of Hannah Arendt*, 84.
24. Todorov, *Facing the Extreme*, 125.
25. Ibid.
26. James Waller captures this characteristic perfectly when he writes: "Arendt reasoned that anyone could have filled Eichmann's role and that his evil was 'banal' because insertion into a social hierarchy committed to such evil made it normal and legitimate. This is why, in her view, Eichmann was not a madman. His deeds were monstrous, but Eichmann himself was thoroughly ordinary." James Waller, *Becoming Evil: How Ordinary People Commit Genocide and Mass Killings* (Oxford and New York: Oxford UP, 2002), 98.
27. Browning, *Ordinary Men*.
28. Todorov, *Facing the Extreme*, 127. Subsequent references to this work are cited in the text.
29. Arendt says: "It is inherent in our entire philosophical tradition that we cannot conceive of a 'radical evil,' and this is true both for Christian theology, which conceded even the Devil himself a celestial origin, as well as for Kant, the only philosopher who, in the word he coined for it, at least must have suspected the existence of this evil even though he immediately rationalized it in the concept of a 'perverted ill will' that could be explained by comprehensible motives." Arendt, *The Origins of Totalitarianism*, 459. Subsequent references to this work are cited in the text.
30. Margaret Canovan argues that "the totalitarian assault upon human nature is an attempt to create something closer to nature than human beings ought to be, and to destroy the specifically human qualities that distinguish human beings from animals, namely their individuality and their capacity to initiate action and thought." Margaret Canovan, *Hannah Arendt: A Reinterpretation of Her Political Thought* (New York: Cambridge UP, 1994), 25.
31. Arendt, *The Origins of Totalitarianism*, 469. Subsequent references to this work are cited in the text.
32. Canovan, Hannah Arendt, 27.
33. Arendt, *The Origins of Totalitarianism*, 474.

34. Ibid., 189.
35. Todorov, *Facing the Extreme*, 131.
36. Mark J. Osiel, *Mass Atrocity, Ordinary Evil, and Hannah Arendt: Criminal Consciousness in Argentina's Dirty War* (New Haven and London: Yale UP, 2001), 83. Subsequent references to this work are cited in the text.
37. Osiel argues that if evil can appear banal, "this is because one of its several forms—perhaps the least noticed—involves the perceptual inability of well-intentioned people to recognize situations where the moral principles are at stake, and the affective inability to care enough about acting upon them." Osiel, *Mass Atrocity, Ordinary Evil, and Hannah Arendt*, 31.
38. Herbert Hirsch, *Genocide and the Politics of Memory: Studying Death to Preserve Life* (Chapel Hill and London: U of North Carolina P, 1995), 100.
39. Hirsch, *Genocide and the Politics of Memory*, 102.
40. Waller, *Becoming Evil*, 245. Subsequent references to this work are cited in the text.
41. Norman Naimark, *Fires of Hatred: Ethnic Cleansing in Twentieth-Century Europe* (Cambridge and London: Harvard UP, 2001), 3. Subsequent references to this work are cited in the text.
42. Naimark argues that "modern racialist nationalism was necessary for ethnic cleansing in the twentieth century but not sufficient. The modern state was a critical part of the story as it organized itself by ethnic criteria, especially after the Balkan Wars and World War I. According to Zygmunt Baumann, this marriage of modern nationalism and the post–World War I state was fatal in particular for the Jews." Naimark, *Fires of Hatred*, 7.
43. Naimark, *Fires of Hatred*, 8.
44. Ibid., 5.
45. See Lara, "Introduction: Contemporary Perspectives," in Lara, ed., *Rethinking Evil*, 1–14.

8. Death and the Maiden

1. See Claudia Card, *The Atrocity Paradigm: A Theory of Evil*.
2. See Hannah Arendt, *Eichmann in Jerusalem: A Report on the Banality of Evil*.
3. I had not read Leora Bilsky's book *Transformative Justice: Israeli Identity on Trial*, where she also focuses on the play *Death and the Maiden* to analyze the enactment of a trial when the main character reencounters her torturer. Needless to say that Bilsky's interpretation is a powerful one and I admired her skill in finding the connection to her main idea in the book, namely, how trials and political understandings help reshape societies. It was good that I had not read her book because my own interpretation is totally different and aims at highlighting a very different aspect of the play. See Bilsky, *Transformative Justice*, 87.
4. See, for example, Annette Insdorf, *Indelible Shadows: Film and the Holocaust* (Cambridge: Cambridge UP, 2003).
5. In addition to several other films that highlight the problem of evil, Roman Polanski also made *The Pianist* (2002), a piece about a Polish survivor of the Holocaust. Polanski claims that he is "much more affected by the past now

than when I was young. When I recently saw the Frédéric Rossif documentary, *Le Temps du Ghetto*, it affected me more than when I lived it." Polanski, quoted in Insdorff, *Indelible Shadows*, 241.

6. For an interesting account of this problem in Chile, see Steve J. Stern, *Remembering Pinochet's Chile: On the Eve of London 1998* (Durham, N.C., and London: Duke UP, 2004).
7. Dorfman argues that he felt "*Death and the Maiden* touched upon a tragedy in almost an Aristotelian sense, a work of art that might help a collective to purge itself, through pity and terror—in other words, to force spectators to confront those predicaments that, if not brought into the light of day, could lead to ruin." Ariel Dorfman, "Afterwords," in *Death and the Maiden* (New York: Penguin, 1991), 71–75 (74).
8. The script was written by Ariel Dorfman and Rafael Yglesias.
9. Dorfman, *Death and the Maiden*, 72.
10. See Larry May, "The Pinochet Case," in *Crimes Against Humanity: A Normative Account*, 148–52.
11. International journalists called this historical episode the "Pinochet effect." The term describes the "multiplying initiatives against authoritarian tyrants since the British police accepted Garzón's claim" (Ignacio Cembrero "The Pinochet Effect," *El País*, February 6, 2000). The Pinochet effect inspired legal scholars to revise their international precedents—as, for example, Human Rights Watch did in their work entitled *The Pinochet Precedent*, an account of procedures for prosecuting former dictators. A legal adviser for the United Nations Commission on Human Rights has also argued that "the message to new democracies is that you can't be afraid; in order to evolve as a nation and as a society, you have *to face the past*. These people cannot be above the law" (Anthony Faiola, "Pinochet Effect Exposes Once-Untouchable Ex- Dictators," *Herald Tribune*, August 7, 2000; emphasis added). Another journalist from the *New York Times* has written that "suddenly, the taboo subjects of disappearances and *torture* became daily grist of the *news media* as journalists covered the charges made against him by prosecutors in Spain, Belgium, France and other quarters. Local rights groups resuscitated themselves and began to organize" (Clifford Krauss, "Pinochet, at Home in Chile: A Real Nowhere Man," *New York Times*, March 5, 2000; emphasis in the original). The Pinochet effect, therefore, led Latin American societies to return to the essential task of connecting their transition to democracy with their authoritarian past. Furthermore, they began such processes by publicly disclosing the identities of the criminals who had led their countries to commit acts of genocide and to violate international law. Since August 8, 2000, Pinochet has been battling the Chilean system against a variety of other charges, among them a charge of corruption which has allowed the judge to strip him of his immunity. Pinochet is currently living in house detention and awaiting the legal course of several other charges during his dictatorship. In mid-November of 2000, former President Bill Clinton ordered the declassification of 16,000 documents that proved the CIA's involvement in the 1973 Chilean coup, and all that agency's secret strategies to make Allende's government fail. The official document explains that this information was also demanded by Judge Garzón.

12. See Stern, *Remembering Pinochet's Chile.*
13. Ibid., xx (emphasis added).
14. Ariel Dorfman argues that "it was not until Chile returned to democracy in 1990 and I myself returned to resettle there with my family after seventeen years of exile, that I finally understood *how the story had to be told.*" Dorfman, *Death and the Maiden*, 71 (emphasis added).
15. Stern, *Remembering Pinochet's Chile*, 108. Subsequent references to this work are cited in the text.

9. The Place of the "Angelus Novus": Between Catastrophes

1. See J. M. Bernstein, *Adorno: Disenchantment and Ethics* (Cambridge: Cambridge UP, 2001).
2. Andreas Huyssen, *Present Pasts: Urban Palimpsests and the Politics of Memory* (Stanford, Calif.: Stanford UP, 2003), 13.
3. Anson Rabinbach claims that "if there was no agreement whatsoever between Jaspers, Heidegger, and Horkheimer and Adorno on the nature of the catastrophe, I will argue that each of these thinkers nonetheless attempted to narrate the event as the apotheosis of a Western tradition and simultaneously to regard it as a deep rupture in that tradition." Anson Rabinbach, *In the Shadow of Catastrophe: German Intellectuals Between Apocalypse and Enlightenment* (Berkeley and London: U of California P, 1997), 19.
4. I was inspired to develop this conclusion while reading Manuel Cruz's essay "La vida entendida como ensayo general: Sobre traumas, catástrofes y calamidades," a paper he presented at a conference in Barcelona in July 2004. I am indebted to him for his insights and for allowing me to cite his paper.
5. Huyssen, *Present Pasts*, 13.
6. The most important judgment coming from this position is owing to Claude Lanzmann's film *Shoah*, which has resulted in an enormous amount of literature and critical essays. One of the most significant of these has been Dominick LaCapra's "Lanzmann's *Shoah*: 'Here There is No Why,'" in *History and Memory After Auschwitz*, 95–138.
7. Tzvetan Todorov, *Memoria del Mal, tentación del bien: Indagación sobre el siglo XX* (Barcelona: Península, 2002), 196; English-language edition: *Hope and Memory: Lessons from the Twentieth Century*, trans. David Bellos (Princeton: Princeton UP, 2003).
8. There already exist various critical views about this particular position. See Tim Cole, *Images of the Holocaust*; see also Peter Novick, *The Holocaust in American Life* (Boston: Houghton Mifflin, 1999).
9. The most important critical argument about politicians and their ways of avoiding responsibility comes from Samantha Powers, *A Problem from Hell: America and the Age of Genocide.*
10. Powers, *A Problem from Hell.*
11. Huyssen, *Present Pasts*, 5.
12. The historical conception of trauma not only conveys the centrality of psychoanalytic thinking in terms of "revival and survival," but it also contributes

to a serious number of epistemological problems when we deal with its reconstructions. See Caruth, ed., *Trauma: Explorations in Memory*.

13. Huyssen, *Present Pasts*, 10.
14. Teitel, *Transitional Justice*, 72.
15. Huyssen, *Present Pasts*, 15. Subsequent references to this work are cited in the text.
16. Teitel, *Transitional Justice*, 85. Subsequent references to this work are cited in the text.
17. Teitel claims that "the attribution of criminal responsibility to prior political leadership for waging unlawful war, or other similar bad state rule, is the thread running through the ancient successor trials of the tyrants of the city-states described by Aristotle and the trials of Kings Charles I and Louis XVI, to the trials in the contemporary period: the Nuremberg trials, the Tokyo war crimes trials, Greece's trial of the military colonels, and Argentina's trial of its military commanders." Teitel, *Transitional Justice*, 29.
18. See Michael Walzer, *Just and Unjust Wars* (New York: Basic Books, 1997). See also Michael Walzer, *Arguing About War* (New Haven and London: Yale UP, 2004).
19. Teitel, *Transitional Justice*, 30.
20. Ibid.
21. It is Leora Bilsky's book, *Transformative Justice: Israeli Identity on Trial*, that proves how important those reflective judgments are for reconceptualizing justice.
22. Teitel argues that this is the reason why "successor trials walk a remarkably thin line between the fulfillment of the potential for a renewed adherence to the rule of law and the risk of perpetuating political justice." Teitel, *Transitional Justice*, 30.
23. Teitel, *Transitional Justice*, 31.
24. Ibid., 31–32.
25. Ibid., 34.
26. Teitel argues that "in rejecting traditional defenses to individual responsibility for atrocities, Nuremberg dramatically expanded the potential individual criminal liability for state wrongs. While, traditionally, heads of state enjoyed sovereign immunity under the Nuremberg Principles, public officials could no longer avail themselves of a 'head of state' defense based on their official positions but, instead, could be held criminally responsible. Although under traditional military rules applicable in command structure, 'due obedience' to orders is a defense, under the Nuremberg Principles, persons acting under orders could be held responsible. In eliminating the 'act of state' and 'superior orders' defenses, the Nuremberg Principles pierce the veil of diffused responsibility characterizing the wrongdoing perpetrated under totalitarian regimes. Under the law of war, the principal of command responsibility affords a basis for attribution of responsibility to superiors for wrongdoing. This basis is reinforced by the Nuremberg Principles' lifting the defense of immunity from the heads of state." Teitel, *Transitional Justice*, 34.
27. Teitel, *Transitional Justice*, 36.
28. Ibid., 60.

29. Ibid., 61.
30. Walter Benjamin, "Theses on the Philosophy of History," in *Illuminations: Essays and Reflections*, 257. Subsequent references to this work are cited in the text.
31. Reinhart Kosselleck, *Future Past: On the Semantics of Historical Time* (Cambridge: MIT Press, 1985), 270.

Epilogue

1. Hannah Arendt, *Responsibility and Judgment*, ed. Jerome Kohn (New York: Schocken, 2003), 22 (emphasis added). Subsequent references to this work are cited in the text.

Bibliography

Agamben, Giorgio. *Homo Sacer: Sovereign Power and Bare Life*. Stanford, Calif.: Stanford UP, 1995.

——. *Remnants of Auschwitz: The Witness and the Archive*. New York: Zone, 1999.

Allison, Henry. *Kant's Theory of Taste: A Reading of the Critique of Aesthetic Judgment*. Cambridge: Cambridge UP, 2001.

Alvis, John E. and Thomas G. West, eds., *Shakespeare as Political Thinker*. Wilmington, Del.: ISI Books, 2000.

Anonymous. *A Woman in Berlin: Eight Weeks in the Conquered City*. With an introduction by Hans Magnus Enzenberger. New York: Metropolitan Books, 2005.

Arendt, Hannah. *Between Past and Future: Eight Exercises in Political Thought*. New York: Penguin, 1968.

——. *Eichmann in Jerusalem: A Report on the Banality of Evil* (1963). New York and London: Penguin, 1992.

——. *Essays in Understanding, 1930–1954*. Edited by Jerome Kohn. New York and London: Harcourt Brace, 1994.

——. *The Human Condition*. Chicago: U of Chicago P, 1958.

——. *Lectures on Kant's Political Philosophy*. Edited by Ronald Beiner. Chicago: U of Chicago P, 1982.

——. *The Life of the Mind*. New York and London: Harcourt Brace Jovanovich, 1971.

——. *Men in Dark Times* (1955). New York and London: Harcourt Brace, 1968.

——. *On Revolution*. New York: Penguin, 1977.

——. *The Origins of Totalitarianism* (1951). New York and London: Harcourt Brace Jovanovich, 1973.

——. *Rahel Varnhagen: The Life of a Jewess*. Edited by Liliane Weissberg. Baltimore and London: Johns Hopkins UP, 1997.

——. *Responsibility and Judgment*. Edited by Jerome Kohn. New York: Schocken, 2003.

Arendt, Hannah and Martin Heidegger. *Briefe (1925–1975)*. Frankfurt am Main: Vittorio Klostermann, 1999.

Baldwin, Peter, ed. *Reworking the Past: Hitler, the Holocaust, and the Historians' Debate*. Boston: Beacon Press, 1990.
Beiner, Ronald and Jennifer Nedelsky, eds. *Judgment, Imagination, and Politics: Themes from Kant and Arendt*. New York and Oxford: Rowman and Littlefield, 2001.
Benhabib, Seyla. *The Reluctant Modernism of Hannah Arendt*. Thousand Oaks, Calif., and London: Sage, 1996.
Benjamin, Walter. *Illuminations: Essays and Reflections*. Edited by Hannah Arendt. New York: Schocken, 1968.
Bernstein, J. M. *Adorno: Disenchantment and Ethics*. Cambridge: Cambridge UP, 2001.
Bernstein, Richard J. *Hannah Arendt and the Jewish Question*. Cambridge: MIT Press, 1996.
——. *Radical Evil: A Philosophical Interrogation*. Cambridge, Eng.: Polity Press, 2002.
Bilsky, Leora. *Transformative Justice: Israeli Identity on Trial*. Ann Arbor: U of Michigan P, 2004.
Bloom, Harold. *Shakespeare: The Invention of the Human*. New York: Riverhead, 1998.
Bohman, James. *Public Deliberation: Pluralism, Complexity, and Democracy*. Cambridge: MIT Press, 1996.
Browning, Christopher R. *Ordinary Men: Reserve Police Battalion 101 and the Final Solution in Poland*. New York: HarperCollins, 1992.
Calhoun, Craig and John McGowan, eds., *Hannah Arendt and the Meaning of Politics*. Minneapolis and London: U of Minnesota P, 1997.
Canovan, Margaret. *Hannah Arendt: A Reinterpretation of Her Political Thought*. New York: Cambridge UP, 1994.
Card, Claudia. *The Atrocity Paradigm: A Theory of Evil*. Oxford and New York: Oxford UP, 2002.
Caruth, Cathy, ed. *Trauma: Explorations in Memory*. Baltimore and London: John Hopkins UP, 1995.
Celan, Paul. *Poems of Paul Celan*. New York: Persea, 1995.
Cembrero, Ignacio. "The Pinochet Effect," *El País*, February 6, 2000.
Cole, Tim. *Images of the Holocaust: The Myth of the "Shoah Business."* London: Duckworth, 1999.
Conrad, Joseph. *Heart of Darkness* (1902). New York: Penguin, 2000.
Disch, Lisa Jane. *Hannah Arendt and the Limits of Philosophy*. Ithaca, N.Y., and London: Cornell UP, 1994.
Dorfman, Ariel. *Death and the Maiden* (play). New York: Penguin, 1991.
Dudziak, Mary L., ed. *September 11 in History: A Watershed Moment?* Durham, N.C., and London: Duke UP, 2003.
Evans, Richard J. *Hitler's Shadows: West German Historians and the Attempt to Escape from the Nazi Past*. New York: Pantheon, 1998.
Faiola, Anthony. "Pinochet Effect Exposes Once-Untouchable Ex- Dictators," *Herald Tribune*, August 7, 2000.
Farias, Victor. *Heidegger and Nazism*. Philadelphia: Temple UP, 1989.
Feilowitz, Marguerite. *A Lexicon of Terror: Argentina and the Legacies of Torture*. Oxford: Oxford UP, 1998.

Felman, Shoshana. *The Juridical Unconscious: Trials and Traumas in the Twentieth Century*. Cambridge and London: Harvard UP, 2002.
Ferrara, Alessandro. "Judgment, Identity, and Authenticity: A Reconstruction of Hannah Arendt's Interpretation of Kant." *Philosophy and Social Criticism* 24.2–3 (1998): 113–36.
Finchelstein, Federico, ed. *The Germans, the Holocaust, and Collective Guilt: The Goldhagen Debate*. Buenos Aires: Eudeba, 1999.
Frye, Northrop. *Anatomy of Criticism: Four Essays*. Princeton: Princeton UP, 1971.
Gadamer, Hans-Georg. *Wahrheit und Methode*. Tübingen: J. C. B. Mohr, 1975.
Gessa-Kurotschka, Vanna. "Lebensform, nachtes Leben, Untaetigkeit ohne Werk." *Deutsche Zeitschrift für Philosophie* 52 (2004): 929–943.
Glover, Jonathan. *Humanity: A Moral History of the Twentieth Century*. London: Jonathan Cape, 1999.
Goldhagen, Daniel J. *Hitler's Willing Executioners: Ordinary Germans and the Holocaust*. New York: Knopf, 1996.
Granja, Dulce María. "El juicio reflexivo en la ética kantiana." *Dianoia* 42 (1996): 125–44.
Gross, Jan Thomas. *Neighbors: The Destruction of the Jewish Community in Jedwabne, Poland*. Princeton and London: Princeton UP, 2002.
Guyer, Paul. *Kant and the Claims of Taste*. Cambridge: Cambridge UP, 1997.
Habermas, Jürgen. *The New Conservatism: Cultural Criticism and the Historians' Debate*. Edited by Shierry Weber Nicholsen. Cambridge: MIT Press, 1989.
——. *Postmetaphysical Thinking: Philosophical Essays*. Cambridge: MIT Press, 1992.
——. *The Postnational Constellation: Political Essays*. Edited by Max Pensky. Cambridge: MIT Press, 2001.
——. *Religion and Rationality: Essays on Reason, God, and Modernity*. Edited by Eduardo Mendieta. Cambridge: MIT Press, 2002.
Habermas, Jürgen, ed. *Observations on "The Spiritual Situation of the Age."* Translated by Andrew Buchwalter. Cambridge: MIT Press, 1987.
Heinrich, Dieter. *Aesthetic Judgment and the Moral Image of the World: Studies in Kant*. Stanford, Calif.: Stanford UP, 1992.
Heller, Agnes. *The Time Is Out of Joint: Shakespeare as Philosopher of History*. New York and Oxford: Rowman and Littlefield, 2002.
Hilberg, Raul. *The Destruction of the European Jews* (1961). New York: Holmes and Meier, 1985.
Hill, Melvyn A., ed., *Hannah Arendt: The Recovery of the Public World*. New York: St. Martin's, 1979.
Hirsch, Herbert. *Genocide and the Politics of Memory: Studying Death to Preserve Life*. Chapel Hill and London: U of North Carolina P, 1995.
Huyssen, Andreas. *Present Pasts: Urban Palimpsests and the Politics of Memory*. Stanford, Calif.: Stanford UP, 2003.
Insdorf, Annette. *Indelible Shadows: Film and the Holocaust*. Cambridge: Cambridge UP, 2003.
Jay, Martin. *Refractions on Violence*. New York and London: Routledge, 2003.
Johnson, Mark. *Moral Imagination: Implications of Cognitive Science for Ethics*. Chicago: U of Chicago P, 1993.

Jonas, Hans. *Mortality and Morality: A Search for the Good After Auschwitz*. Edited by Lawrence Vogel. Evanston, Ill.: Northwestern UP, 1996.

Kant, Immanuel. *Critique of Judgment* (1790). Indianapolis and Cambridge, Eng.: Hackett, 1987.

——. *Observations on the Feeling of the Beautiful and the Sublime.*(1764) Berkeley: U of California P, 1960.

——. *Political Writings*. Edited by H. S. Reiss. Cambridge: Cambridge UP, 1970.)

——. *Religion and Rational Theology*. New York: Cambridge UP, 1996.

——. *Religion within the Boundaries of Mere Reason*. Edited by Robert Merrihew Adams. New York: Cambridge UP, 1998.

Katznelson, Ira. *Desolation and Enlightment: Political Knowledge After Total War, Totalitarianism, and the Holocaust*. New York and Chichester, Eng.: Columbia UP, 2003.

Kearney, Richard. *The Poetics of Imagining: Modern and Postmodern*. New York: Fordham UP, 1998.

——. *Strangers, Gods, and Monsters*. London and New York: Routledge, 2003.

——. *The Wake of Imagination*. London: Routledge, 1994.

Kennedy, Ellen. *Constitutional Failure: Carl Schmitt in Weimar*. Durham, N.C., and London: Duke UP, 2004.

Kershaw, Ian. *The Nazi Dictatorship: Problems and Perspectives in Interpretation*. London and New York: Edward Arnold Editors, 1989.

Kosselleck, Reinhart. *Future Past: On the Semantics of Historical Time*. Cambridge: MIT Press, 1985.

Krauss, Clifford. "Pinochet, at Home in Chile: A Real Nowhere Man." *New York Times*, March 5, 2000.

Kristeva, Julia. *Powers of Horror: An Essay on Abjection*. New York: Columbia UP, 1982.

LaCapra, Dominick. *History and Memory After Auschwitz*. Ithaca, N.Y., and London: Cornell UP, 1998.

——. *History in Transit: Experience, Identity, Critical Theory*. Ithaca, N.Y., and London: Cornell UP, 2004.

Lacoue-Labarthe, Philippe. *Heidegger, Art, and Politics*. Oxford: Blackwell, 1990.

Lang, Berel. *Heidegger's Silence*, Ithaca, N.Y., and London: Cornell UP, 1996.

Langer, Lawrence L. *Preempting the Holocaust*. New Haven: Yale UP, 1998.

Lara, María Pía. *Moral Textures: Feminist Narratives in the Public Sphere*. Berkeley: U of California P, 1998.

Lara, María Pía, ed. *Rethinking Evil: Contemporary Perspectives*. Berkeley: U of California P, 2001.

Lemkin, Rafael. *Axis Rule in Occupied Europe*. Washington D.C.: Lawbook Exchange, 2005.

Levi, Primo. *The Drowned and the Saved* (1986). New York: Vintage, 1989.

——. *La Tregua* (1963). Mexico: Océano, 1998. (English-language edition: *"If This Is a Man" and "The Truce."* Translated by Stuart Woolf. Grand Rapids, Mich.: Abacus, 1991.)

——. *The Search for Roots: A Personal Anthology*. Chicago: Ivan R. Dee, 1981.

——. *The Voices of Memory: Primo Levi Interviews, 1961–1987*. New York: New York UP, 2001.

Lyotard, Jean François. *The Inhuman*. Stanford, Calif.: Stanford UP, 1988.
Maier, Charles, S. *The Unmasterable Past: History, Holocaust, and German National Identity*. Cambridge: Harvard UP, 1988.
Makkreel, Rudolf A. *Imagination and Interpretation in Kant: The Hermeneutical Import of the Critique of Judgment*. Chicago and London: U of Chicago P, 1990.
May, Larry. *Crimes Against Humanity: A Normative Account*. New York: Cambridge UP, 2005.
Meron, Theodor. *Bloody Constraint: War and Chivalry in Shakespeare*. Oxford and New York: Oxford UP, 1998.
——. *Henry's Wars and Shakespeare's Laws: Perspectives on the Law of War in the Later Middle Ages*. Oxford and New York: Oxford UP, 1993.
Müller, Jan-Werner. *A Dangerous Mind: Carl Schmitt in Postwar European Thought*. New Haven: Yale UP, 2003.
Naimark, Norman. *Fires of Hatred: Ethnic Cleansing in Twentieth-Century Europe*. Cambridge and London: Harvard UP, 2001.
Neier, Aryeh. *War Crimes: Brutality, Genocide, Terror, and the Struggle for Justice*. New York: Random House, 1998.
Neiman, Susan. *Evil in Modern Thought: An Alternative History of Philosophy*. Princeton: Princeton UP, 2002.
Ne'eman, Arad, ed. *History and Memory. Passing into History: Nazism and the Holocaust Beyond Memory*. Bloomington: Indiana UP, 1997.
Nietzsche, Friedrich. *The Birth of Tragedy*. New York: Vintage, 1967.
Nino, Carlos Santiago. *Radical Evil on Trial*. New Haven and London: Yale UP, 1996.
Norris, Andrew, ed. *Politics, Metaphysics, and Death: Essays on Giorgio Agamben's "Homo Sacer."* Durham, N.C., and London: Duke UP, 2005.
Novick, Peter. *The Holocaust in American Life*. Boston: Houghton Mifflin, 1999.
Nussbaum, Martha. *The Fragility of Goodness: Luck and Ethics in Greek Tragedy and Philosophy*. Cambridge and New York: Cambridge UP, 1986.
Osiel, Mark J. *Mass Atrocity, Ordinary Evil, and Hannah Arendt: Criminal Consciousness in Argentina's Dirty War*. New Haven and London: Yale UP, 2001.
Pirro, Robert C. *Hannah Arendt and the Politics of Tragedy*. DeKalb: Northern Illinois UP, 2001.
Powers, Samantha. *A Problem from Hell: America and the Age of Genocide*. New York: Basic Books, 2001.
Rabinbach, Anson. *In the Shadow of Catastrophe: German Intellectuals Between Apocalypse and Enlightenment*. Berkeley and London: U of California P, 1997.
Ricoeur, Paul. *Freud and Philosophy: An Essay on Interpretation*. New Haven and London: Yale UP, 1970.
——. *The Symbolism of Evil*. Boston: Beacon Press, 1967.
Ricoeur, Paul. *Time and Narrative*. Chicago: U of Chicago P, 1984.
Safranski, Rüdiger. *Martin Heidegger: Between Good and Evil*. Translated by Ewald Osers. Cambridge and London: Harvard UP, 1998.
Schmitt, Carl. *Political Theology: Four Chapters on the Concept of Sovereignty*. Cambridge: MIT Press, 1988.
Sebald, W.G. *On the Natural History of Destruction*. New York: Random House, 2003.

Shklar, Judith. *Ordinary Vices*. Cambridge: Harvard UP, 1984.
——. *Political Thought and Political Thinkers*. Edited by Stanley Hoffman. Chicago: U of Chicago P, 1998.
Skinner, Anthony, ed. *Gershom Scholem: A Life in Letters, 1914–1982*. Cambridge and London: Harvard UP, 2002.
Steiner, George. *Martin Heidegger*. Chicago: U of Chicago P, 1987
Stern, Steve J. *Remembering Pinochet's Chile: On the Eve of London 1998*. Durham, N.C., and London: Duke UP, 2004.
Strawson, P. F. *Freedom and Resentment and Other Essays*. London and New York: Methuen, 1974.
Teitel, Ruti G. *Transitional Justice*. Oxford and New York: Oxford UP, 2000.
Todorov, Tzvetan. *Facing the Extreme: Moral Life in the Concentration Camps*. New York: Holt/Metropolitan Books, 1996.
——. *Memoria del Mal, tentación del bien: Indagación sobre el siglo XX*. Barcelona: Península, 2002. (English-language edition: *Hope and Memory: Lessons from the Twentieth Century*. Trans. David Bellos. Princeton: Princeton UP, 2003.)
Villa, Dana R. *Arendt and Heidegger: The Fate of the Political*. Princeton: Princeton UP, 1996.
——. *Politics, Philosophy, Terror: Essays on the Thought of Hannah Arendt*. Princeton: Princeton UP, 1999.
Waller, James. *Becoming Evil: How Ordinary People Commit Genocide and Mass Killing*. Oxford and New York: Oxford UP, 2002.
Walzer, Michael. *Arguing About War*. New Haven and London: Yale UP, 2004.
——. *Just and Unjust Wars*. New York: Basic Books, 1997.
Warnock, Mary. *Imagination and Time*. Oxford and Cambridge: Blackwell, 1994.
Wellmer, Albrecht. *Endgames*. Cambridge: MIT Press, 1998.
Williams, Bernard. *Shame and Necessity*. Berkeley: U of California P, 1993.
Wittgenstein, Ludwig. *Philosophische Untersuchungen*. Edited G. E. M. Anscombe and R. Rhees. London: Blackwell, 1958.
Young, James E. *Writing and Rewriting the Holocaust: Narrative Consequences of Interpretation*. Bloomington: Indiana UP, 1990.
Žižek, Slavoj. *The Plague of Fantasies*. London: Verso, 1997.

Index